# Mastering Repo Markets

# Mastering Repo Markets

A step-by-step guide to the
products, applications, and risks

BOB STEINER

FT
PITMAN
PUBLISHING

market editions

PITMAN PUBLISHING
128 Long Acre, London WC2E 9AN
Tel: +44 (0)171 447 2000
Fax: +44 (0)171 240 5771

A Division of Pearson Professional Limited

First published in Great Britain 1997

© Pearson Professional Limited 1997

ISBN 0 273 62589 6

*British Library Cataloguing in Publication Data*
A CIP catalogue record for this book can be obtained from the British Library

10 9 8 7 6 5 4 3 2 1

Typeset by Pantek Arts, Maidstone, Kent.
Printed and bound in Great Britain by Bell and Bain Ltd, Glasgow.

*The Publishers' policy is to use paper manufactured from sustainable forests.*

# About the Author

**Bob Steiner** is Managing Director of Markets International Ltd, an independent company specializing in providing advice to finance directors and treasurers of international companies on foreign exchange, money markets, and other treasury matters. This ranges from written studies reviewing existing management policies and procedures, through the development of appropriate hedging strategies, to short-term market advice. Bob also spends a considerable amount of time training bankers, corporate staff and others involved in the financial markets.

Bob was previously treasurer and fund manager of H P Bulmer Holdings PLC and English and American Insurance Group PLC, active in currency and interest rate management. Prior to this he was senior consultant with HongKong and Shanghai Banking Corporation, where he worked in London and New York advising major US and European companies on currency and interest rate risk management. He has thus been closely involved in treasury management as consultant, practitioner, and trainer. He has also worked in the Overseas Department of the Bank of England, and with the European Commission in Brussels. In addition to his own experience as a corporate treasurer, his close involvement with his clients gives Bob a "hands-on" understanding of the practical problems facing the treasury department of an international company. He encourages companies to understand fully the mechanics of the currency and interest rate risks to which they are exposed, and to manage these risks appropriately.

Bob spends a considerable amount of time training bankers, corporate staff, and others involved in the financial markets. In particular, he personally runs courses for several of the ACI exams – the ACI Diploma, the "Pre-Diploma," Financial Calculations, and Repos.

His academic background is an honors degree in mathematics from Cambridge University followed by further studies in economics with London University. He is a member of the Association of Corporate Treasurers and an associate member of Forex Association London.

TO BARBARA
(*who never wanted to know anything
about repos in the first place*),

RICHARD AND LOLLY
(*who still don't*)

# CONTENTS

## 9 The Legal and Regulatory Framework      173

# Part 4: PRACTICE ACI EXAM, HINTS, AND ANSWERS

## 10 A Complete Practice ACI Exam      193

## 11 Hints and Answers to Exercises and Practice Exam      207

# FOREWORD

The ACI Institute is the educational arm of the ACI. It was founded in London in 1994. The ACI is the Financial Markets Association, an international organization with more than 25,000 members in 54 countries which began life in 1956.

In late 1994 and early 1995 the ACI Institute conducted a survey of its members to find out what they would like to study, what they thought their colleagues needed to study, and how they would like to study it. It is slightly embarrassing to have to admit that the repo market was not included in the initial list of subjects suggested to the membership. However, there was an open-ended question at the end of the questionnaire which asked respondents to tell us what we had missed. And they told us: they wanted to learn about the repo markets.

The repo markets are not new, they have an 80-year history in the US. But the international repo market and its dramatic growth are new. A recent estimate of the size of the market was $7,300bn of net repo purchases in 1995 (quoted in the *Financial Times* Survey of March 1, 1996) which makes it one of the biggest financial markets in the world. So it is hardly surprising that our members told us about its omission in our survey and perfectly understandable that they wanted to learn about it.

The task of the ACI Institute is simple to state: it is to use the skills of its members to make a clear statement of what a market professional needs to know and to what level they need to know it. The Institute is benchmarking the acquisition of knowledge in the rapidly changing wholesale financial markets – a task which is both challenging and exciting. To this end we encourage authors, publishers and tutors to provide as wide a variety of routes to our exams as possible.

For this reason, I am delighted that Bob Steiner and *FT* Pitman have produced *Mastering Repo Markets*. It captures the knowledge necessary to pass one of the ACI's second level examinations: "The Repo Market", one of the stepping stones to ACI Fellowship/ Associateship status. The examination board is provided by a group led by highly experienced practitioners from Forex Luxembourg, in partnership with staff from IFBL (Institut de Formation Bancaire, Luxembourg) and the clearing houses Cedel and Euroclear.

I am sure that the volume will be appreciated by a wider audience than candidates for the ACI examination. Anyone looking for a source of information about the activities of professionals in these markets will find it here, and they can use it with the comforting knowledge that the "specification" was drawn up by practitioners for practitioners.

*Michael J Osborne*
*Director, ACI Institute*

# INTRODUCTION

The repo markets have grown very rapidly in the last few years for a variety of reasons. Among them are the increasing need to be able to take and hedge short positions in the capital and derivative markets, growing concern over counterparty credit risk, and the favorable capital adequacy treatment given to repos. Last but not least is the growing awareness among market participants of the flexibility of repos and wide range of circumstances in which they can be of benefit.

## The aim of the book

Because repos are used by so many different players in the market, this book is necessarily aimed at a wide audience – dealers in bonds, money markets, and futures, treasurers, investors, and fund managers, those involved in hedging derivatives, and of course repo dealers. It will also be of interest to those in the associated areas of systems and risk management.

It is worth stating, however, that it was inspired by the new exam on the repo market, promoted by the ACI and first set in June 1996. This is, as far as we are aware, the only exam specific to repos, and there appeared to be a need to provide a book for the student who chooses to undertake the exam without any formal tuition course. Much of the book has in fact been developed from a course given at the request of the Forex Club of Luxembourg, which is responsible for setting the ACI syllabus and exam for this subject. It has therefore been conceived as a workbook rather than simply a reference book, with strong emphasis on examples and exercises.

## The structure of the book

The book is in four parts:

### The market background

This covers the various financial markets which underlie the uses of repos – money markets, bonds, and derivatives – and takes the reader through the basic financial arithmetic necessary for a complete understanding of the book. These chapters are included for two reasons. First, repos are inextricably linked with each of these other markets and the reader interested in repos is likely also to be interested in the interrelationship with them. Second, experience suggests that if the reader is not familiar with these areas he or she will probably find it much harder to understand other parts of the book, precisely because of these relationships.

### Repos and how to use them

This is the central part of the book, covering the various forms of repo, their terminology, structure, and pricing, as well as the wide range of uses to which repos are put in the financial markets.

### Market details and documentation

This looks in more detail at the differences between some of the domestic repo markets, where circumstances and conventions are not always the same as in the international market. It goes on to consider the details of repo documentation, which is key to the growth of the repo market because of its implications for risk management and favorable capital adequacy treatment. This part also considers some CAD (Capital Adequacy Directive), accounting, and tax aspects of repos.

### Practice ACI exam, hints and answers

This includes a full mock exam for those readers studying for the ACI repos exam. There are also hints and answers to the calculation exercises which are found throughout the book.

# Key features of the book

### Key points

Throughout the technical areas, key points have been highlighted for emphasis.

### Calculation summaries

The procedures for all the necessary calculations have been summarized in the text to ensure the reader's understanding. These have also been collected together into a reference section in Appendix 3.

### Glossary

The repo market has its own terminology, which is explained through-out the text, with a glossary for reference.

### Market interest conventions

A constant source of confusion is the range of different conventions used for interest and coupon calculations in different markets. These are detailed in Appendix 2 for various countries' markets.

### Examples

The technical areas of the book contain a number of examples and diagrams to help the reader's understanding. In the central chapter (5) on repo structures, many of the examples are linked by using the same basic data.

### Exercises

Answers are provided at the end of the book for each chapter's calculation exercises. For readers who are struggling with a particular question but who wish to persevere, there is a section of hints, which will lead them through the procedure to be followed for each calculation question.

### Documentation

The documentation used domestically varies from country to country, but the PSA/ISMA agreement is used internationally and is also increasingly the standard on which different countries' domestic documentation is based. This has therefore been included in full in Appendix 1, together with the annex to the agreement used in the UK gilt market.

## How to use the book

The book has been designed as a useful reference work for everyone involved in the market, as well as a workbook. The book therefore deliberately covers rather more than is strictly required for the ACI exam. An exam candidate can therefore read the first four chapters on associated financial markets and instruments less intently, if he or she already feels familiar with those areas. On the other hand, our hope is that most readers will benefit from reading through them rather more thoroughly

For the exam student, then, a few preliminary suggestions. First, we encourage you to follow through all the examples and diagrams and try all the exercises throughout the book. Worked answers are provided in chapter 11 for all the calculation exercises. If you feel uncertain about how to go about a particular calculation, try the "hints" section at the beginning of chapter 11 first. All the questions which have been marked with an ACI logo are relevant to the ACI exam and should be tried. The exercises without a logo are outside the scope of the exam but have been included for completeness to cover the material in this book. Finally, when you have read through the book, do try your hand at the practice exam given in chapter 10.

## A final word

However hard one tries, inaccuracies inevitably creep into a book such as this, not least because the subject is a moving target as the market is developing and conventions and market practice are changing. I apologize for any such inaccuracies and welcome comments or suggestions from readers.

# ACKNOWLEDGEMENTS

I would like to thank various people for their help and suggestions for the book, notably:

Claude Schon, Banque Internationale à Luxembourg
William Webster, Banca Nacional Financiera
Simon Keogh, Applied Financial Projects

Thanks also go to Pitman Publishing for never complaining that the manuscript arrived so late and, most importantly, to my wife Barbara for all her help.

The publishers would like to thank the International Securities Market Association and the Public Securities Association for allowing them to reproduce the PSA/ISMA Agreement which appears in Appendix 1.

The publishers are also grateful to the Bank of England for agreement to reproduce the gilt annex to this document, which was produced by the Gilt Repo Legal Agreement Working Party convened by the Bank of England.

Part 1

# The Market
# Background

■ ■ ■

*"Any given amount of money is worth more sooner than it is later . . ."*

# Mastering Financial Arithmetic

Some opening remarks on formulas

Simple and compound interest

Future value/present value; time value of money

Cashflow analysis

Interpolation

Exercises

# SOME OPENING REMARKS ON FORMULAS

It is probably worthwhile beginning with two remarks concerning many of the formulas in this book. These remarks have nothing to do with the business of finance, but, rather, with how mathematical formulas are written in all areas of life.

First, consider the expression "$1 + 0.08 \times \frac{92}{365}$." In this, you must do the multiplication *before* the addition. It is a convention of the way mathematical formulas are written that any exponents ($5^4$, $x^2$, $4.2^{\frac{1}{4}}$ etc.) must be done first, followed by multiplication and division ($0.08 \times 92$, $x \div y$, $\frac{17}{38}$ etc.) and addition and subtraction last. This rule is applied first to anything inside brackets "(...)" and then to everything else. This means that "$1 + 0.08 \times \frac{92}{365}$" is the same as "$1 + (0.08 \times \frac{92}{365})$" and is equal to 1.0202. This is *not* the same as "$(1 + 0.08) \times \frac{92}{365}$," which is equal to 0.2722. If I mean to write this latter expression, I *must* write the brackets. If I mean to write the first expression, I do not need to write the brackets and it is in fact usual to leave them out.

Second, the expression "percent" strictly means "divided by 100." When writing a formula which involves an interest rate – 4.7 percent, for example – the formula will often include 0.047 rather than $\frac{4.7}{100}$, simply because 0.047 is neater.

# SIMPLE AND COMPOUND INTEREST

## Simple interest

On short-term financial instruments, interest is "simple" rather than "compound". Suppose, for example, that I place £1 on deposit at 8 percent for 92 days. As the 8 percent is generally quoted as if for a whole year rather than for only 92 days, the interest I expect to receive is the appropriate proportion of 8 percent:

$$£0.08 \times \frac{92}{365}$$

The total proceeds after 92 days are therefore the return of my principal, plus the interest:

$$£(1 + 0.08 \times \frac{92}{365})$$

If I place instead £73 on deposit at 8 percent for 92 days, I will receive a total of:

$$£73 \times \left(1 + 0.08 \times \tfrac{92}{365}\right)$$

> **Key Point**
>
> *Total proceeds of short-term investment =*
>
> $$principal \times \left(1 + \ interest\ rate \times \frac{days}{year}\right)$$

## Compound interest

Now consider an investment of 1 made for two years at 10 percent per annum. At the end of the first year, the investor receives interest of 0.10. At the end of the second year he receives interest of 0.10, plus the principal of 1. The total received is 0.10 + 0.10 + 1 = 1.20. However, the investor could in practice reinvest the 0.10 received at the end of the first year, for a further year. If he could do this at 10 percent, he would receive an extra 0.01 (= 10% × 0.10) at the end of the second year, for a total of 1.21.

In effect, this is the same as investing 1 for one year at 10 percent to receive 1 + 0.10 at the end of the first year and then reinvesting the whole (1 + 0.10) for a further year, also at 10 percent, to give (1 + 0.10) × (1 + 0.10) = 1.21.

The same idea can be extended for any number of years, so that the total return after $N$ years, including principal, is:

$$Principal \times \left(1 + \frac{interest\ rate}{100}\right)^{N}$$

This is "compounding" the interest, and assumes that all interim cashflows can be reinvested at the same original interest rate. "Simple" interest is the expression used when the interest is not reinvested in this way.

> **Key Point**
>
> *Total proceeds of long-term investment for N years =*
>
> $$principal \times \left(1 + \ interest\ rate\right)^{N}$$

# FUTURE VALUE/PRESENT VALUE; TIME VALUE OF MONEY

## Short-term investments

If I deposit 100 for one year at 10 percent per annum, I receive:

$$100 \times (1 + 0.10) = 110$$

at the end of the year. In this case 110 is said to be the "future value" after one year of 100 now. In the same way, 100 is said to be the "present value" of 110 in a year's time. Future and present values clearly depend on both the interest rate used and the length of time involved.

Similarly, the future value after 98 days of £100 now at 10 percent per annum would be £100 × (1 + 0.10 × $\frac{98}{365}$) = £102.68.

The expression above can be turned upside down, so that the present value now of 102.68 in 98 days' time, using 10 percent per annum, is:

$$\frac{102.68}{(1 + 0.10 \times \frac{98}{365})} = 100$$

In general, the present value of a cashflow $C$ occurring after $d$ days using an interest rate $i$ is:

$$\frac{C}{\left(1 + i \times \frac{d}{\text{year}}\right)}$$

We can therefore now generate a future value from a present value, and vice versa, given the number of days and the interest rate. The third calculation needed is the answer to the question: if we know how much money we invest at the beginning (= the present value) and we know the total amount at the end (= the future value), what is our rate of return, or yield, on the investment (= the interest rate)? This is found by turning round the formula above again, to give:

$$\text{Yield} = \left(\frac{\text{future value}}{\text{present value}} - 1\right) \times \frac{\text{year}}{d}$$

The calculation of present value is sometimes known as "discounting" a future value to a present value and the interest rate used is sometimes known as the "rate of discount."

In general, these calculations demonstrate the "time value of money." Any given amount of money is worth more sooner than it is later because, if you have it sooner, you can place it on deposit to earn interest on it. The extent to which it is worthwhile having the money sooner depends on the interest rate and the time period involved.

### For short-term investments

$$FV = PV \times \left(1 + i \times \frac{days}{year}\right)$$

$$PV = \frac{FV}{\left(1 + i \times \frac{days}{year}\right)}$$

$$i = \left(\frac{FV}{PV} - 1\right) \times \frac{year}{days}$$

## Long-term investments

The formulas above are for investments where no compound interest is involved. For periods of more than a year where compounding is involved, this compounding must be taken into account.

The future value in three years' time of 100 now, using 10 percent per annum is:

$$100 \times (1 + 0.10)^3 = 133.10$$

This expression can again be turned upside down, so that the present value now of 133.10 in three years' time, using 10 percent per annum, is:

$$\frac{133.10}{(1 + 0.10)^3} = 100$$

In general, the present value of a cashflow $C$ in $N$ years' time, using an interest rate $i$ is:

$$\frac{C}{(1 + i)^N}$$

| Key Point | **For long-term investments over _N_ years** |
|---|---|

$$FV = PV \times (1 + i)^N$$

$$PV = \frac{FV}{(1 + i)^N}$$

**Example 1.1** What is the future value in 5 years' time of £120 now, using 8% per annum?

$$120 \times (1.08)^5 = 176.32$$

(The interest rate is compounded because interest is paid each year and can be reinvested.)

*Answer*: £176.32

**Example 1.2** What is the future value in 92 days' time of £120 now, using 8% per annum?

$$120 \times (1 + 0.08 \times \tfrac{92}{365}) = 122.42$$

(Simple interest rate, because there is only one interest payment, at maturity.)

*Answer*: £122.42

**Example 1.3** What is the present value of £270 in 4 years' time, using 7% per annum?

$$\frac{270}{(1.07)^4} = 205.98$$

(The interest rate is compounded because interest is paid each year and can be reinvested.)

*Answer*: £205.98

Example 1.4

What is the present value of £270 in 180 days' time, using 7% per annum?

$$\frac{270}{(1 + 0.07 \times \frac{180}{365})} = 260.99$$

(Simple interest rate, because there is only one interest payment, at maturity.)

*Answer*: £260.99

Example 1.5

I invest £138 now. After 64 days I receive back a total (principal plus interest) of £139.58. What is my yield on this investment?

$$\text{Yield} = \left(\frac{139.58}{138.00} - 1\right) \times \frac{365}{64} = 0.0653$$

*Answer*: 6.53%

# CASHFLOW ANALYSIS
## NPV

Suppose that we have a series of future cashflows, some of which are positive and some negative. Each will have a present value, dependent on the time to the cashflow and the interest rate used. The sum of all the positive and negative present values added together is the *net* present value or NPV.

Example 1.6

What is the NPV of the following future cashflows, discounting at a rate of 7.5%?

After 1 year      + $83
After 2 years     – $10
After 3 years     + $150

$$\frac{83}{(1.075)} - \frac{10}{(1.075)^2} + \frac{150}{(1.075)^3} = 189.30$$

*Answer*: +$189.30

Key Point

*NPV = sum of all the present values*

# IRR

An internal rate of return (IRR) is the one single interest rate which it is necessary to use when discounting a series of future values to achieve a given net present value. This is equivalent to the interest rate which it is necessary to use when discounting a series of future values *and* an opposite cashflow *now*, to achieve a *zero* present value. Suppose the following cashflows, for example, which might arise from some project:

| | | |
|---|---|---|
| Now | – | 87 |
| After 1 year | + | 25 |
| After 2 years | – | 40 |
| After 3 years | + | 60 |
| After 4 years | + | 60 |

What interest rate is needed to discount +25, –40, +60 and +60 back to a net present value of +87? The answer is 5.6 percent. It can therefore be said that an initial investment of 87 produces a 5.6 percent internal rate of return if it generates these subsequent cashflows. This is equivalent to saying that, using 5.6 percent, the net present value of –87, +25, –40, +60, and +60 is zero.

Calculating an NPV is relatively simple: calculate each present value separately and add them together. Calculating an IRR, however, requires a repeated "trial and error" method and is therefore generally done using a specially designed calculator.

---

**Example 1.7**    What is the IRR of the following cashflows?

| | |
|---|---|
| Now | –$164 |
| After 1 year | +$45 |
| After 2 years | +$83 |
| After 3 years | +$75 |

*Answer*: 10.59% (If you do not have a calculator able to calculate this, try checking the answer by working "backwards": the NPV of all the future values, using the rate of 10.59%, should come to + $164).

---

**Key Point**    *The internal rate of return is the rate which discounts all the known future values to a given NPV*

# INTERPOLATION

In the money market, prices are generally quoted for standard periods such as one month, two months, etc. If a dealer needs to quote a price for an "odd date" between these periods, he needs to "interpolate."

Suppose for example that the one-month rate (30 days) is 8.0 percent and that the two-month rate (61 days) is 8.5 percent. The rate for one month and nine days (39 days) assumes that interest rates increase steadily from the one-month rate to the two-month rate – a *straight-line* interpolation. The increase from 30 days to 39 days will therefore be a $\frac{9}{31}$ proportion of the increase from 30 days to 61 days. The 39-day rate is therefore:

$$8.0\% + \tfrac{9}{31} \times (8.5\% - 8.0\%) = 8.15\%$$

The same process can be used for interpolating exchange rates.

---

The 2-month (61 days) rate is 7.5% and the 3-month rate (92 days) is 7.6%.    **Example 1.8**

What is the 73-day rate?

$$7.5 + (7.6 - 7.5) \times \tfrac{12}{31} = 7.5387$$

*Answer*: 7.5387%

# EXERCISES

1. What is the future value after 120 days of £43 invested at 7.5%?

2. I will receive a total of £89 after 93 days. What is the present value of this amount discounted at 10.1%?

3. I invest £83 now and receive a total of £83.64 back after 28 days. What is the yield on my investment?

4. What is the future value in 10 years' time of 36 now, using 9% per annum?

5. If I invest 342 for 5 years at 6% per annum (interest paid annually), how much interest do I receive at the end of 5 years assuming that all interim cashflows can be reinvested also at 6%?

6. What is the present value, using a rate of discount of 11%, of a cashflow of DEM 98.00 in 5 years' time?

7. The 30-day DEM interest rate is 5.2% and the 60-day rate is 5.4%. Interpolate to find the 41-day rate.

■ ■ ■

"The 'money market' is the term used to include all short-term financial instruments which are based on an interest rate, whether the interest rate is actually paid or just implied in the way the instrument is priced."

# Money Market Basics

# OVERVIEW

The "money market" is the term used to include all *short-term* financial instruments which are based on an interest rate (whether the interest rate is actually paid or just implied in the way the instrument is priced).

The underlying instruments are essentially those used by one party (borrower, seller, or issuer) to borrow and by the other party (the lender, buyer, or investor) to lend. The main such instruments are:

- Treasury bill – borrowing by government.

- Time deposit.
  Certificate of deposit (CD) } – borrowing by banks.

- Commercial paper – borrowing by companies (or in some cases banks).

- Bill of exchange – borrowing by companies.

Each of these instruments is essentially an obligation on the borrower to repay the amount borrowed at maturity, plus interest if appropriate. As well as these underlying borrowing instruments, there are other money market instruments which are linked to these, or at least to the same interest rate structure, but which are not direct obligations on the issuer in the same way:

- Repurchase agreement – used to borrow short term but using another instrument (such as a bond) as collateral.

- Futures contract
  Forward rate agreement (FRA) } – used to trade or hedge short-term interest rates for future periods.

The money market is linked to other markets though arbitrage mechanisms. Arbitrage occurs when it is possible to achieve the same result in terms of position and risk through two alternative mechanisms which have a slightly different price; the arbitrage involves achieving the result via the cheaper method and simultaneously reversing the position via the more expensive method – thereby locking in a profit which is free from market risk (although still probably subject to credit risk). For example, if I can buy one instrument cheaply and simultaneously sell at a higher price another instrument or combination of instruments which has identical characteristics, I am arbitraging. In a completely free market with no other price considerations involved, the supply and demand effect of arbitrage tends to drive the two prices together.

The money market is linked in this way to the forward foreign exchange market, through the theoretical ability to create synthetic deposits in one currency, by using foreign exchange deals combined with money market instruments. Similarly, it is linked to the capital markets (long-term financial instruments) through the ability to create longer-term instruments from a series of short-term instruments (such as a two-year swap from a series of three-month FRAs).

Because of the size of deals in the money market, it is essentially a market between professional participants – banks, brokers, companies, and institutional investors – rather than private individuals. It is thus a "wholesale" rather than a "retail" market. The market is extremely liquid, with huge volumes traded continually. This is due partly to the relatively fine spreads (between bid and offer) available compared with, say, the market in equities, and partly to the high credit standing of many of the organizations which issue the instruments in the first place.

There is of course a tiering of creditworthiness, as not all issues are of equal standing. In major markets, government issues (i.e. T-bills) will be of the highest rating and hence command the lowest yield and highest price. Below the government come the highest-rated banks and companies, followed by those seen as being less creditworthy. Companies which are not seen as having a very high creditworthiness will, for example, find it difficult to issue commercial paper because no one will wish to invest in it. Such a company could issue a trade bill, but only with the backing of a bank prepared to "accept" the bill – that is, act as a guarantor.

**Terminology**

**Euro currency** The term "euro" is used to describe any instrument which is held outside the country whose currency is involved. The term does not imply "European" specifically. For example, a sterling deposit made by a UK resident in London is domestic sterling, but a sterling deposit made in New York is eurosterling. Similarly, US dollar commercial paper issued outside the US is eurocommercial paper while US dollar commercial paper issued inside the US is domestic commercial paper.

**Coupon/yield** A certificate of deposit (CD) pays interest at maturity as well as repaying the principal. For example, a CD might be issued with a face value of £1 million which is repaid on maturity together with interest of say, 10 percent calculated on the number of days between issue and maturity. The 10 percent interest rate is called the "coupon." The coupon is fixed once the CD is issued. This should not be confused with the "yield," which is the current rate available in the market when buying and selling an instrument, and varies continually.

**Discount** 1. An instrument which does not carry a coupon is a "discount" instrument. Because no interest is paid on the principal, a buyer will only ever buy it for less than its face value – that is, "at a discount" (unless yields are negative!). For example, all Treasury bills are discount instruments.

2. The word "discount" is also used in the very specialized context of a "discount rate" quoted in the US and UK markets on certain instruments. This is explained in detail below.

**Bearer/registered** A "bearer" security is one where the issuer pays the principal (and coupon if there is one) to whoever is holding the security at maturity. This enables the security to be held anonymously. A "registered" security, by contrast, is one where the owner is considered to be whoever is registered centrally as the owner; this registration is changed each time the security changes hands

# DAY/YEAR CONVENTIONS

As a general rule in the money markets, the calculation of interest to be paid takes account of the exact numbers of days in the period in question, as a proportion of a year. Thus:

> *Interest rate paid = "annualized" interest rate quoted × days in period/days in year*

A variation between different money markets arises, however, in the conventions used for the number of days assumed to be in the base "year." Domestic UK instruments, for example, assume that there are 365 days in a year, even when it is a leap year. Thus a sterling time deposit at 10 percent which lasts exactly one year, but includes February 29 in its period (a total of 366 days), will actually pay slightly more than 10 percent – in fact:

$$10\% \times \frac{366}{365} = 10.027\%$$

This convention is usually referred to as "ACT/365" – that is, the "actual" number of days in the period concerned, divided by 365. Some money markets, however, assume that each year has a conventional 360 days. For example, a eurodollar time deposit at 10 percent which lasts exactly 365 days pays:

$$10\% \times \frac{365}{360} = 10.139\%$$

This convention is usually referred to as "ACT/360." Many important money markets assume a conventional year of 360 days. The major European exceptions, which assume a year of 365 days, are the euro and domestic markets in sterling, Belgian and Luxembourg francs, Irish pounds, Portuguese escudos and Greek drachmas, and the domestic (but not euro) market in Italian lire.

In order to convert interest $i$ per cent quoted on a 360-day basis to interest $i^*$ percent quoted on a 365-day basis:

$$i^* = i \times \frac{365}{360}$$

Similarly,

$$i = i^* \times \frac{360}{365}$$

---

**Key Point**

*Interest on 360-day basis = interest on 365-day basis* $\times \dfrac{360}{365}$
*and vice versa*

**Example 2.1** The yield on a security on an ACT/360 basis is 10.5%. What is the equivalent yield expressed on an ACT/365 day basis?

$$10.5 \times \frac{365}{360} = 10.6458$$

*Answer:* 10.6458%

There are some exceptions to the general approach above. Yields on Swedish T-bills, for example, are calculated in the same way as eurobonds (discussed in chapter 3).

*We give a list of the conventions used in some important markets in Appendix 2.*

# MONEY MARKET INSTRUMENTS

## Time deposit/loan

A time deposit or "clean" deposit is a deposit placed with a bank. This is not a security which can be bought or sold (that is, it is not "negotiable"), and it must normally be held to maturity.

| | |
|---|---|
| *term* | from one day to several years, but usually less than one year |
| *interest* | usually all paid on maturity, but deposits of over a year (and sometimes those of less than a year) pay interest more frequently – commonly each six months or each year |
| *quotation* | as an interest rate |
| *currency* | any domestic or euro currency |
| *settlement* | generally same day for domestic, two working days for euro |
| *registration* | there is no registration |
| *negotiable* | no |

## Certificate of deposit (CD)

A CD is a security issued to a depositor by a bank or building society, to raise money in the same way as a time deposit. A CD can, however, be bought and sold (that is, it is "negotiable").

| | |
|---|---|
| *term* | generally up to one year, although longer-term CDs are issued |
| *interest* | usually pay a coupon, although occasionally sold as a discount instrument. Interest usually all paid on maturity, but CDs of over a year (and sometimes those of less than a year) pay interest more frequently – commonly each six months or each year. Some CDs pay a "floating" rate (FRCD), which is paid and refixed at regular intervals |
| *quotation etc.* | as a yield |
| *currency* | any domestic or euro currency |
| *settlement* | generally same day for domestic, two working days for euro |
| *registration* | usually in bearer form |
| *negotiable* | yes |

## Treasury bill

Treasury bills are domestic instruments issued by governments to raise short-term finance.

| | |
|---|---|
| *term* | generally 13, 26, or 52 weeks; in France also 4 to 7 weeks; in the UK generally 13 weeks |
| *interest* | non-interest bearing, issued at a discount |
| *quotation* | in US, UK, and Ireland, quoted on a "discount rate" basis, but elsewhere on a true yield basis |
| *currency* | usually the currency of the country; however, the UK and Italian governments, for example, also issue ECU T-bills |
| *registration* | bearer security |
| *negotiable* | yes |

## Commercial paper (CP)

CP is issued usually by a company (although some banks also issue CP) in the same way that a CD is issued by a bank. CP is, however, usually not interest-bearing. A company generally needs to have a rating from a credit agency for its CP to be widely acceptable. Details vary between markets:

### US CP

| | |
|---|---|
| *term* | from one day to 270 days; usually very short term |
| *interest* | non-interest bearing, issued at a discount |
| *quotation* | on a "discount rate" basis |
| *currency* | domestic US$ |
| *settlement* | same day |
| *registration* | in bearer form |
| *negotiable* | yes |

### Euro commercial paper (ECP)

| | |
|---|---|
| *term* | from two to 365 days; usually between 30 and 180 days |
| *interest* | usually non-interest bearing, issued at a discount |
| *quotation* | as a yield, calculated on the same year basis as other money market instruments in that euro currency. |
| *currency* | any euro currency but largely US$ |
| *settlement* | two working days, through Euroclear or Cedel |
| *registration* | in bearer form |
| *negotiable* | yes |

## Bill of exchange

A bill of exchange is essentially used by a company to borrow short-term money for trade purposes. The party owing the money is the "drawer of the bill". If a bank stands as guarantor

to the drawer, it is said to "accept" the bill by indorsing it appropriately, and is the "acceptor". A bill accepted in this way is a
"banker's acceptance" (BA).

In the UK, if the bank accepting the bill is one on a specific
list of banks published by the Bank of England, the bill
becomes an "eligible bill" which means it is eligible for discounting by the Bank of England itself, and will therefore
command a slightly lower yield than an ineligible bill.

| | |
|---|---|
| *term* | from one week to one year but usually less than six months |
| *interest* | non-interest bearing, issued at a discount |
| *quotation* | in US and UK, quoted on a "discount rate" basis, but elsewhere on a true yield basis |
| *currency* | mostly domestic, although it is possible, for example, to draw US$ and DEM in the UK |
| *settlement* | available for discount immediately on being drawn |
| *registration* | none |
| *negotiable* | yes, although in practice banks often tend to hold the bills they have discounted until maturity, rather than pass them round the market |

## MONEY MARKET CALCULATIONS

For any instrument, the price an investor is prepared to pay is essentially the present value, or NPV, of the future cashflow(s) which he or
she will receive as a result of owning it. This present value depends on
the interest rate (the "yield"), the time to the cashflow(s), and the size
of the cashflow(s).

| |
|---|
| *Price = present value* |

**Key Point**

For an instrument such as a CD which has a coupon rate, the price in
the secondary market will therefore depend not only on the current

yield but also on the coupon rate because the coupon rate affects the size of the cashflow received at maturity.

Consider first a CD paying only one coupon (or in its last coupon period). The maturity proceeds of the CD are given by:

$$F \times (1 + \text{coupon rate} \times \frac{d}{\text{year}})$$

where   $F$ = face value of the CD
$d$ = number of days in the coupon period
"year" = either 360 (e.g. in the US) or 365 (e.g. in the UK).

The price $P$ of this CD now is the investment needed at the *current* yield $i$ to achieve this amount on maturity – in other words, the present value now of the maturity proceeds:

$$P = \frac{F \times \left(1 + \text{coupon rate} \times \frac{d}{\text{year}}\right)}{\left(1 + i \times \frac{d_{pm}}{\text{year}}\right)}$$

where: $d_{pm}$ = number of days from purchase to maturity.

In chapter 1 we saw that the simple return on any investment can be calculated as:

$$\left(\frac{\text{total proceeds at maturity}}{\text{initial investment}} - 1\right) \times \frac{\text{year}}{\text{days held}}$$

Following this, the yield $E$ earned on a CD purchased after issue and sold before maturity will be given by:

$$E = \left(\frac{\text{Price achieved on sale}}{\text{Price achieved on purchase}} - 1\right) \times \left(\frac{\text{year}}{\text{days held}}\right)$$

From the previous formula, this is:

$$E = \left[\frac{\left(1 + i_p \times \frac{d_{pm}}{\text{year}}\right)}{\left(1 + i_s \times \frac{d_{sm}}{\text{year}}\right)} - 1\right] \times \left(\frac{\text{year}}{\text{days held}}\right)$$

where: $i_p$   = yield on purchase
$i_s$   = yield on sale
$d_{pm}$   = number of days from purchase to maturity
$d_{sm}$   = number of days from sale to maturity.

Example 2

A CD is issued for \$1 million on March 17 for 90 days (maturity June 15) with a 6.0 percent coupon. On April 10 the yield is 5.5 percent. What are the total maturity proceeds? What is the secondary market cost on April 10?

$$\text{Maturity proceeds} = \$1\text{million} \times (1 + 0.06 \times \tfrac{90}{360}) = \$1,015,000.00$$

$$\text{Cost} = \frac{\$1,015,000.00}{(1 + 0.055 \times \tfrac{66}{360})} + \$1,004,867.59$$

On May 10, the CD is sold at a yield of 5.0 percent. What is the rate of return earned on holding the CD for the 30 days from April 10 to May 10?

$$\text{Return} = \left[\frac{1 + 0.055 \times \tfrac{66}{360}}{1 + 0.050 \times \tfrac{66}{360}} - 1\right] \times \frac{360}{30} = 6.07\%$$

Key Point

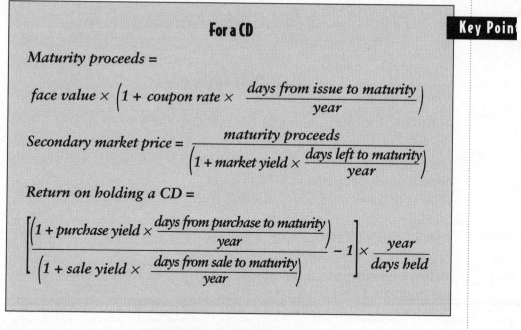

### For a CD

*Maturity proceeds =*

$$\textit{face value} \times \left(1 + \textit{coupon rate} \times \frac{\textit{days from issue to maturity}}{\textit{year}}\right)$$

*Secondary market price =*

$$\frac{\textit{maturity proceeds}}{\left(1 + \textit{market yield} \times \dfrac{\textit{days left to maturity}}{\textit{year}}\right)}$$

*Return on holding a CD =*

$$\left[\frac{\left(1 + \textit{purchase yield} \times \dfrac{\textit{days from purchase to maturity}}{\textit{year}}\right)}{\left(1 + \textit{sale yield} \times \dfrac{\textit{days from sale to maturity}}{\textit{year}}\right)} - 1\right] \times \frac{\textit{year}}{\textit{days held}}$$

## DISCOUNT INSTRUMENTS

Some instruments are known as "discount" instruments. This means that only the face value of the instrument is paid on maturity, without interest, in return for a smaller amount paid originally (instead of the face value paid originally in return for a larger amount on maturity). Treasury bills, for example, are discount instruments.

Consider, for example, a Belgian Treasury bill for BEF 10 million issued for 91 days. On maturity, the investor receives only the face value of BEF 10 million. If the yield on the bill is 10 percent, the price the investor will be willing to pay now for the bill is its present value calculated at 10 percent:

$$\text{Price} = \frac{\text{BEF 10 million}}{(1 + 0.10 \times \frac{91}{365})} = \text{BEF } 9,756,749.53$$

**Example 2.3** A French T-bill with face value FRF 10 million matures in 74 days. It is quoted at 8.4 percent. What is the cost of the bill?

$$\frac{\text{FRF 10 million}}{(1 + 0.084 \times \frac{74}{360})} = \text{FRF } 9,830,264.11$$

**Key Point**    *Secondary market proceeds = present value (again!)*

# DISCOUNT/TRUE YIELD

In the US, UK, and Ireland, a further complication arises in the way the interest rate is quoted on discount instruments – as a "discount rate" instead of a yield. If you invest 98.436 in a sterling time deposit or CD at 10 percent for 58 days, you expect to receive the 98.436 back at the end of 58 days, together with interest calculated as:

$$98.436 \times 0.10 \times \frac{58}{365} = 1.564$$

In this case, the total proceeds at maturity – principal plus interest – are 98.436 + 1.564 = 100.00.

This means that we invested 98.436 to receive (98.436 + 1.564) = 100 at the end of 58 days. If the same investment were made in a discount instrument, the *face value* of the instrument would be 100, and the *amount of discount* would be 1.564. In this case, the *discount rate* is the discount expressed as an annualized percentage of the face value – paid at maturity – rather than as a percentage of the original amount paid. In this case, the discount rate is therefore:

$$(1.564 \div 100) \times \frac{365}{58} = 9.84\%$$

The discount rate is always less than the corresponding yield. In general, the discount rate $D$ is given by:

$$D = \frac{i}{1 + i \times \frac{days}{year}}$$

where $i$ is the yield.
Similarly,

$$i = \frac{D}{1 - D \times \frac{days}{year}}$$

If the discount rate on an instrument is $D$, then the amount of discount to be paid is:

$$F \times D \times \frac{days}{year}$$

where $F$ is the face value of the instrument.
The price $P$ to be paid is the face value less the discount:

$$P = F \times \left(1 - D \times \frac{days}{year}\right)$$

Similarly,

$$D = \left(1 - \frac{P}{F}\right) \times \frac{year}{days}$$

Instruments quoted on a discount basis in the US and UK include Treasury bills, and trade bills, while a yield basis is used for loans, deposits, and CDs. US CP is also quoted on a discount rate basis, while ECP and sterling CP are quoted on a yield basis.

---

**Example 2.4**

A US Treasury bill of $1 million is issued for 91 days at a discount rate of 6.5 percent. What is the amount of the discount and the price paid?

Amount of discount = $1 million $\times 0.065 \times \frac{91}{360}$ = $16,430.56

Price paid = face value − discount = $ 983,569.44

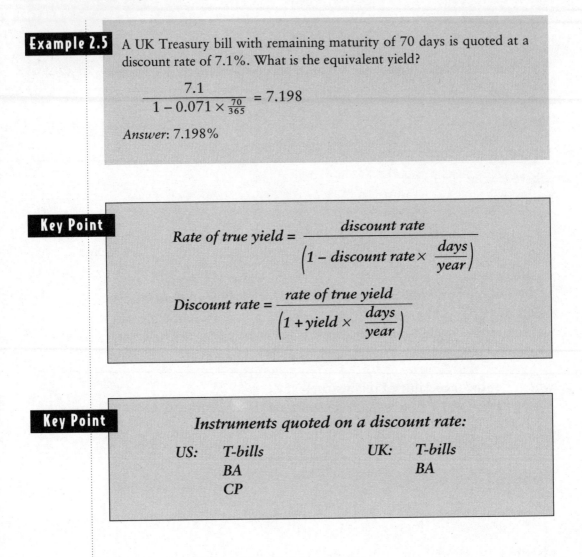

**Example 2.5** A UK Treasury bill with remaining maturity of 70 days is quoted at a discount rate of 7.1%. What is the equivalent yield?

$$\frac{7.1}{1 - 0.071 \times \frac{70}{365}} = 7.198$$

*Answer: 7.198%*

**Key Point**

$$Rate\ of\ true\ yield = \frac{discount\ rate}{\left(1 - discount\ rate \times \dfrac{days}{year}\right)}$$

$$Discount\ rate = \frac{rate\ of\ true\ yield}{\left(1 + yield \times \dfrac{days}{year}\right)}$$

**Key Point**

*Instruments quoted on a discount rate:*

| US: | T-bills | UK: | T-bills |
|-----|---------|-----|---------|
|     | BA      |     | BA      |
|     | CP      |     |         |

# FORWARD-FORWARDS, FRAS, AND FUTURES

## Overview

Forward-forwards, forward rate agreements (FRAs), and futures are very similar and closely linked instruments, all relating to an interest rate applied to some period which starts in the future. We shall first define them here and then examine each more closely.

A **forward-forward** is a cash borrowing or deposit which starts on one forward date and ends on another forward date. The term, amount, and interest rate are all fixed in advance.

An **FRA** is an off-balance sheet instrument which can achieve the same economic effect as a forward-forward. Someone who expects to borrow cash in the future can buy an FRA to fix in advance the interest rate on the borrowing. When the time to borrow arrives, he or she borrows the cash in the usual way. Under the FRA, which remains quite separate, the borrower receives or pays the difference between the cash borrowing rate and the FRA rate, so achieving the same net effect as with forward-forward borrowing.

A **futures** contract is similar to an FRA – an off-balance sheet contract for the difference between the cash borrowing rate and the agreed futures rate. Futures are traded only on an exchange, however, and differ from FRAs in a variety of technical ways.

## Pricing a forward-forward

Suppose that the three-month sterling interest rate is 13.0 percent and the six-month rate is 13.1 percent. If I borrow £100 for six months and simultaneously deposit it for three months, I have created a *net* borrowing which begins in three months and ends in six. The position over the first three months is a net zero one. If I undertake these two transactions at the same time, I have created a forward-forward borrowing – that is, a borrowing which starts on one forward date and ends on another.

If I deposit £1 for 91 days at 13 percent, then at the end of the 91 days I receive:

$$£1 + 0.13 \times \frac{91}{365} = £1.03241$$

If I borrow £1 for 183 days at 13.1 percent, then at the end of the 183 days I must repay:

$$£1 + 0.131 \times \frac{183}{365} = £1.06568$$

My cashflows are: an inflow of £1.03241 after 91 days and an outflow of £1.06568 after 183 days. What is the cost of this forward-forward borrowing? The calculation is exactly the same as when working out a yield in chapter 1:

$$\text{cost} = \left(\frac{\text{cash outflow at the end}}{\text{cash inflow at the start}} - 1\right) \times \frac{\text{year}}{\text{days}} = \left(\frac{1.06568}{1.03241} - 1\right) \times \frac{365}{92} = 12.79\%$$

In general:

**Key Point**

$$\textit{Forward} - \textit{Forward rate} = \left[\frac{\left(1 + R_L \times \dfrac{d_L}{Y}\right)}{\left(1 + R_S \times \dfrac{d_S}{Y}\right)} - 1\right] \times \left(\frac{Y}{d_L - d_S}\right)$$

where $R_L$     =     interest rate for longer period
$R_S$     =     interest rate for shorter period
$d_L$     =     number of days in longer period
$d_S$     =     number of days in shorter period
$Y$     =     number of days in conventional year.

# Forward rate agreements (FRAs)

An FRA is an off-balance sheet agreement to make a settlement in the future with the same economic effect as a forward-forward.

**An FRA is therefore an agreement to pay or receive, on an agreed future date, the difference between an agreed interest rate and the interest rate actually prevailing on that future date, calculated on an agreed notional principal amount. It is settled against the actual interest rate prevailing at the beginning of the period to which it relates, rather than paid as a gross amount.**

## Pricing

In calculating a theoretical FRA price, we can apply exactly the same ideas as in the forward-forward calculation above. As we are not actually borrowing cash with the FRA, however, we will use middle rates for both the six-month and the three-month periods – rather than separate bid and offered rates. Conventionally, FRAs are always

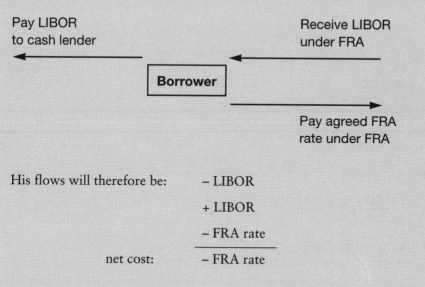

Example 2.6

A borrower intends to borrow cash at LIBOR from 91 days forward to 183 days forward, and he fixes the cost with an FRA. His costs will be as follows:

Pay LIBOR to cash lender

Receive LIBOR under FRA

Borrower

Pay agreed FRA rate under FRA

His flows will therefore be:

    – LIBOR

    + LIBOR

    – FRA rate

net cost:    – FRA rate

If the cash is actually borrowed at a different rate – say LIBOR + $\frac{1}{4}$% – then the net cost will be (FRA rate + $\frac{1}{4}$%), but the all-in cost is still fixed.

settled against LIBOR. We will therefore need to make an adjustment – generally around $\frac{1}{16}$ percent – to this theoretical "middle price" forward-forward.

## Settlement

In the example of pricing a forward-forward (*see* page 30), the FRA rate could be calculated as 12.79 percent + 0.06 percent = 12.85 percent. Suppose that the actual three-month LIBOR, in three months' time, is 11.5 percent. Settlement then takes place between these two rates. On a principal of £100, the effective interest settlement would be:

$$£100 \times (0.1285 - 0.1150) \times \tfrac{92}{365} = £0.3403$$

Conventionally however, this settlement takes place at the *beginning* of the three-month borrowing period. It is therefore discounted to a present value at the *current* three-month rate for this settlement:

$$\frac{£100 \times (0.1285 - 0.1150) \times \frac{92}{365}}{1 + 0.1150 \times \frac{92}{365}} = £0.3307$$

In general, the settlement amount is:

**Key Point**

$$\frac{P \times (R - L) \times \dfrac{d}{y}}{\left(1 + L \times \dfrac{d}{y}\right)}$$

Alternatively:

$$\frac{P \times (R - L) \times d}{L \times d + y}$$

where (in either case):

| | | |
|---|---|---|
| $P$ | = | notional principal |
| $R$ | = | FRA rate |
| $L$ | = | interest rate prevailing at the beginning of the period to which the FRA relates |
| $d$ | = | number of days in the FRA period |
| $y$ | = | number of days in the conventional year. |

## Interest rate futures

In general, a futures contract in any market is a contract in which the commodity being bought and sold is to be delivered (at least theoretically) not immediately but at some future date – hence the name. The significant differences between a "futures contract" and a "forward" arise in two ways. First, a futures contract is always traded on a particular exchange (although two or more exchanges might trade identically specified contracts). A forward, however, which is also a deal for delivery on a future date, is dealt "over the counter" (OTC) – a deal made between any two parties, not on an exchange. Second, futures contracts are generally standardized, while forwards are not. The specifications of each futures contract are laid down precisely by the relevant exchange and vary from commodity to commodity and from exchange to exchange. Some contracts, for example, specifically do not allow for the commodity to be delivered; although their prices are calculated as if future delivery takes place, the contracts must be reversed before the notional delivery date, thereby capturing a profit or a loss. Interest rate futures, for example, cannot be delivered, whereas bond futures can.

The theory underlying the pricing of a futures contract depends on the underlying "commodity" on which the contract is based. For a futures contract based on three-month interest rates, for example, the pricing is based on forward-forward pricing theory, in the same way as FRAs. Bond futures pricing theory is explained in chapter 3.

The principle – and the different characteristics – of interest rate and currency futures are most easily understood by an example:

---

Three-month euro-DEM interest rate futures contract traded on LIFFE **Example 2.7**

**Exchange** LIFFE (London International Financial Futures and Options Exchange), where a variety of futures and options contracts on interest rates, bonds, and equities is traded.

**Commodity** The basis of the contract is a deposit of DEM 1 million (euro-DEM) lasting for 90 days.

**Delivery** It is not permitted for this contract to be delivered; a trader who buys such a contract cannot insist that, on the future delivery date, the counterparty makes arrangements for the trader to have a deposit for 90 days from then onwards at the interest rate agreed. Rather, the trader must reverse the futures contract before delivery, thereby taking a profit or loss.

**Delivery date** The contract must be based on a notional delivery date. In this case, the delivery date must be the first business day before the third Wednesday of March, June, September, or December.

**Trading** It is possible to trade the contract until 11:00 am on the last business day before the delivery day. Trading hours are from 08:00 to 16:10 each business day in London for "open outcry" (physical trading, face to face on the exchange), and from 16:29 to 17:59 for "APT" (automated pit trading – computerized trading outside the exchange).

**Price** The price is determined by the free market and is quoted as an index rather than an interest rate. The index is expressed as 100 minus the implied interest rate. Thus a price of 93.52 implies an interest rate of 6.48 percent (100 – 93.52 = 6.48).

**2.7 Cont'd**

**Price movement** Prices are quoted to two decimal places and can move by as little as 0.01. This minimum movement is called a "tick" and is equivalent to a profit or loss of DEM 25. This is calculated as:

$$\text{Amount of contract} \times \text{price movement} \times \frac{\text{days}}{\text{year}}$$

$$= \text{DEM 1 million} \times 0.01\% \times \frac{90}{360} = \text{DEM 25}$$

**Settlement price** At the close of trading, LIFFE declares an "Exchange Delivery Settlement Price" (EDSP), which is the closing price at which any contracts still outstanding will be automatically reversed. The EDSP is 100 minus the BBAISR (British Bankers' Association Interest Settlement Rate).

In practice, an FRA trader will in fact generally take his price from the futures market (which may not be precisely in line with the theoretical calculations), rather than directly from the forward-forward calculation. This is because FRA traders would use the futures market rather than a forward-forward to hedge their FRA book – because of both the balance sheet implications and the transaction costs. In practice, therefore, the FRA rate will be (100 – futures price).

One important practical difference between FRAs and futures is in the settlement mechanics. The FRA settlement is paid at the beginning of the notional borrowing period, and is discounted to a present value. The futures "settlement" – the profit or loss on the contract – is also all settled by the same date, via "margin" payments (discussed below) made during the period from transaction until the futures delivery date. However, in most futures markets this settlement is *not discounted*. A 90-day FRA cannot therefore be exactly matched by an offsetting futures contract, even if the amounts and dates are the same.

A second important difference is that FRAs and futures are "in opposite directions." A *buyer* of an FRA will profit if interest rates rise. A *buyer* of a futures contract will profit if interest rates fall. A trader selling an FRA to a counterparty must therefore also *sell* a futures contract to cover the position.

# OTC v. exchange-traded

It is worthwhile summarizing the differences between OTC contracts, such as an FRA, and futures contracts.

**Comparison**

**Amount** The amount of a futures contract is standardized. The amount of an OTC deal is entirely flexible.

**Delivery date** The delivery date of a futures contract is standardized. The delivery date of an OTC deal is entirely flexible.

**Margin** Dealing in futures requires the payment of collateral (called "initial margin") as security. When trading OTC, professional traders usually deal on the basis of credit lines, with no security required. In addition, "variation margin" is paid or received each day to reflect the day's loss or profit on futures contracts held.

**Settlement** Settlement on an instrument such as an FRA is discounted to a present value. Settlement on a futures contract, because it is paid through variation margin, is not discounted.

**Credit risk** The margin system ensures that the exchange clearing house is generally fully protected against the risk of default. As the counter-party to each futures contract is the clearing house, there is therefore usually virtually no credit risk in dealing futures. OTC counterparties are generally not of the same creditworthiness.

**Delivery** Some futures contracts are not deliverable and must be cash set-tled. It is generally possible to arrange any OTC deal to include delivery.

**Liquidity and spread** Standardization and transparency generally ensure a liquid market in futures contracts, together with narrower spreads between bid and offer than in OTC deals. For delivery dates far in the future, on the other hand, there may be insufficient liquidity in the futures market, where an OTC price may be available.

**Underlying commodity** Futures contracts are not available in all underlying commodities. For example, there is no ringgit/peseta futures contract but a ringgit/peseta forward is easily available.

# The short-term yield curve

A "yield curve" shows how interest rates vary with term to maturity. For example, a Reuters screen might show the following rates:

| | |
|---|---|
| 1 month | 9.5% |
| 2 months | 9.7% |
| 3 months | 10.0% |
| 6 months | 10.0% |
| 12 months | 10.2% |
| 2 years | 10.5% |

In a free market these rates show where the market on average believes rates "should" be, as supply and demand would otherwise tend to move the rates up or down. Clearly the rates at some maturity level or levels are influenced by central bank policy. If the market believes that the central bank is about to change official three-month rates, for example, this expectation will already have been factored into the market three-month rate.

If the three-month maturity is indeed the rate manipulated by the central bank for this particular currency, a more logical curve to look at might be one that shows what the market expects three-month rates to be at certain times in the future. For example, what is the three-month rate now, what will it be after one month, after two months, after three months, etc. Given enough such rates, it is possible to work "backwards" to construct the yield curve shown above.

Suppose, for example that the three-month rate now is 10.0 percent and the market expects that there will be a 0.25 percent cut in rates during the next three months – so that at the end of three months, the three-month rate will be 9.75 percent. Given these data, what should the six-month rate be now?

The answer must be the rate achieved by taking the three-month rate now, compounded with the expected three-month rate in three months' time; otherwise there would be an expected profit in going long for three months and short for six months or vice versa, and the market would tend to move the rates. In this way, the six-month rate now could be calculated as:

$$\left[\left(1 + 0.10 \times \frac{91}{360}\right) \times \left(1 + 0.0975 \times \frac{92}{360}\right) - 1\right] \times \frac{360}{183} = 10.00\%$$

This rate is in fact the rate shown in the "screen list" above. If we now work in the other direction, we would find that the forward-forward rate from three months to six months ("3 v. 6") would be 9.75 percent as expected:

$$\left[\frac{(1 + 0.10 \times \frac{183}{360})}{(1 + 0.10 \times \frac{91}{360})} - 1\right] \times \frac{360}{92} = 9.75\%$$

This shows that a "flat" short-term yield curve – in our example, the three-month and six-month rates are the same at 10.0 percent – does not imply that the market expects interest rates to remain stable. Rather, it expects them to fall.

The important point here is to consider the question of which comes first. Are forward-forward rates (and hence futures prices and FRA rates) the mathematical result of the yield curve? Or are the market's expectations of future rates (i.e. forward-forwards, futures, and FRAs) the starting point, and from these it is possible to create the yield curve? The question is a circular one to some extent, but market traders increasingly look at constructing a yield curve from expected future rates for various periods and maturities.

## Applications of FRAs and futures

As with any instrument, FRAs and futures may be used for hedging, speculating, or arbitrage, depending on whether they are taken to offset an existing underlying position or taken as new positions themselves.

### Hedging

A company has a five-year borrowing with three-monthly rollovers – that is, every three months, the interest rate is refixed at the prevailing three-month LIBOR. The company expects interest rates to rise before the next rollover date. It therefore buys an FRA to start on the next rollover date and finish three months later. If the next rollover date is two months away, this would be a "2 v. 5" FRA. If the company is correct and interest rates do rise, the next rollover will cost more, but the company will make a profit on the FRA settlement to offset this. If rates fall, however, the next rollover will be cheaper but the company will make an offsetting loss on the FRA settlement. The FRA settlement profit or loss will of course depend on how the three-month rate stands after two months compared with the FRA rate now, not compared with the cash rate now. Either way, the net effect will be that the company's borrowing cost will be locked in at the FRA rate (plus the normal margin which it pays on its credit facility):

**Example 2.8**

**2.8 Cont'd**

| Company pays | LIBOR + margin | to lending bank |
|---|---|---|
| Company pays | FRA rate | to FRA counterparty |
| Company receives | LIBOR | from FRA counterparty |
| Net cost | FRA rate + margin | |

The FRA payments are in practice netted and also settled at the beginning of the borrowing period after discounting. The economic effect is still as shown.

**Example 2.9**

A company expects to make a six-month deposit in two weeks' time and fears that interest rates may fall. The company therefore sells a 2-week v. $6\frac{1}{2}$ month FRA. Exactly as in Example 2.8, but in reverse, the company will thereby lock in the deposit rate. Although the company may expect to receive LIBID on its actual deposit, the FRA will always be settled against LIBOR:

| Company receives | LIBID | from deposit |
|---|---|---|
| Company receives | FRA rate | from FRA counterparty |
| Company pays | LIBOR | to FRA counterparty |
| Net return | FRA rate – (LIBOR – LIBID) | |

As the FRA rate is theoretically calculated to be comparable to LIBOR, it is reasonable to expect the net return to be correspondingly lower than the FRA rate by the (LIBID – LIBOR) spread.

## Speculation

The most basic trading strategy is to use an FRA or a futures contract to speculate on the cash interest rate on maturity of the futures contract being higher or lower than the interest rate implied in the futures price now. If traders expect interest rates to rise, they buy an FRA or sell the futures contract; if they expect rates to fall, they sell an FRA or buy the futures contract.

**Example 2.10**

A bank with no position expects interest rates to rise. The bank therefore buys an FRA. If rates rise above the FRA rate it will make a profit; otherwise it will make a loss.

## Arbitrage

Example 2.11

Market prices are currently as follows:

| | |
|---|---|
| 2 v. 5 FRA | 7.22–7.27% |
| 3-month futures | 92.67–92.68 |

A bank can arbitrage between these two prices by dealing at 7.27% in the FRA and at 92.68 in the futures market. It buys the FRA and is therefore effectively paying an agreed 7.27% in two months' time. It also buys the futures contract and is therefore effectively receiving (100 − 92.68)% = 7.32%. The bank has therefore locked in a profit of 5 basis points.

In practice, Example 2.11 will be complicated by several factors. First, there is the problem that the FRA settlement is discounted but the futures settlement is generally not. The bank needs to decrease slightly the number of futures contracts traded to adjust for this.

Second, the period of the 2 v. 5 FRA might be, for example, 92 days, while the futures contract specification is 90 days and the two settlements will reflect this. The bank needs to increase slightly the number of futures contracts traded to adjust for this.

Third, the futures delivery date is unlikely to coincide with the start date of the 2 v. 5 FRA period, which gives rise to a "basis" risk. The bank will therefore need to adjust for this also. If the nearest futures date is earlier than two months, it could buy some futures for the nearest futures date and some for the following date, in a ratio dependent on the time between the two futures dates and the two-month date. If the nearest futures date is later than two months, the bank could buy all the futures for that date and then superimpose another futures trade as an approximate hedge against the basis risk. This hedge involves buying more futures for the nearest date and selling futures for the following date.

# EXERCISES

**8.** I invest in a 181-day sterling CD with a face value of £1,000,000 and a coupon of 11%, when it is issued. What are the total maturity proceeds?

**9.** Instead of buying the CD in Question 8 when it is issued, I buy it 47 days after issue, for a yield of 10%. What amount do I pay for the CD?

**10.** I buy the CD in Question 9 and then sell it again after holding it for only 63 days (between purchase and sale), at a yield to the new purchaser of 9.5%. What yield have I earned on my whole investment?

**11.** I purchase some sterling euro-commercial paper as follows:

| | |
|---|---|
| Purchase value date: | July 2, 1996 |
| Maturity value date: | September 2, 1996 |
| Yield: | 8.2% |
| Amount: | £2,000,000.00 |

What do I pay for the paper?

**12.** An investor seeks a yield of 9.5% on a sterling 1 million 60-day BA. What is the discount rate and the amount of this discount?

**13.** If the discount rate were in fact 9.5%, what would the yield and the amount paid for the BA be?

**14.** If the amount paid is in fact £975,000.00, what is the discount rate?

**15.** The rate quoted for a 91-day US Treasury bill is 6.5%.

a. What is the amount paid for US$1,000,000.00 of this T-bill?

b. What is the equivalent true yield?

**16.** I buy a US Treasury bill 176 days before it matures at a discount rate of 7% and sell it again at a discount rate of 6.7% after holding it for 64 days. What yield have I achieved on a 365-day year basis? (US Treasury bills are traded on a 360-day basis.)

**17.** The rate quoted for a 91-day T-bill is 5% in the US, UK, Belgium, and France. Each T-bill has a face value of 1 million of the local currency. What is the amount paid for the bill in each country?

**18.** Place the following instruments in descending order of yield, working from the rates quoted:

| | |
|---|---|
| 30-day UK T-bill (£) | $8\frac{1}{4}\%$ |
| 30-day UK CP (£) | $8\frac{3}{16}\%$ |
| 30-day ECP (£) | $8\frac{1}{8}\%$ |
| 30-day US T-bill | $8\frac{5}{16}\%$ |
| 30-day interbank deposit (£) | $8\frac{1}{4}\%$ |
| 30-day US CP | $8\frac{1}{2}\%$ |
| 30-day US$ CD | $8\frac{5}{8}\%$ |
| 30-day French T-bill | $8\frac{1}{2}\%$ |

**19.** Current market rates are as follows for the Swedish krona (SEK).

| | SEK |
|---|---|
| 3 months (91 days) | 9.87–10.00% |
| 6 months (182 days) | 10.12–10.25% |
| 9 months (273 days) | 10.00–10.12% |

What is the theoretical FRA 3 v. 9 for SEK now (based on cash market middle rates)?

■ ■ ■

*"Bonds are long-term – hence 'capital market' – debt instruments, typically with maturities from 5 years to 30 years . . ."*

# Bond Market Basics

# OVERVIEW

We have already considered short-term securities issued in the money market. Long-term securities are considered as "capital market" instruments rather than money market ones. Capital market issues share with commercial paper the feature that they normally involve lending directly from the investor to the borrower without the inter-mediation of a credit analysis specialist – that is, a bank. As a result of this disintermediation, only companies of very high creditworthiness – or governments, quasi-governmental bodies, and supranational bodies – can usually borrow from the capital markets. Those that do so, however, can raise finance more cheaply than they could on the same terms from a bank, because of investor demand for the securities.

# BOND PRICING

**Bonds are long-term – hence "capital market" – debt instruments, typically with maturities from 5 years to 30 years, although some are issued with maturities of less than 5 years and (rarely) with greater than 30 years.**

We have already seen that for a given interest rate every future cashflow $C$ has a present value, equal to:

$$\frac{C}{(1+i)^N}$$

where $i$ is the annual interest rate and $N$ is the number of years ahead that the cashflow occurs.

Given a series of cashflows – some of which could in theory be negative and some positive – the "net present value" of the whole series is the sum of all the present values.

The principles of pricing in the bond market are the same as the principles of pricing in other financial markets – the price paid for a bond now is the net present value now of all the bond's future cashflows which arise from holding the bond. The price is in fact always expressed as the price for 100 units of the bond.

In general, therefore, the theoretical price $P$ of a straightforward bond should be given by:

$$P = \sum_k \frac{C_k}{\left(1 + \dfrac{i}{n \times 100}\right)^{\frac{d_k \times n}{y}}}$$

where
$\begin{aligned}
C_k &= &&\text{the } k^{\text{th}} \text{ cashflow arising} \\
d_k &= &&\text{number of days until } C_k \\
i &= &&\text{yield on the basis of } n \text{ interest payments per year} \\
y &= &&\text{number of days in the conventional year.}
\end{aligned}$

If this formula looks frightening, don't worry! Bond prices are not normally calculated by hand – generally a host of computerized sources of prices is available. The important thing to note here is the concept that the all-in price of a bond equals the NPV of its future cashflows.

---

*All-in price of a bond = NPV of the bond's future cashflows*   **Key Point**

---

There are four small but significant differences in practice between pricing calculations for a bond price and the price of a money market instrument such as a CD. Again, you do not need to be able to make these calculations by hand, but the differences are instructive in understanding the ideas behind bond pricing:

1. The coupon actually paid on a CD is calculated on the basis of the exact number of days between issue and maturity. With a bond, the coupons paid each year or half-year (or occasionally each quarter) are paid as fixed "round" amounts. For example, if a 10 percent coupon bond pays semi-annual coupons, exactly 5 percent will be paid each half-year regardless of the exact number of days involved (which will change according to weekends and leap years, for example).

---

*Bond coupons are paid in round amounts, unlike CD coupons which are calculated to the exact day*   **Key Point**

---

2. When discounting to a present value, it is again assumed that the time periods between coupons are "round" amounts – 0.5 years, 1 year, etc. – rather than an odd number of days.

3. When discounting back to a present value from the next coupon payment date, the yield calculation is made on the basis of compound rather than simple interest. Suppose, for example there is a cashflow of 105 occurring 78 days in the future, the yield is 6 percent and the year-count basis is 360. The present value calculation for a CD would be $\frac{105}{(1 + 0.06 \times \frac{78}{360})}$, which uses the 6 percent yield for 78 days on a simple basis. The corresponding calculation for a bond would be $\frac{105}{(1 + 0.06)^{\frac{78}{360}}}$, which compounds the 6 percent yield for $\frac{78}{360}$ of a year.

4. The day/year count basis for money market instruments and bonds is generally different. The first have been described earlier. The day/year counts for bonds are described later in this chapter.

Given these differences, it is possible to give an equation for a bond price as follows:

$$P = \frac{100}{A^Q} \left( \frac{R}{n} \times \frac{(1 - \frac{1}{A^N})}{(1 - \frac{1}{A})} + \frac{1}{A^{(N-1)}} \right)$$

where  $R$ = the annualized coupon rate paid $n$ times per year
$Q$ = the fraction of an interest period between purchase and the first coupon received
$N$ = the number of coupon payments outstanding
$A$ = $\left(1 + \frac{i}{n}\right)$
$i$ = annualized yield based on $n$ payments per year.

## Accrued coupon

The price we have calculated so far is in fact known as the "dirty" price of the bond and represents the *total* amount of cash paid now by the buyer. The seller, however, expects to receive "accrued" coupon on the bond.

**The accrued coupon is the coupon which the seller of a bond has "earned" so far by holding the bond since the last coupon date.**

Clearly the seller feels entitled to this portion of the coupon and therefore insists on the bond buyer paying it. The buyer, however, will pay no more in total than the NPV of all the future cashflows. Therefore the *total* price paid is the dirty price but this is effectively considered as two separate amounts, the "clean" price and the accrued coupon. The price quoted in the market is the "clean" price, which is equal to dirty price *minus* the accrued coupon.

In this book we usually refer to the "accrued coupon" on a bond, but to "accrued interest" on money market instruments, including repos. This is because in repo calculations the two need to be distinguished. In the market generally, however, "accrued coupon" is often called "accrued interest" also.

---

Example 3.1

A bond pays a 9% coupon annually. Maturity is on August 15, 2003. The current market yield for the bond is 8%. Interest is calculated on a 30(E)/360 basis (see later in this chapter for an explanation of this convention.) What are the accrued coupon, dirty price, and clean price for settlement on June 12, 1996?

*Answer*:

Time from August 15, 1995 to June 12, 1996 is 297 days on a 30(E) basis:

$$\text{Accrued coupon} = 9 \times \frac{297}{360} = 7.4250$$

Time from June 12, 1996 to August 15, 1996 is 63 days on a 30(E) basis:

$$\text{Dirty price} = \frac{100}{1.08^{63/360}} \times \left( 0.09 \times \frac{\left(1 - \dfrac{1}{1.08^8}\right)}{\left(1 - \dfrac{1}{1.08}\right)} + \frac{1}{1.08^7} \right) = 112.6785$$

Clean price = 112.6785 – 7.4250 = 105.25

---

Key Point

*Dirty price = NPV of cashflows*

*Accrued coupon = proportion of coupon since last coupon payment*

*Clean price = dirty price – accrued coupon*

---

## Price sensitivity and zero-coupon bonds

In the money markets a Treasury bill is a short-term instrument which pays no coupon and is therefore always priced at a discount to the face value. In the same way, in the capital markets it is possible to have a bond which pays no coupon and is similarly priced at a discount to face value. This is a zero-coupon bond.

A zero-coupon bond can of course be used as the security in a repo. One slight drawback, however, is that a zero-coupon bond is more price-sensitive than a coupon-paying bond of the same maturity. Generally, the following are true:

- For a given coupon rate, the shorter the maturity of a bond the less volatile the bond's price.

- For a given maturity, the higher the coupon, the less volatile the bond's price.

As a result, the lender of cash in a repo transaction may wish to take a greater amount of collateral if it is a long-maturity bond paying a low or zero coupon, than if it is a short-maturity bond paying a high coupon.

# DAY/YEAR CONVENTIONS

Accrued coupon and fractional periods of a year are calculated according to different conventions in different markets, and generally expressed in the form "$d/y$" where $d$ is the conventional number of days in a particular period and $y$ is the conventional number of days in a year.

In general, the convention for accrued coupon in a particular market is the same as the convention used in that market for calculating the fraction of a year for the yield formula. This is not always so, however. In Italy, for example, accrued coupon is calculated on a 30(E)/360 basis, but yield is calculated on an ACT/365 basis.

## Calculation of days in the period ("$d$")

**ACT** The actual number of days in the period. This method is used for gilts and JGBs (Japanese government bonds).

**30(E)** Calculate the number of days between the two dates $d_1/m_1/y_1$ and $d_2/m_2/y_2$ assuming 30-day months, as follows:

   If $d_1$ is 31, change to 30.
   If $d_2$ is 31, change to 30.

Then the number of days between the two dates is given by:

$$(y_2 - y_1) \times 360 + (m_2 - m_1) \times 30 + (d_2 - d_1)$$

Thus there are 29 days between May 1 and May 30 and also 29 days between May 1 and May 31. This method is used in the Euromarkets and some European domestic markets.

**30(A)** This method is used for US Federal Agency and corporate bonds. It is similar to 30(E), but with the following difference:

If $d_2$ is 31 and $d_1$ is 30 or 31, change $d_2$ to 30.
Otherwise leave $d_2$ at 31.

The number of days between the two dates is then again given by:

$$(y_2 - y_1) \times 360 + (m_2 - m_1) \times 30 + (d_2 - d_1)$$

Thus there are 29 days between May 1 and May 30 but 30 days between May 1 and May 31.

## Calculation of year basis ("$y$")

**365** Assume 365 days in a year. This method is used for gilts and JGBs.

**360** Assume 360 days in a year. This method is used for Eurobonds.

**ACT** Takes the actual number of days in the current coupon period multiplied by the number of coupon payments per year. This method is used for US Treasury notes and bonds, which always pay coupons semi-annually, and results in a value for ACT of 362, 364, 366 or 368 (twice the coupon period of 181, 182, 183, or 184). It is also used for French government bonds, which pay coupons annually, resulting in a value for ACT of 365 or 366.

---

**Example 3.2**

Consider a bond whose last coupon was due on January 15, 1997 and whose next coupon is due on July 15, 1997. The number of days in the current coupon period is 181. The day/year calculation under the various conventions is shown below for accrued coupon from January 15 up to March 30, March 31 and April 1 respectively:

|  | March 30 | March 31 | April 1 |
|---|---|---|---|
| ACT/365 | 74/365 | 75/365 | 76/365 |
| ACT/360 | 74/360 | 75/360 | 76/360 |
| 30(E)/360 | 75/360 | 75/360 | 76/360 |
| 30(A)/360 | 75/360 | 76/360 | 76/360 |
| ACT/ACT | 74/362 | 75/362 | 76/362 |

---

*We give a list of the conventions used in some important markets in Appendix 2.*

# BOND FUTURES

**A bond futures contract is an agreement whereby the seller must deliver to the buyer an agreed amount of a bond at an agreed time, for an agreed price.**

In practice, bond futures contracts are generally closed out before maturity in the same way that short-term futures contracts are, and the profit/loss is captured through variation margins. In theory, however, a bond futures buyer can insist on delivery of a bond at maturity of the futures contract. There are several complications which do not arise in the case of short-term interest rate futures.

## Bond specification

For practical reasons, a bond futures contract must be based on a precisely specified bond, in the same way that a short-term interest rate futures contract is based precisely on a 90-day deposit. Such a precisely defined bond cannot exist, however, as any such bond, if it existed on one day, would not exist the next day because its maturity would have altered slightly. Furthermore, coupons of actual bonds tend to change with each issue. Bond futures prices are therefore based on a *notional* bond index rather than an actual one, which means that the specification can remain unchanged over time. In the case of a US T-bond futures, for example, the bond specified is a fictional 8 percent bond of at least 15 years' maturity.

## Deliverable bonds and conversion factors

The seller of the futures contract cannot of course deliver this fictional bond. Instead, the seller is usually entitled to deliver any one of a range of bonds which is defined in the specifications for the futures contract. In this case, it is the seller who chooses which bond to deliver to the buyer. In the case of US T-bond futures, for example, the seller may deliver any bond maturing at least 15 years from the first day of the delivery month if the bond is not callable. If it is callable, the earliest call date must be at least 15 years from the first day of the delivery month.

Because the different deliverable bonds have different coupons and maturities, they need to be put on a common basis. The futures exchange therefore publishes a "price factor" or "conversion factor" for each deliverable bond. In the case of a T-bond, this is the price per $1 nominal value of the specific bond at which the bond has a gross redemption yield of 8 percent on the first day of the delivery month (i.e. it has the same yield as the fictional coupon underlying the contract). The maturity of the deliverable bond is found by measuring the time from the first day of the delivery month to the maturity of the bond (first call day if callable) and rounding down to the nearest quarter.

On the delivery day, the specific bond nominated by the seller will be delivered and the seller will receive from the buyer the relevant invoicing amount. The invoicing amount is based on the "Exchange Delivery Settlement Price" (EDSP) and the size of the futures contract ($100,000 in the case of a T-bond futures):

Invoicing amount =

$$(\frac{EDSP}{100} \times \text{conversion factor} \times \$100,000) + \text{accrued coupon}$$

This choice of deliverable bonds also gives rise to the concept of "cheapest to deliver": sellers will always choose to deliver whichever bond is the cheapest for them to do so – known as the "cheapest to deliver" or "CTD" bond.

> *A bond futures contract is based on a notional bond index. The real bonds deliverable into the contract are made comparable by their conversion factors*

**Key Point**

## Delivery date

Delivery specifications vary between futures contracts and exchanges. In the case of a T-bond futures, for example, the seller is entitled to deliver on any business day in the delivery month. Clearly the seller will deliver later if the coupon is higher than the cost of funding the position and earlier if the coupon is lower.

## Dividends

If there is an intervening dividend payment on the actual bond which the futures seller expects to deliver, this will be taken into account in calculating the futures price.

## Pricing

The theoretical futures price depends on the elimination of arbitrage. The seller of a futures contract, if delivering a bond at maturity of the

Basics

tures contract, will receive the invoicing amount on delivery. The ler will also receive any interim coupon plus interest earned on the upon between receipt of the coupon and delivery of the bond to the futures buyer.

In order to hedge themselves, futures sellers must buy the bond in the cash market at the same time as they sell the futures contract. For this they must pay the current bond price plus accrued coupon. This total amount must be funded from the time they buy the bond until the time they deliver it to the futures buyer. Combining these various cashflows, and assuming that the futures seller makes zero profit/loss, the following should hold:

(Bond price now + accrued coupon now) funded at $i$ for $d$ days

= ([futures price × conversion factor] + accrued coupon at maturity of futures) + (any interim coupon + interest earned on it)

From this, it follows that the theoretical futures price equals:

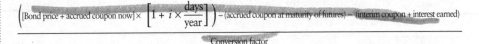

$$\frac{\left([\text{Bond price} + \text{accrued coupon now}] \times \left[1 + i \times \dfrac{\text{days}}{\text{year}}\right]\right) - (\text{accrued coupon at maturity of futures}) - (\text{interim coupon} + \text{interest earned})}{\text{Conversion factor}}$$

**Example 3.3**

What is the theoretical September T-bond futures price on June 18 if the cheapest-to-deliver bond is the Treasury $12\frac{3}{4}$% 2020, trading at 142-09 (i.e. $142\frac{9}{32}$)? The conversion factor for the 2020 is 1.4546. Coupon dates are May 15 and November 15. Short-term funds can be borrowed at 6.45%.

*Answer*:

Payment for the bond purchased by the futures seller to hedge the futures sale is made on June 19. Coupon on the purchase of the bond is accrued for 35 days. The current coupon period is 184 days. Therefore:

Accrued coupon now = 12.75 × 35/368 = 1.212636

Assume that delivery of the bond to the futures buyer requires payment to the futures seller on September 30. The futures seller must then fund his or her position from June 19 to September 30 (103 actual days) and coupon on the sale of the bond will then be accrued for 138 days.

3.3 Cont'd

Therefore:

Accrued coupon then $= 12.75 \times \dfrac{138}{368} = 4.781250$

Theoretical futures price $=$

$$\dfrac{(142.281250 + 1.212636) \times (1 + 0.0645 \times \frac{103}{360}) - 4.781250}{1.4546}$$

$$= \quad 97.1818$$

$$= \quad 97\text{-}06 \text{ (i.e. } 97\tfrac{6}{32})$$

# EXERCISES

**20.** I buy the following bond for settlement on a coupon payment date. What is the cost of the bond?

| | |
|---|---|
| Amount: | FRF 100,000,000.00 |
| Remaining maturity: | 3 years |
| Coupon: | 8.0% |
| Yield: | 7.0% |

**21.** What is the accrued coupon on July 28, 1997 on the following bonds?

**a.** 7.5% gilt 2005 — Maturity December 7, 2005
**b.** 5.625% US Treasury bond 2005 — Maturity August 15, 2005
**c.** 6.25% Bund 2005 — Maturity October 26, 2005
**d.** 7.25% OAT 2005 — Maturity October 25, 2005
**e.** 3.00% JGB 2005 number 182 — Maturity September 20, 2005
**f.** 7.00% OLO 2005 — Maturity November 15, 2005
**g.** 8.80% Bono 2005 — Maturity October 28, 2005
**h.** 9.50% BTP 2005 — Maturity August 1, 2005

**22.** What is the theoretical September Bund futures price on April 23 if the cheapest-to-deliver bond is the 7.375% 2005, trading at 106.13? The conversion factor for the 7.375% 2005 is 1.1247. The last coupon date was January 3. Short-term funds can be borrowed at 3.35%. Futures delivery would be on September 10. Spot settlement for a Bund traded on April 23 would be April 25.

■ ■ ■

*"An interest rate swap is an exchange of one set of interest flows for another, with no exchange of principal.*

*An option is a deal for forward delivery, where the buyer can choose whether the transaction will be consummated, and pays a premium for this advantage."*

# Swaps and Options Basics

# INTEREST RATE SWAPS

## The concept of a swap

**The concept of an interest rate swap is similar to an FRA, but is applied to a series of cashflows over a longer period of time, rather than to a single borrowing period.**

Consider, for example, the case we examined in chapter 2, of a borrower who uses an FRA to hedge the cost of a single three-month borrowing due to begin in two months' time, by buying a 2 v. 5 FRA, shown diagramatically in Figure 4.1.

Fig 4.1

### Hedging with a 2 v. 5 FRA

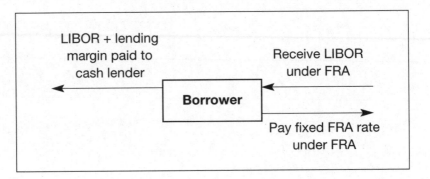

In this case, the borrower's *net* cost is (fixed FRA rate + lending margin).

Now consider the case of a borrower which takes a five-year loan now. The cost of the first three-month period of the loan is fixed at LIBOR now. The borrower will pay LIBOR refixed at three-monthly intervals throughout the life of the loan. This borrower could fix the cost of the second three-month period of the loan with a 3 v. 6 FRA. Or it could fix the cost of the third three-month period with a 6 v. 9 FRA. However, if the borrower wishes to hedge the cost of all the three-month LIBOR settings throughout the five years, it would use an interest rate swap, which achieves exactly this (*see* Figure 4.2).

## Hedging with an interest rate swap

Fig 4.2

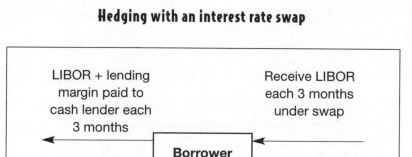

In this case, the borrower's net cost is (fixed swap rate + lending margin). The fixed rate quoted to the borrower by the swap dealer applies throughout the five-year period of the swap including the first period which starts now. The fixed rate may be paid three-monthly, six-monthly, or annually, depending on the exact terms of the swap. For our purposes here, it is sufficient to know that a fixed rate can be quoted.

> *An interest rate swap is an exchange of one set of interest flows for another, with no exchange of principal*

**Key Point**

The comparison between an FRA and a swap can be taken further in considering the applications of a swap. As with an FRA, a bank swap dealer can use a swap in essentially three ways: hedging a borrowing cost as above, speculating, or arbitraging.

As a swap is a long-term instrument, swap rates are generally linked to capital market yields rather than short-term money market rates. A dealer deliberately taking a position with a swap is therefore speculating that long-term yields will move up or down. If yields are expected to rise, the dealer will undertake a swap which entails paying out the fixed interest rate. If correct, the dealer can later offset this with a swap, for the same period, which entails receiving the fixed interest rate – which will then be at a higher level, giving the dealer a profit (as shown in Figure 4.3).

Fig 4.3 **Taking a position with an interest rate swap**

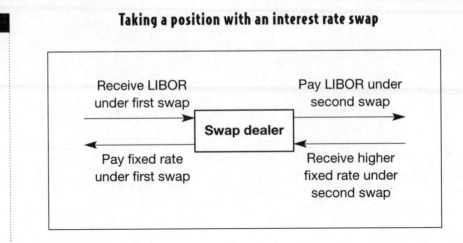

On relatively short-term swaps – say one to two years in maturity – the fixed rate is linked to short-term rates, and it is possible, for example, to consider arbitrage between such swaps and FRAs or futures.

# Hedging an interest rate swap

As with every instrument, dealers may find they have a position which they do not want – either because they have changed their minds about the direction of interest rates, or because they have made a price and been taken up on it. They are therefore exposed to movements in the swap rate and will want to hedge themselves. This they can do in any of several ways:

- Deal an exactly offsetting swap.
- Deal in a different instrument which will give offsetting flows. Suppose, for example, that under the existing swap, the dealer is paying out a fixed interest rate for five years. As a hedge, the dealer might buy a five-year bond. This will give a fixed income to match the fixed payment on the swap. In order to buy the bond, the dealer can fund himself or herself at LIBOR or a rate linked to LIBOR, as shown in Figure 4.4.

## Hedging an interest rate swap

Fig 4.4

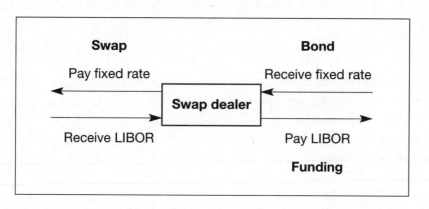

In this way the dealer is hedged for as long as he or she holds the bond. If the dealer does subsequently deal a second swap which offsets the first one, but five-year rates have fallen, a loss will result. However, the bond will have increased in value correspondingly.

- Deal in bond futures or options. These may provide a liquid hedge, but the hedge could be less perfect, as the specifications of the futures or options contracts may imply a rather different maturity from the swap, so that the hedge does not respond to yield changes in the same way as the swap.

# OPTIONS

## The concept of an option

An option is a contract whereby one party has the right to complete a transaction in the future (with a previously agreed amount, date, and price) if it so chooses, but is not obliged to do so. The counterparty has no choice: it must transact if the first party wishes and cannot otherwise.

For the first party, an option is therefore similar to a forward deal, with the difference that it can subsequently decide whether or not to fulfill the deal. For the second party, an option is similar to a forward deal with the difference that it does not know whether or not it will be required to fulfill it. Clearly, the contract will be fulfilled only if advantageous to the first party and disadvantageous to the second. In return for this flexibility allowed to the first party, a "premium" must be paid up front to compensate the second party for the latter's additional risk.

For someone using an option as a hedge rather than as a trading instrument, it can be considered as a form of insurance. An insurance policy is not called upon if circumstances are satisfactory. The insured person is willing to pay an insurance premium, however, in order to be able to claim on the insurance policy if circumstances are not satisfactory. An option as a hedge is similar. If an option enables a hedger to buy something at a certain rate but it is in fact now cheaper in the market than that rate, the hedger does not need the option. If, however, it is in fact now more expensive than the option rate, the hedger can "claim" on the option. The hedger thus has "insurance protection" at the option rate, for which he or she pays a premium.

For the trader selling the option, the situation is similar to that of the insurer – the seller is exposed to the risk of being obliged to deliver at the agreed rate but only being able to cover his or her position in the market only at a worse rate.

Options are available in a wide range of underlying instruments, including currencies, interest rates, bonds, and commodities. Our concern is essentially with options where the underlying instrument is a bond.

**Key Point**

*An option is a deal for forward delivery, where the buyer can choose whether the transaction will be consummated, and pays a premium for this advantage*

# Basic terminology

As the terminology used in the options markets is specific to those markets, it is worthwhile rehearsing the terms here.

**Terminology**

The first party described in the previous section is the purchaser or **holder** of the option. The second party (the seller of the option who receives the premium) is called the **writer** of the option.

To **exercise** an option is to use it, rather than allow it to expire unused when it matures.

With a **European** option, the holder can exercise the option only when it matures. With a three-month option, for example, you can only choose at the end of three months whether or not to exercise. With an **American** option, however, the holder can choose to exercise at any time between the purchase of the option and its maturity (or **expiry**). European and American options are both available everywhere; the terms are technical rather than geographical.

The price agreed in the transaction – the **strike price** or **strike rate** – is not necessarily the same as the forward rate for the same future date, but is chosen to suit the option buyer. If it is more advantageous than the forward rate to the option buyer, the option is referred to as **in-the-money**. If it is less advantageous than the forward rate to the option buyer, it is **out-of-the-money**. If the strike is the same as the forward rate, the option is **at-the-money** (ATM). As the market moves after the option has been written, the option will move in- and out-of-the-money.

A **put** option is an option to sell something. A **call** option is an option to buy something. The "something" which is being bought or sold is referred to as the **underlying**. Thus in a bond option, the bond is the underlying. In a USD/DEM option, the exchange rate is the underlying. In a short-term interest rate option, the underlying is an FRA or an interest rate futures contract.

It is always possible to exercise an in-the-money option at an immediate profit or, in the case of a European option, to lock in a profit immediately by reversing it with a forward deal and exercising it later. The locked-in profit – the difference between the strike price and the current market price – is known as the **intrinsic value** of the option. The remaining part of the premium paid for the option is known as the **time value**.

## Some option pricing concepts

The pricing of an option depends on probability. In principle, ignoring bid–offer spreads, the premium paid to the writer should represent his or her expected loss on the option assuming the option sale is not hedged. The loss arises from the fact that, if unhedged, the writer will need to deliver on options which expire in-the-money, and simultane-ously cover himself or herself in the market at a worse price. The writer will never be obliged to deliver at a profit. As with insurance premiums, assuming that option writers can accurately assess the probability of each possible outcome, their total payment on expiry of a portfolio of options should approximate to the premiums received. Option pricing theory therefore depends on assessing these probabili-ties and deriving from them a fair value for the premium.

The factors on which these probabilities depend are as follows:

**Factors**

**The strike price** The more advantageous the strike is to the buyer at the time of pricing, the greater the probability of the option being exercised, at a loss to the writer, and hence the greater the option premium.

**Volatility** Volatility is a measure of how much the price fluctuates. The more volatile the bond price, the greater the probability that it will become of value to the buyer at some time. This measurement is for-malized in traditional option pricing theory as the annualized standard deviation of the logarithm of relative price movements.

**The maturity** The longer the maturity of the option, the greater the probability that it will become of value to the buyer at some time, because the price has a longer time in which to fluctuate.

**Interest rates** Premiums represent the probability of the buyer making a profit when the option is exercised, but are payable up front and are therefore discounted to a present value. This therefore affects the pre-mium to some extent. The forward price – and hence the relationship between the strike and the forward – is also affected by interest rate movements. Most importantly, in the case of an option on a bond or other interest rate instrument, the interest rate itself also directly affects the underlying price.

# Delta hedging

In order to manage a portfolio of options, option writers must know how the value of the options they have sold will vary with changes in the vari-ous factors affecting their price, so that they can hedge the options.

An option's delta ($\Delta$) measures how the option's value (which is the same as its current premium) varies with changes in the underlying price. It is (change in option's value ÷ change in underlying's value). If an option has a delta of 0.7, for example, a $100 increase in the value of the underlying will cause a $70 increase in the value of the option.

For a call option which is deep out-of-the-money, the premium will increase very little as the underlying improves – essentially the option will remain worth almost zero. For an option deep in-the-money, an improvement in the underlying will be reflected completely in the premium. The delta is therefore close to zero for deep out-of-the money call options and close to 1 for deep in-the-money call options. For at-the-money call options, the delta is 0.5. This can be seen as reflecting the fact that at-the-money, there is a 50 percent probability of the underlying price rising or falling.

For put options, delta is close to zero deep out-of-the-money, −0.5 at-the-money and close to −1 deep in-the-money.

An option trader wishing to hedge an option has several choices:

- Buy or sell an exactly matching option.
- Buy or sell the underlying. In this case, the trader will buy or sell enough of the underlying so that, if the price changes, he or she will make a profit or loss which exactly offsets the loss or profit on the option position. In general, the amount of the hedge is equal to (delta × the amount of the option). This is known as "delta hedging" and demonstrates the importance of knowing the delta.
- Buy or sell another instrument with the same (but opposite) value for (delta × amount), so that again any change in the underlying price gives rise to a change in the hedge value which exactly offsets the change in the option value. Such a hedge might be the purchase of an option with a different strike price – say a larger amount of an option which is more out-of-the-money (and hence has a smaller delta).

A trader who is short of a call or long of a put has a negative delta and needs to buy the underlying to hedge. If long of a call or short of a put, the trader has a positive delta and needs to sell the underlying to hedge.

---

**Key Point**

*Delta hedging an option can be achieved by buying or selling the correct amount of the underlying so that any change in the option's P & L is offset by a change in the underlying position's P & L*

# Put/call parity and risk reversal

Suppose that I pay a premium of $C$ to buy a European bond call option with a strike price of $X$. Suppose that, at the same time, I also receive a premium $P$ to sell a put option on the same bond, also with a strike of $X$. Third, suppose that I also sell the bond for forward delivery at a forward price $F$. If the bond price is above $X$ at expiry, I will exercise my call option at $X$. If it is below $X$ at maturity, my counterparty will exercise the put option which I have sold. Either way, I buy the bond at a price $X$. However, I also sell the bond at a price $F$, because of the forward deal. I therefore have a profit $(F - X)$. On the basis that arbitrage minimizes "free profits", this must offset my net payment $(C - P)$. However, $(F - X)$ is received/paid at maturity while $(C - P)$ is paid/received up front. Therefore:

$$(C - P) = (F - X) \text{ discounted to a present value}$$

If the strike price is set equal to the forward price, $(C - P)$ must be zero. Therefore, with an option struck at the forward price (at-the-money), the put and call premiums are equal. This is the "put/call parity."

This relationship is important because it is related to the creation of synthetic positions. From the above analysis, which is essentially a zero-sum game, it can be seen that for any strike price $X$, it is true that:

sell forward *plus* buy call *plus* sell put = 0

This is the same as saying:

buy forward    =    buy call *plus* sell put

This can be expressed in a variety of ways to synthesize positions, as follows:

| | | |
|---|---|---|
| sell forward | = | sell call *plus* buy put |
| buy call | = | buy put *plus* buy forward |
| sell call | = | sell put *plus* sell forward |
| buy put | = | buy call *plus* sell forward |
| sell put | = | sell call *plus* buy forward |

Thus, for example, a trader can either buy a call at a particular strike or, if priced more efficiently, he can buy a put at the same strike and buy forward simultaneously. Viewed from a different standpoint, this is known as "risk reversal." If, for example, a trader already has a position where he or she is long of a put, this position can be reversed to become effectively long of a call instead, by buying forward.

*Buying a call and selling a put at the same strike creates a synthetic forward purchase*

**Key Point**

# Part 2

# Repos and How to Use Them

■ ■ ■

*". . . all repos are driven by either the need to lend or borrow cash . . . or the need to borrow specific securities."*

# The Different Repo Structures

# OVERVIEW

"Repo" is short for "sale and repurchase agreement" and is essentially a transaction whereby the two parties involved agree to do two deals as a package. The first deal is a purchase or sale of a security – often a government bond – for delivery straight away (the exact settlement date will vary according to the market convention for the security involved). The second deal is a reversal of the first deal, for settlement on some future date.

> *A repo is a purchase or sale of a security now, together with an opposite transaction later*

Key Poin

Because it is understood from the outset that the first deal will be reversed, it is clear that both parties intend the transfer of securities (in one direction) and the transfer of cash (in the other direction) to be temporary rather than permanent. The transaction is therefore exactly equivalent to a loan of securities in one direction and a loan of cash in the other. The repo is structured so that the economic benefit of owning the securities – income and capital gains/losses – remains with their original owner. These are in fact the driving forces behind the repo market; all repos are driven by either the need to lend or borrow cash, which is collateralized by securities, or the need to borrow specific securities. The prices for both the original sale and the subsequent repurchase are agreed at the outset. The difference between the two prices is calculated to be equivalent to the cost of borrowing secured money, as shown in Figure 5.1.

> *All repos are driven by either the need to lend or borrow cash, or the need to borrow a specific security*

Key Poir

**A repo**

Fig 5.1

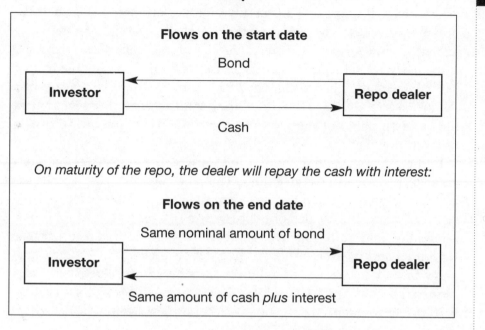

**Flows on the start date**

Bond

Investor ← Repo dealer

Cash

*On maturity of the repo, the dealer will repay the cash with interest:*

**Flows on the end date**

Same nominal amount of bond

Investor → Repo dealer

Same amount of cash *plus* interest

For lenders of cash, a repo has the advantage of double security – if a counterparty defaults, they can rely on the collateral. They can therefore look to the creditworthiness of both the counterparty and the issuer of the collateral. For borrowers of cash, the advantage is that they can make use of an investment in their portfolio to borrow funds either more cheaply, or which they might not otherwise be able to borrow at all.

It is important to note that we are not using the word "collateral" in its usual sense here. Collateral normally means something which is given temporarily as a guarantee, but which does not actually change ownership. In a repo, however, ownership of the securities does pass from one party to the other. The securities are nevertheless generally referred to as collateral, both in the market and in the standard legal agreements for repos.

A repo is defined as an initial sale of securities followed by a subsequent repurchase. A "reverse repo" is the opposite – an initial purchase of securities followed by a subsequent resale. Because the two parties involved are of course doing opposite transactions, a "repo" to one party is a "reverse" to the other. For this purpose, the deal is generally considered from the repo dealer's point of view. If the dealer is effectively borrowing cash, the deal is a repo; if effectively lending cash, the deal is a reverse. In a repo the "seller" (or "lender") is the party selling securities at the outset and repurchasing them later. The "buyer" (or "borrower" or "investor") is the other party. It is important to note that the terminology is taken from the viewpoint of the bond market, not the money market: the party borrowing cash is usually known as the lender in the repo.

In the same way, "bid" and "offer" are used in most repo markets according to the same convention. Thus if a rate of "5.20 – 5.30 percent" is quoted in the interbank deposit market, 5.30 percent is the "offered" rate (the dealer offers cash at 5.30 percent) and 5.20 percent is the "bid" rate (the dealer bids for cash at 5.20 percent). In the repo market, however, although the rates still mean the same to each party in *cash* terms, the terminology is generally reversed: 5.30 percent is the "bid" rate (the dealer bids for securities against cash at 5.30 percent) and 5.20 percent is the "offered" rate (the dealer offers securities against cash at 5.20 percent).

> *Repo terminology is based on the securities side of the deal, not the cash side*   **Key Poin**

The repo market involves three very similar types of transaction: the classic repo (or "US-style repo"), the buy/sell-back, and securities lending.

# CLASSIC REPO

## Agreement

An important point about a classic repo, particularly compared with a traditional buy/sell-back as we shall see later, is that both legs of the repo are transacted under one agreement. In the US this is the PSA agreement. In Europe the PSA/ISMA General Master Repo Agreement (GMRA) is the standard increasingly used, adapted for local market conditions in the case of domestic repos.

# Legal title

Legal title (ownership) to the collateral passes to the buyer for the period of the repo. The effect of this is that if the seller defaults on the cash repayment, the buyer does not need to establish his or her right to the collateral. As a consequence, the legal rights relating to the collateral also pass to the buyer; for example, the buyer receives any coupons or partial redemptions due. On the other hand, as explained below, the buyer is obliged under the repo agreement to make compensating payments to the seller.

> *Legal title in the collateral passes from lender to borrower* **Key Point**

# Coupon payment

If a coupon is payable on the security during the term of the repo, the buyer, who is holding the security (except in the case of a hold-in-custody repo – see below), will receive the coupon. However, although the buyer has legal title, from an economic point of view he or she is holding the security only as collateral; the financial reward from the transaction comes from the interest on the cash loan, which the buyer is effectively receiving through the difference in prices between the first and second legs of the repo. The coupon is therefore passed back to the seller. The payment back to the seller, due on the same date as the buyer receives the coupon, is known as a "manufactured dividend."

Repos in the international market generally involve gross-paying securities – that is, securities where the issuer pays the coupons gross, without deduction of income tax. The GMRA, for example, is designed for gross-paying securities. Under the GMRA, a buyer who does receive any payments net of tax is still liable to pay the gross amount to the seller. Clearly the two parties involved can instead establish a different agreement for net-paying securities if they choose.

> *Any coupon during a classic repo is received by the borrower, who must, however, make a matching payment to the lender* **Key Point**

# Price calculation

The total price at which the first leg of the repo is transacted is the straightforward current market price for the security, plus accrued coupon, taking into account any margin (see below) if agreed. The total price for the second leg, however, reflects only the repo interest rate and not the accrued coupon due on the security at that time. This is because the security is in reality only playing the part of collateral. The repo interest rate is calculated according to the normal convention in the relevant money market. On a DEM repo, for example, this would be calculated on an ACT/360 basis; this is unaffected by the fact that the coupon on the collateral might be calculated on a 30(E)/360 basis.

> **Key Point**
>
> *The price on the first leg of a classic repo is the market price.*
> *The price on the second leg is the first price plus the repo interest*

**Example 5.1**

Currency: DEM

Deal date: July 15, 1996

Settlement date: July 17, 1996

Term: 28 days (August 14, 1996)

Repo rate: 4.0% (ACT/360 basis)

Collateral: DEM 60,000,000 nominal 8.5% bond with maturity March 26, 2004 and annual coupons (30(E)/360 basis)

Clean bond price: 108.95

Clean price of bond for value July 17, 1996 is 108.95

Accrued coupon on bond on July 17, 1996 = $\dfrac{111}{360} \times 8.5 = 2.62083333$

Total purchase price = 111.57083333

Purchase amount = DEM $60,000,000 \times \dfrac{111.57083333}{100} =$ DEM 66,942,500.00

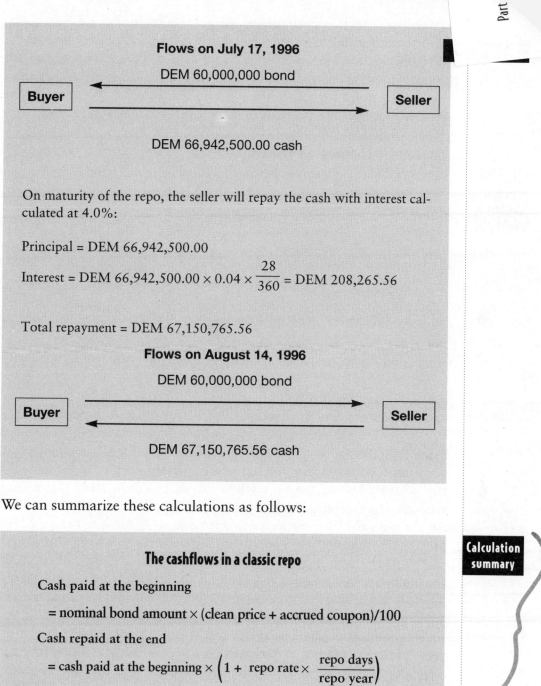

**Flows on July 17, 1996**

DEM 60,000,000 bond

Buyer ←——————————————————— Seller

——————————————————————→

DEM 66,942,500.00 cash

On maturity of the repo, the seller will repay the cash with interest calculated at 4.0%:

Principal = DEM 66,942,500.00

Interest = DEM 66,942,500.00 $\times 0.04 \times \dfrac{28}{360}$ = DEM 208,265.56

Total repayment = DEM 67,150,765.56

**Flows on August 14, 1996**

DEM 60,000,000 bond

Buyer ——————————————————→ Seller

←——————————————————

DEM 67,150,765.56 cash

We can summarize these calculations as follows:

**The cashflows in a classic repo**

Cash paid at the beginning

= nominal bond amount × (clean price + accrued coupon)/100

Cash repaid at the end

= cash paid at the beginning $\times \left(1 + \text{repo rate} \times \dfrac{\text{repo days}}{\text{repo year}}\right)$

Calculation
summary

In Example 5.1, we started the calculation by assuming that the deal was to be based on a particular amount of security – in this case DEM 60 million. This would be the case, for example, if the seller wished to fund this particular holding or if, as discussed below, the buyer wished to borrow this particular amount of stock as a "special."

The deal could alternatively be based on a particular amount of cash to be borrowed. That is, the deal could be "cash-driven" rather than "security-driven" (or "stock-driven"). In this case the nominal amount of security would be arrived at by reversing the original calculation:

$$\text{nominal amount of security} = \frac{\text{cash amount at start}}{\text{dirty price at start}}$$

Calculation summary

### Cash-driven deals

$$\text{nominal bond amount} = \frac{\text{cash paid at the beginning}}{(\text{clean price} + \text{accrued coupon})/100}$$

**Cash repaid at the end**

$$= \text{cash paid at the beginning} \times \left(1 + \text{repo rate} \times \frac{\text{repo days}}{\text{year}}\right)$$

All the examples throughout this chapter could be set out as either cash-driven or security-driven examples. In order to help the reader follow each step through clearly, however, we have built them up using the same basic information in each one rather than changing it each time. We have therefore chosen to set out each example as security-driven. The adjustment when starting with a particular round amount of cash rather than a particular round amount of securities should not cause any difficulty and is covered in some of the exercises at the end of the chapter.

A further point worth mentioning about the examples here concerns precision. In order to show all the calculations as clearly as possible, we have used more decimal places in calculating prices than is sometimes done. In practice, the level of precision will vary between markets and also between dealers. This precision can be seen in two areas of the calculations. First, in calculating the price of a security – for example, 111.57083333 in Example 5.1 – this precision is not necessary. If the price were rounded down to 111.57, for example, the result would be only that the cash borrowed against the collateral would have been very slightly less (or, in a cash-driven deal, the nominal amount of collateral would need to be very slightly higher). In a cash-driven deal, for example, dealers sometimes approximate in practice by rounding up the amount of security to a convenient nominal amount. This affects only the level of collateralization, and not the economics of the deal.

Second, however, in calculating the cash interest, precision is necessary. Once the amount of cash to be borrowed has been determined (DEM 66,942,500.00 in Example 5.1), the repo interest calculation should be precise, in the same way that it would be in any money market interest calculation. If this is not done precisely, the economics of the deal are changed slightly. The same is true when calculating forward prices for buy/sell-backs later in the chapter.

## General collateral v. special

Where a repo is driven by the buyer's need – or at least willingness – to invest cash, the exact nature of the collateral is not important. Clearly it needs to be of adequate quality, and government or quasi-government securities are by far the most widely used. It is not, however, important to the buyer exactly which government bond is received as collateral.

In some cases, however, a repo is driven on the buyer's side by the need to borrow a particular bond as a result of being short of that bond. In this case the collateral delivered must be that particular bond rather than any other and is called "special," as opposed to "general collateral" (or simply "GC"). The extent to which any particular security becomes special depends on the supply of, and demand for, that security in the market generally.

A seller who is aware that the security being requested by the buyer is in particularly short supply is able to negotiate a lower interest rate for the cash he or she is taking through the repo. The more special the security, the lower the repo interest rate. Thus, if a particular security is "expensive" for the buyer to borrow, this implies a lower rather than a higher repo rate.

In the Bank ABC screen shown in Figure 5.2, for example, the rate for a Deutschmark (DEM) repo dealt against general collateral is quoted at 3.33–3.28 percent for 1 week (that is, 3.33 percent if the market maker is borrowing the security and 3.28 percent if lending the security). Repo for specific bonds, however, is quoted at lower rates. In the case of one bond, the "Bond Z," the dealer is prepared to borrow the bond and lend cash for only 1.50 percent, because the bond is in such short supply.

Fig 5.2

## Examples of repo rates

```
Bank ABC - DEM repo rates
All prices out of spot
             1 week      1 month     3 months    6 months
GC           3.33-28     3.35-30     3.39-34     3.42-37
Bond X       3.10-00     3.15-05     3.20-10     3.30-20
Bond Y       3.30-25     3.32-27     3.36-31     3.39-34
Bond Z       1.50-40     2.00-90     2.50-40     2.70-60
```

**Key Point**    *A "special" is a security in demand by borrowers. The more special the security, the lower the repo rate*

# Settlement

Settlement of each leg of the repo is by the same delivery method that is used for a straightforward security sale or purchase. This is often – and preferably – by "delivery versus payment" (DVP). In this, the settlement is effected through a third party clearing house which undertakes to pass the collateral in one direction only as the cash is passed in the other direction – and vice versa on maturity of the repo. For international securities, for example, the clearing house will often be Euroclear or Cedel.

# Margin

For the collateral to be of adequate value, it is important that the buyer recalculates the value of the collateral continually in order to ensure that it is at least equal to the cash lent. This recalculation is called "marking to market" and is customarily done at the end of each day. If the value of the collateral has fallen, the buyer may make a "margin call," requiring the seller to transfer more collateral. This is often a transfer of more securities but, depending on the agreement, the seller may choose to transfer cash instead to make up the correct value of collateral. In this case, again depending on the agreement, the buyer would normally pay the seller interest on this cash collateral.

If the value of the collateral rises rather than falls, the seller can similarly make a margin call, requiring the buyer to return some of the collateral. Because bond prices are constantly changing, there would be small transfers of collateral every day if the collateral value were always to be marked to market precisely. To avoid the administrative costs and burden of this, the two parties agree a threshold, below which changes in the collateral's value do not trigger a margin call.

> *Margin calls are made to keep the value of the collateral in line with the value of the cash loan*
>
> **Key Point**

Because of the risk that the value of the collateral will fall before there is time to ensure that the seller has increased it, the buyer often requires that the collateral value is always slightly higher – by 2 percent, for example – than the cash loan. This extra margin is called an "initial margin" or "haircut." Whether a haircut is applied depends on the relative creditworthiness of the two parties. A seller of greater creditworthiness than the buyer may insist on having no haircut, or even the opposite – that the cash loan is a few percent greater than the collateral.

> *Initial margin protects against adverse movements which may arise before a margin call can be paid*
>
> **Key Point**

Internationally, the term "variation margin" is used to mean "margin transfer" – the amount of margin transferred from seller to buyer or buyer to seller in response to a margin call. "Initial margin" and "variation margin" are therefore used in the same way as in the futures markets. Confusingly, however, in the UK gilt repo market "variation margin" is used instead to mean the threshold below which a margin call is not made.

When marking to market the collateral, it is the dirty price including accrued coupon which is considered, because this is the amount of money which could be realized by the buyer by selling the collateral if necessary. Similarly, the amount of cash which is secured by the collateral takes account of accrued interest on the cash.

**Key Point**

*Marking to market includes both accrued coupon on the security and accrued interest on the cash*

**Example 5.2**

With the same information as Example 5.1:

Currency: DEM

Deal date: July 15, 1996

Settlement date: July 17, 1996

Term: 28 days (August 14, 1996)

Repo rate: 4.0% (ACT/360 basis)

Collateral: DEM 60,000,000 nominal 8.5% bond with maturity March 26, 2004 and annual coupons (30(E)/360 basis)

Clean bond price: 108.95

Haircut: 2%

Clean price of bond for value July 17, 1996 is 108.95

Accrued coupon on bond on July 17, 1996 $= \dfrac{111}{360} \times 8.5 = 2.62083333$

Market dirty price = 111.57083333

Dirty price adjusted for 2% haircut $= \dfrac{111.57083333}{1.02} = 109.38316993$

Purchase amount = DEM $60{,}000{,}000 \times \dfrac{109.38316993}{100} =$ DEM 65,629,901.96

**Flows on July 17, 1996**

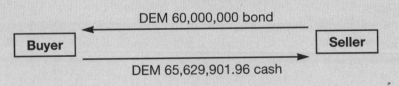

Buyer ← DEM 60,000,000 bond ← Seller

Buyer → DEM 65,629,901.96 cash → Seller

On maturity of the repo, the seller again repays the cash with interest calculated at 4.0%:

Principal = DEM 65,629,901.96

Interest = DEM 65,629,901.96 × 0.04 × $\dfrac{28}{360}$ = DEM 204,181.92

Total repayment = DEM 65,834,083.88

**Flows on August 14, 1996**

DEM 60,000,000 bond

| Buyer | → | Seller |

DEM 65,834,083.88 cash

We can summarize these calculations as follows:

### Haircut calculations

**Cash paid at the beginning**

$$= \frac{\text{nominal bond amount} \times (\text{clean price} + \text{accrued coupon})/100}{(1 + \text{haircut rate})}$$

**Cash repaid at the end**

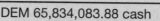

$$= \text{cash consideration at the beginning} \times \left(1 + \text{repo rate} \times \frac{\text{repo days}}{\text{year}}\right)$$

In Example 5.2, the amount of the cash loan is DEM 65,629,901.96 and the *market value of the collateral is 2 percent greater than the cash*, at DEM 60 million × $\dfrac{111.57083333}{100}$ = DEM 66,942,500. That is:

market value of collateral = cash amount × 1.02

If the *seller* were in a position to demand the haircut, the amount of the cash loan would be 2 percent greater than the market value of the collateral:

cash amount = market value of collateral × 1.02

If this had been the case in Example 5.2, we would have had:

$$\text{cash amount} = \text{DEM } 60 \text{ million} \times 111.57083333/100 \times 1.02$$

$$= \text{DEM } 68,281,350.00$$

In the GMRA it is suggested that "margin ratio" be expressed as:

$$\text{margin ratio} = \frac{\text{market value of collateral}}{\text{amount of cash loan}}$$

In Example 5.2, the margin ratio is therefore 1.02. If the margin had been demanded by the seller instead, the margin ratio would have been $1/1.02 = 0.9804$.

It is important to note, however, that dealers often consider the margin to be expressed the other way round. A buyer may demand a "2 percent haircut," meaning that he or she intends to transfer *cash which is 2 percent less than the market value of the collateral*. In other words:

$$\text{cash amount} = \text{market value of collateral} \times 0.98$$

This gives a result which is similar to our example, but not exactly the same because $(1 \div 1.02)$ is not exactly 0.98. If we followed this approach, the cash amount in Example 5.2 would be:

$$\text{DEM } 60 \text{ million} \times \frac{111.57083333}{100} \times 0.98 = \text{DEM } 65,603,650.00$$

instead of DEM 65,629,901.96. This would not affect the economics of the deal – interest would still be calculated at the same repo rate of 4 percent, but on a slightly smaller amount.

In the case of small haircuts, the difference is very slight. It is important to be aware that different dealers take different approaches, however. All our examples here have used the terminology consistently.

## Margin payments

In practice, there are various ways of settling a margin call, and which method is to be used needs to be agreed between the two parties.

### Method 1: Margin call transferred in securities
- Leave the cash loan unchanged.
- Add the accrued interest to the amount of the cash loan.

- Calculate the nominal amount (A) of collateral now required, adjusted for the haircut.
- Compare with the nominal amount (B) of the existing collateral.
- Transfer the difference (A − B) in securities from seller to buyer (or buyer to seller if B is greater than A).

**Example 5.3**

With the same information as Example 5.2, we have the same initial exchange at the beginning:

**Flows on July 17, 1996**

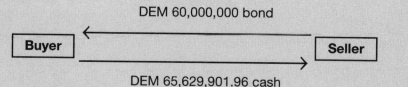

DEM 60,000,000 bond

Buyer ←———————— Seller

DEM 65,629,901.96 cash

Suppose now that on July 24 the bond price falls to 107.15

Accrued coupon on bond on July 24, 1996 $= \dfrac{118}{360} \times 8.5 = 2.78611111$

Total new dirty market price = 109.93611111

Cash originally lent plus interest accrued so far at 4.0% =

$$\text{DEM } 65{,}629{,}901.96 \times \left(1 + 0.04 \times \frac{7}{360}\right) = \text{DEM } 65{,}680{,}947.44$$

Allowing for the 2% haircut, the buyer will require that the collateral is now worth DEM 65,680,947.44 × 1.02 = DEM 66,994,566.39

At the new price, the new total nominal amount of security must therefore be:

$$\text{DEM } \frac{66{,}994{,}566.39}{109.93611111/100} = \text{DEM } 60{,}939{,}545.44$$

As the buyer currently has DEM 60,000,000 bond, the seller must transfer another DEM 939,545.44. Assuming a minimum denomination for the bond of DEM 1000, the seller will transfer at least DEM 940,000 nominal.

**5.3 Cont'd**

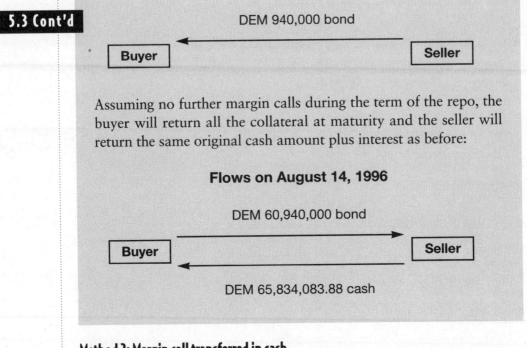

DEM 940,000 bond

Buyer ← Seller

Assuming no further margin calls during the term of the repo, the buyer will return all the collateral at maturity and the seller will return the same original cash amount plus interest as before:

**Flows on August 14, 1996**

DEM 60,940,000 bond

Buyer → Seller

DEM 65,834,083.88 cash

## Method 2: Margin call transferred in cash

Similar to Method 1, but the difference $(A - B)$ is settled in cash rather than securities, by transferring the current dirty market cash value of $(A - B)$.

The buyer pays interest on this cash collateral on an agreed basis – for example at the existing repo rate, or at an accepted benchmark rate.

**Example 5.4**

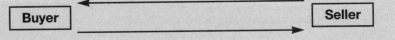

**Flows on July 17, 1996**

DEM 60,000,000 bond

Buyer ← Seller

DEM 65,629,901.96 cash

With the same information as before, on July 24 we still want the value of the collateral to be DEM 66,994,566.39.

If we do not wish to transfer any more bonds as collateral, however, we must transfer cash instead.

At the new dirty price, the existing collateral is worth:

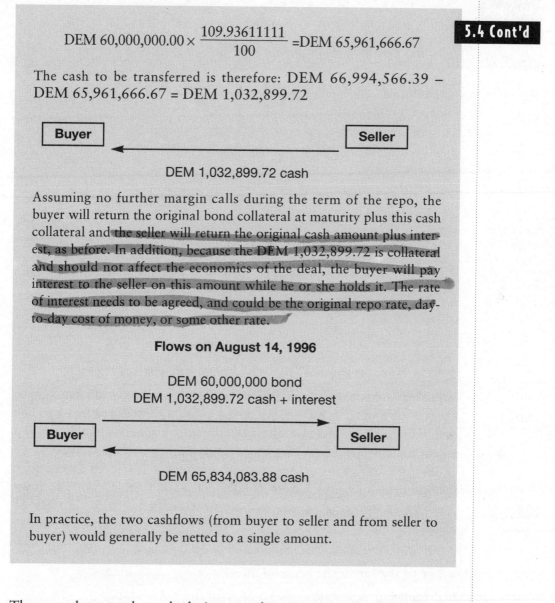

$$\text{DEM } 60,000,000.00 \times \frac{109.93611111}{100} = \text{DEM } 65,961,666.67$$

The cash to be transferred is therefore: DEM 66,994,566.39 – DEM 65,961,666.67 = DEM 1,032,899.72

| Buyer | ← | Seller |
|---|---|---|

DEM 1,032,899.72 cash

Assuming no further margin calls during the term of the repo, the buyer will return the original bond collateral at maturity plus this cash collateral and the seller will return the original cash amount plus interest, as before. In addition, because the DEM 1,032,899.72 is collateral and should not affect the economics of the deal, the buyer will pay interest to the seller on this amount while he or she holds it. The rate of interest needs to be agreed, and could be the original repo rate, day-to-day cost of money, or some other rate.

**Flows on August 14, 1996**

DEM 60,000,000 bond
DEM 1,032,899.72 cash + interest

| Buyer | → | Seller |
|---|---|---|

DEM 65,834,083.88 cash

In practice, the two cashflows (from buyer to seller and from seller to buyer) would generally be netted to a single amount.

These mark-to-market calculations can be summarized as follows:

## Marking to market

New value of cash loan =

$$\text{cash paid at the beginning} \times \left(1 + \text{ repo rate } \times \frac{\text{days so far}}{\text{year}}\right)$$

(A) New nominal amount of collateral required

$$= \frac{\text{new value of cash loan}}{(\text{new clean price} + \text{new accrued coupon})/100} \times \left(1 + \text{haircut rate}\right)$$

(B) Margin call = difference between (A) and the collateral previously transferred.

If the margin call is settled in cash rather than securities, then cash transferred

$$= B \times (\text{new clean price} + \text{new accrued coupon})/100$$

## Method 3: "Close out and repricing" with adjustment of securities amount

Repay the original deal plus accrued interest so far and open a new one with the same maturity date and based on the same repo rate. The cash loan amount remains the same but the collateral is adjusted to reflect the current price. As with Method 1, this method is likely to be used if the deal is driven by the cash amount of the deal rather than the securities – in which case the original repo is more likely to have been dealt for a round amount of cash rather than a round amount of securities. Again, however, we have used the same details as in the previous example for a clear comparison.

- Pay to the buyer the accrued interest on the cash loan.
- Establish a new cash loan of exactly the same amount as the original loan at the same repo rate, to the same maturity date.
- Calculate the nominal amount of collateral needed (C) for the cash loan amount at the new dirty market price, adjusted for the haircut.
- Settle the difference between C and the original nominal collateral amount, in securities.

Example 5.5

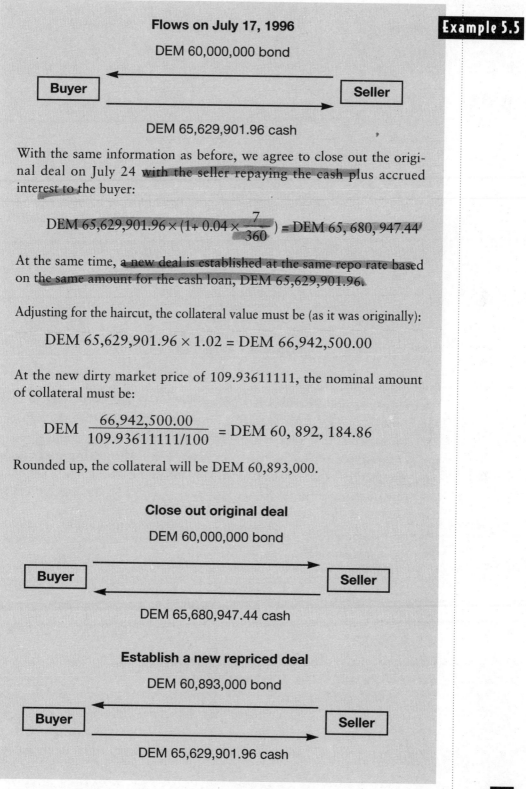

**Flows on July 17, 1996**

DEM 60,000,000 bond

Buyer ← Seller

DEM 65,629,901.96 cash

With the same information as before, we agree to close out the original deal on July 24 with the seller repaying the cash plus accrued interest to the buyer:

$$\text{DEM } 65,629,901.96 \times (1 + 0.04 \times \frac{7}{360}) = \text{DEM } 65,680,947.44$$

At the same time, a new deal is established at the same repo rate based on the same amount for the cash loan, DEM 65,629,901.96.

Adjusting for the haircut, the collateral value must be (as it was originally):

$$\text{DEM } 65,629,901.96 \times 1.02 = \text{DEM } 66,942,500.00$$

At the new dirty market price of 109.93611111, the nominal amount of collateral must be:

$$\text{DEM } \frac{66,942,500.00}{109.93611111/100} = \text{DEM } 60,892,184.86$$

Rounded up, the collateral will be DEM 60,893,000.

**Close out original deal**

DEM 60,000,000 bond

Buyer → Seller

DEM 65,680,947.44 cash

**Establish a new repriced deal**

DEM 60,893,000 bond

Buyer ← Seller

DEM 65,629,901.96 cash

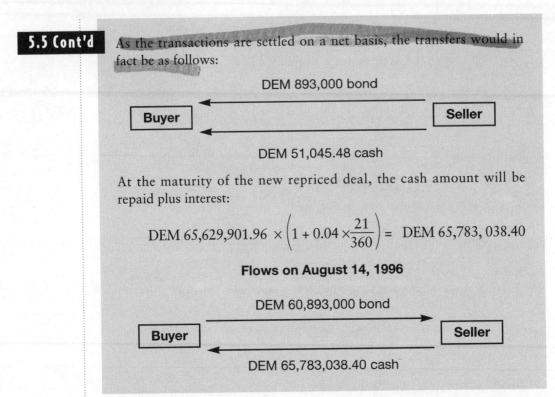

**5.5 Cont'd**  As the transactions are settled on a net basis, the transfers would in fact be as follows:

DEM 893,000 bond

Buyer ← ← Seller

DEM 51,045.48 cash

At the maturity of the new repriced deal, the cash amount will be repaid plus interest:

$$\text{DEM } 65,629,901.96 \times \left(1 + 0.04 \times \frac{21}{360}\right) = \text{DEM } 65,783,038.40$$

**Flows on August 14, 1996**

DEM 60,893,000 bond

Buyer → Seller

DEM 65,783,038.40 cash

The net effect of Method 3 is slightly less beneficial to the seller than Methods 1 and 2. In Method 3, because the seller has closed out the deal and re-established it at the same rate for a shorter period, he or she is effectively paying some interest early on the cash without any compensation – that is, compound interest on the cash borrowed instead of simple interest. If we suppose that the seller needs to refinance the interim cashflow of DEM 51,045.48 somehow until August 14, and can do this at 4 percent, the total cost of this cashflow is:

$$\text{DEM } 51,045.48 \times \left(1 + 0.04 \times \frac{21}{360}\right) = \text{DEM } 51,164.59$$

The seller's total cash outflows on August 14, would then be:

$$\text{DEM } 65,783,038.40 + \text{DEM } 51,164.59 = \text{DEM } 65,834,202.99$$

This is slightly greater than the amount of DEM 65,834,083.88 repaid at the end under Methods 1 and 2.

In order not to change the economics of the deal in this way, it would be necessary to agree to defer the interest payment of DEM 51,045.48 until August 14, to avoid the compounding effect. In this case, the collateral amount would need to be increased to take account of the extra exposure this represents for the buyer. With the 2 percent margin and the new market dirty bond price of 109.93611111, the collateral would need to be increased by a further nominal amount of:

$$\frac{DEM\ 51,045.48}{109.93611111/100} \times 1.02 = DEM\ 47,360.59$$

This would give a total new nominal collateral amount of:

DEM 60,892,184.86 + DEM 47,360.59 = DEM 60,939,545.45

which rounds up to DEM 60,940,000.

## Method 4: "Close out and repricing" with adjustment of cash amount

Repay the original deal plus accrued interest so far and open a new one with the same maturity date and based on the same repo rate but valuing the collateral at current prices. The amount of collateral remains the same but the cash is adjusted.

- Add the accrued interest on the original cash loan to the amount of the original cash loan to give what must be now repaid ($D$) to close it out.
- Calculate the new dirty market value of the existing collateral.
- Calculate the new cash loan ($E$) which can now be made based on this collateral value, adjusted for the haircut.
- Settle the difference ($E - D$) in cash.

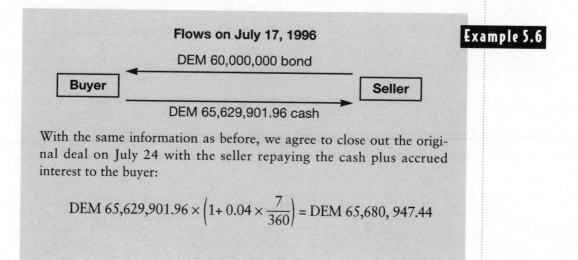

**Flows on July 17, 1996**

**Example 5.6**

DEM 60,000,000 bond

Buyer ← Seller

DEM 65,629,901.96 cash →

With the same information as before, we agree to close out the original deal on July 24 with the seller repaying the cash plus accrued interest to the buyer:

$$DEM\ 65,629,901.96 \times \left(1 + 0.04 \times \frac{7}{360}\right) = DEM\ 65,680,947.44$$

**5.6 Cont'd**  At the same time, a new deal is established at the same repo rate based on the same collateral but reducing the amount of the cash loan to equate to the new value of the collateral after adjustment for the haircut – which is:

$$\text{DEM} \ \frac{60,000,000 \times 109.93611111/100}{1.02} = \text{DEM } 64,668,300.65$$

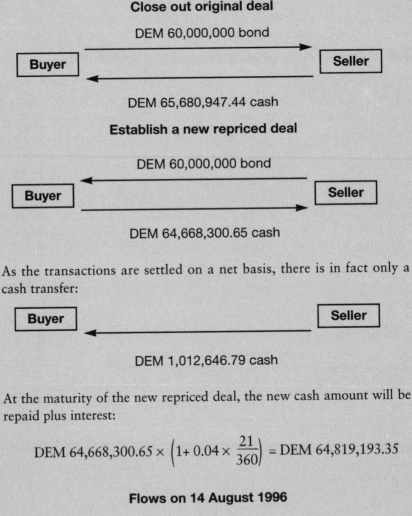

**Close out original deal**

DEM 60,000,000 bond

Buyer → Seller

DEM 65,680,947.44 cash

**Establish a new repriced deal**

DEM 60,000,000 bond

Buyer ← Seller

DEM 64,668,300.65 cash

As the transactions are settled on a net basis, there is in fact only a cash transfer:

Buyer ← Seller

DEM 1,012,646.79 cash

At the maturity of the new repriced deal, the new cash amount will be repaid plus interest:

$$\text{DEM } 64,668,300.65 \times \left(1 + 0.04 \times \frac{21}{360}\right) = \text{DEM } 64,819,193.35$$

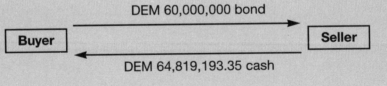

**Flows on 14 August 1996**

DEM 60,000,000 bond

Buyer → Seller

DEM 64,819,193.35 cash

The economics of Method 4 are exactly the same as Method 3 – that is, slightly less beneficial for the seller – for the same reason that the seller is effectively paying some interest early.

Calculation summary

## Close out and repricing (adjusting the securities amount)

Cash interest is paid on loan so far

$$= \text{cash paid at the beginning} \times \left( \text{repo rate} \times \frac{\text{days so far}}{\text{year}} \right)$$

Nominal bond amount now required as collateral

$$= \frac{\text{cash paid at the beginning}}{(\text{new bond price} + \text{new accrued coupon})/100} \times (1 + \text{haircut rate})$$

The difference between this and the original collateral is transferred in order to change the nominal amount of security lodged as collateral, and a new repo is then in place for the same cash amount from the new start date.

Calculation summary

## Close out and repricing (adjusting the cash amount)

Close-out amount on original repo

$$= \text{cash paid at the beginning} \times \left( 1 + \text{repo rate} \times \frac{\text{days so far}}{\text{year}} \right)$$

New cash amount = new value of collateral adjusted for haircut

$$= \frac{\text{nominal bond amount} \times (\text{new bond price} + \text{new accrued coupon})/100}{1 + \text{haircut rate}}$$

The cash difference between the two amounts is transferred and a new repo is then in place for the new cash amount from the new start date.

# Substitution

In the case of general collateral, the repo may include the right for the seller to change the exact security used as collateral during the period of the repo – a right of "substitution" – as long as the new collateral is equally acceptable. The maximum number of such substitutions is agreed in advance. With special collateral such substitution is clearly not possible, as this would negate the purpose of the repo for the buyer. In calculating the nominal amount of the new collateral, the same approach is taken as with making a margin call – the cash amount is marked to market, any haircut added and then collateral is transferred with this value.

**Example 5.7**  Suppose we start with the same deal as before, using the same collateral:

**Flows on July 17, 1996**

DEM 60,000,000 bond

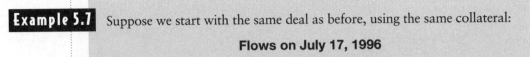

DEM 65,629,901.96 cash

For settlement on July 24, the seller wishes to replace the existing collateral by the following:

New collateral: 6.2% bond with maturity August 16, 2001 and annual coupons (30(E)/360 basis)

Clean bond price: 97.85
Accrued coupon on new bond on July 24 = 338/360 × 6.2 = 5.82111111

Current dirty price of new bond = 103.67111111

Current value of cash loan:

$$\text{DEM } 65,629,901.96 \times \left(1 + 0.04 \times \frac{7}{360}\right) = \text{DEM } 65,680,947.44$$

After adjustment for the haircut, the collateral must be worth:

$$\text{DEM } 65,680,947.44 \times 1.02 = \text{DEM } 66,994,566.39$$

The nominal amount of the new bond must therefore be:

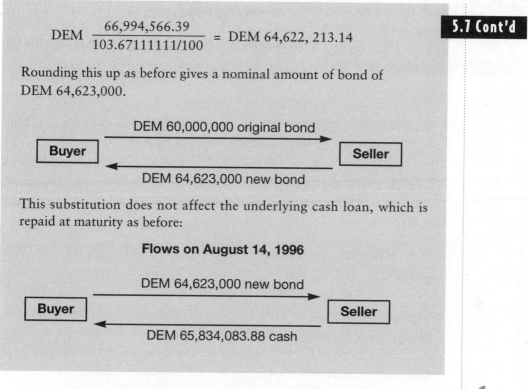

$$\text{DEM } \frac{66,994,566.39}{103.67111111/100} = \text{DEM } 64,622,213.14$$

Rounding this up as before gives a nominal amount of bond of DEM 64,623,000.

DEM 60,000,000 original bond

**Buyer** ⟶ **Seller**

DEM 64,623,000 new bond

This substitution does not affect the underlying cash loan, which is repaid at maturity as before:

**Flows on August 14, 1996**

DEM 64,623,000 new bond

**Buyer** ⟶ **Seller**

DEM 65,834,083.88 cash

## Bilateral v. triparty v. hold-in-custody repos

A repo as we have described it so far is a "bilateral" repo; that is, only the two parties are involved. A "triparty" or "third party" repo involves another organization (the "triparty agent") to act as custodian for the collateral. In this case the collateral is delivered by the seller to the third party and held by that third party in a separate account on the buyer's behalf. The custodian's duties include:

- Arranging the DVP settlement at each end of the repo.
- Providing daily reports to both parties confirming the value of the collateral.
- Ensuring that the collateral satisfies the buyer's criteria regarding:
  – haircut
  – credit rating
  – tradability/liquidity
  – currency.
- Marking to market daily to ensure that the collateral is adequate.
- Overseeing any substitutions.

Such an arrangement requires a separate agreement between all three parties regarding the custody arrangements, which is separate from and in addition to the repo agreement between the two main parties. The third party's fees are paid by the seller. The major triparty custodians are Euroclear and Cedel in Europe, and Bank of New York and Chemical Bank in the US.

A disadvantage for the buyer of a triparty repo is the seller's ability to effect multiple substitutions. This means that the buyer cannot repo out the collateral on the other side. The buyer is unlikely anyway to receive a special as collateral, because the seller is likely to make a substitution if the existing collateral becomes special. The advantages for the buyer are:

- The administrative simplicity and lack of administrative and legal costs, particularly for companies, which can avoid the systems needed by banks dealing regularly in repos.

- The ability to adjust daily the amount of cash lent through a triparty open reverse repo; the settlement costs involved in daily changes where delivery is involved could make it uneconomic for the seller to enter such a transaction on a bilateral basis.

- The seller is prepared to pay a slightly higher repo rate because a triparty repo facilitates substitutions.

If a repo is of very short duration, or if the seller wishes to effect many substitutions, the administrative burden of transferring the collateral, either to the counterparty or to a third party, becomes increasingly costly in relative terms and could make a repo uneconomic. One solution is a "hold-in-custody" ("HIC") repo, where the seller continues to hold the collateral, but on the buyer's behalf, in a segregated account. For the buyer, this clearly entails a significantly greater credit risk, in return for which he expects a higher return on his cash. As with a triparty repo however, the buyer is unable to use the collateral in a repo himself. For the seller, a HIC repo offers reduced costs and administration, and ease of substitution. The seller in a HIC repo is of course not permitted to use the same collateral in more than one repo. This illegal practice is called "double-dipping."

**Bilateral repo v. triparty and hold-in-custody**

Fig 5.3

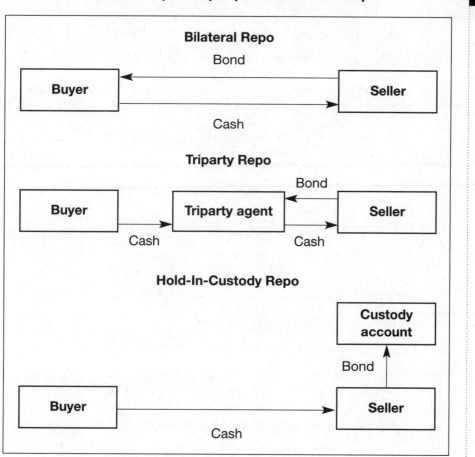

# Cross-currency repo

It may be that the seller in the repo wishes to borrow cash in one currency but has a security to offer in a different currency. This is acceptable as the security is being offered essentially as collateral, and is known as a cross-currency repo. In this case, however, the buyer is exposed to greater potential volatility in the value of the collateral – it is vulnerable to changes in both yields and exchange rates. The buyer may therefore require a larger haircut for a cross-currency repo.

**Example 5.8**

The seller wishes to borrow DEM 60,000,000 cash

Deal date: July 15, 1996

Settlement date: July 17, 1996

Term: 28 days (August 14, 1996)

Repo rate: 4.0% (ACT/360 basis)

Collateral: UK gilt 10.7% with maturity April 24,1999 and semi-annual coupons (ACT/365 basis)

Clean bond price: 106.40

Haircut: 5%

Spot £/DEM exchange rate: 2.3150

Clean price of bond is 106.40

Accrued coupon on bond on July 17, 1996 $= \dfrac{84}{365} \times 10.7 = 2.46246575$

Total purchase price = 108.86246575

Allowing for the haircut, the collateral must have a value of DEM 60,000,000 × 1.05 = DEM 63,000,000

Converted to sterling at the spot exchange rate, this is equivalent to:

$$£ \frac{63,000,000}{2.3150} = £27,213,822.89$$

The nominal amount of bond to be transferred is therefore:

$$£ \frac{27,213,822.89}{108.86246575/100} = £24,998,352.46$$

(UK gilts can in fact be transacted in denominations of £0.01.)

### Flows on July 17, 1996

£24,998,352.46 bond

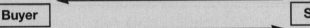

| Buyer | ← | Seller |

DEM 60,000,000 cash

On maturity of the repo, the seller will repay the cash with interest calculated at 4.0%:

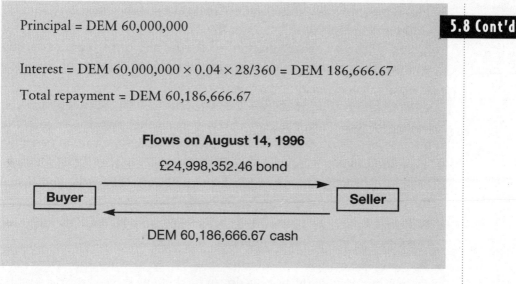

Principal = DEM 60,000,000

Interest = DEM 60,000,000 × 0.04 × 28/360 = DEM 186,666.67

Total repayment = DEM 60,186,666.67

**Flows on August 14, 1996**

£24,998,352.46 bond

| Buyer | → | Seller |

DEM 60,186,666.67 cash

## Maturity

Repos can in theory be transacted for any length of time. In practice, the period (or "term") is usually short – generally from one day (an "overnight" repo) to several months – because the market is driven largely by bond dealers' positions, which tend not to be established with a long time horizon. If the period is fixed and agreed in advance it is a "term repo." The alternative is an "open repo," where either party may call for the repo to be terminated at any time, although often requiring two days' notice. In an open repo, the repo interest rate changes each day – effectively the repo is rolled over each day. Another name for an open repo is a "day-to-day" repo.

## Rate considerations

In general, the rate at which it is possible to borrow through a repo is lower than for an unsecured (or "clean") interbank loan. This is because the credit risk on which the buyer is relying is improved. First, there is a second line of defence in that, if the buyer defaults, the seller can look to the collateral to recover the money. Second, the credit quality of the collateral – usually but not always government bonds – is often higher than the credit quality of the seller.

Other factors also affect the repo rate:

- To the extent that the collateral quality is reduced by using lesser credits, the repo rate will be relatively higher.

- The repo rate should be higher when the market in the particular collateral is less liquid – generally reflected by a higher bid/offer spread in the securities market – because the buyer can less easily realize the value of the collateral in the event of default.

- A right of collateral substitution provides a convenience for the seller and an administrative burden and loss of flexibility for the buyer, for which the seller must be willing to pay; the higher the number of substitutions allowed, the higher the repo rate in general.

- A hold-in-custody repo is more expensive than a bilateral repo because of the greater credit risk to the buyer. The risk, and hence the rate, for a triparty repo lies between these two.

- Willingness on the buyer's part to accept a lower haircut and/or a cross-currency repo will tend to increase the repo rate.

- The most dramatic effect on repo rates can arise when the collateral is special. In this case, the price is driven by the buyer's need for the specific security. If the security is in very short supply in the market, the repo rate can be several percentage points below the normal cost of funds.

- The baseline for repo rates is of course provided by comparable money market rates – clean deposit, CDs, etc. – for the same term, rather than bond yields.

- Bond market conditions do affect repo rates, however. In a generally bearish bond market, when dealers are shorting bonds and need to borrow them, repo rates will tend to be lower. Conversely, in a bull market for bonds, dealers need to finance their positions, which tends to raise repo rates.

- An open repo on which the rate is re-set daily, for example at an agreed spread compared to overnight interest rates, should be cheaper than an overnight repo. Although the open repo can be closed at a day's notice, and the collateral can be substituted, the costs incurred each day with overnight repos through transferring cash and securities are avoided.

## Variations on the basic structure

There are several variations on the basic structure of a repo.

### Dollar repo

In a dollar repo the buyer is permitted, within agreed parameters, to return different securities from those originally purchased, provided that they have the same all-in value.

### Forward start repo

The first leg of a repo is normally settled on the usual settlement date for the security involved. It is possible to deal a repo where the first leg settles on a different date – a forward start repo – equivalent to a forward-forward borrowing or deposit.

### Flex repo

In a flex repo, the cash is repaid to the buyer in stages. This is useful, for example, when the seller is using the repo to finance the purchase of an amortizing asset such as a mortgage-backed security.

### Floating rate repo

In this, generally a longer-term repo, the repo interest rate is re-set at pre-determined intervals according to some benchmark, such as LIBOR. In France, floating-rate repos based on the domestic TMP index are common.

### Reverse to maturity

In a reverse to maturity, the maturity date of the repo is the same as the maturity date of the security used as collateral.

## BUY/SELL-BACK

A buy/sell-back is similar to a classic repo but the two legs of the deal, although dealt simultaneously, are treated as two separate transactions rather than one. The economics of the deal are the same, however, and in a straightforward deal the amounts of cash which pass at the beginning and the end are the same.

In the example given above of a classic repo, the cash amount passing in the second leg of the repo was calculated as "principal plus interest" on the cash loan and expressed as a single amount. In a straightforward buy/sell-back, the same total amount of cash passes on the second leg as in a repo. The difference is that this amount is then expressed as two parts – a forward clean price for the security and the accrued coupon on it.

**Example 5.**

With the same information as Example 5.1:

Currency: DEM

Deal date: July 15, 1996

Settlement date: July 17, 1996

Term: 28 days (August 14, 1996)

Repo rate: 4.0% (ACT/360 basis)

Collateral: DEM 60,000,000 nominal 8.5% bond with maturity March 26, 2004 and annual coupons (30(E)/360 basis)

Clean bond price: 108.95

Clean price of bond for value July 17, 1996 is 108.95

Accrued coupon on bond on July 17, 1996 $= \dfrac{111}{360} \times 8.5 = 2.62083333$

Total purchase price = 111.57083333

### Flows on July 17, 1996

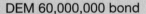

DEM 60,000,000 bond

| Buyer | | Seller |

DEM 66,942,500.00 cash

On maturity of the repo, the seller will repay the cash with interest calculated at 4.0%:

Principal = DEM 66,942,500.00

Interest = DEM 66,942,500.00 × 28/360 × 0.04 = DEM 208,265,56

Total repayment = DEM 67,150,765.56

Note that so far, the calculations are identical to a classic repo.

Now the total repayment must be converted to a forward price for the bond:

Forward dirty price

$$= \frac{\text{total cash repayment}}{\text{nominal bond amount}} \times 100 = \frac{\text{DEM } 67,150,765.56}{\text{DEM } 60,000,000} \times 100$$

$$= 111.91794260$$

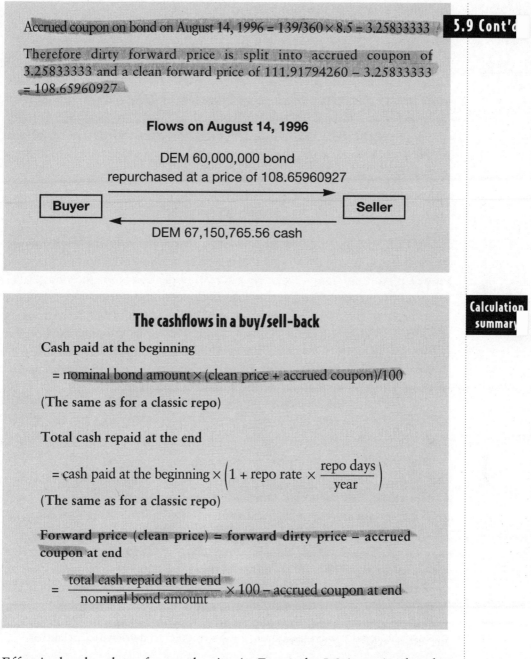

Accrued coupon on bond on August 14, 1996 = 139/360 × 8.5 = 3.25833333

Therefore dirty forward price is split into accrued coupon of 3.25833333 and a clean forward price of 111.91794260 − 3.25833333 = 108.65960927

**Flows on August 14, 1996**

DEM 60,000,000 bond
repurchased at a price of 108.65960927

Buyer → Seller

DEM 67,150,765.56 cash

**Calculation summary**

## The cashflows in a buy/sell-back

**Cash paid at the beginning**

= nominal bond amount × (clean price + accrued coupon)/100

(The same as for a classic repo)

**Total cash repaid at the end**

= cash paid at the beginning × $\left(1 + \text{repo rate} \times \frac{\text{repo days}}{\text{year}}\right)$

(The same as for a classic repo)

**Forward price (clean price) = forward dirty price − accrued coupon at end**

= $\frac{\text{total cash repaid at the end}}{\text{nominal bond amount}}$ × 100 − accrued coupon at end

Effectively, the clean forward price in Example 5.9 is arrived at by taking the starting price, adding interest at the repo rate, and then adjusting for the difference in accrued coupon between start and finish. In fact (ignoring the complication arising from the fact that the day/year count for the repo rate and coupon rate may be different):

Forward clean price =

$$\text{starting clean price} + \left(\text{repo rate} \times \text{starting dirty price} - \text{coupon rate} \times 100\right) \times \frac{\text{days}}{\text{year}}$$

As a result it is usually true that the forward clean price is greater than the starting clean price if the repo rate is greater than the coupon rate, and vice versa. This is not always true, however, if the dirty price of the bond is significantly different from 100 – either because the bond is trading at a large discount or because it is trading at a large premium or has significant accrued coupon at the start.

## Coupon payments

If there is a coupon payment on the security during the term of the buy/sell-back, it is received by the buyer in the same way as in a classic repo. Unlike in a classic repo, however, it is typically not then paid over to the counterparty. Clearly this affects the economics of the deal, as the counterparty needs to be compensated. The amount of the coupon is therefore taken into account in the same way as in the calculation of a theoretical bond futures price where an interim coupon may arise.

We know that without a coupon during the repo, the total amount of money repaid at the end of the buy/sell-back is:

$$(\text{original purchase price} + \text{accrued coupon}) \times \left(1 + \text{repo rate} \times \frac{\text{days}}{\text{year}}\right)$$

If now we include a coupon payment during the repo, the buyer will receive the benefit of that payment. In order to restore the economics of the deal, the value of that payment is deducted from the cash amount repaid by the seller at maturity. Furthermore, as the buyer is also able to invest the coupon payment itself, we also deduct the investment income that can be earned on it from coupon date until maturity of the repo. A usual assumption is that the coupon can be invested at the original repo rate; although unlikely to be correct, the effect of using a different rate would generally be very small.

The total amount of money repaid at the end of the buy/sell-back is therefore adjusted to become:

$$(\text{original purchase price} + \text{accrued coupon}) \times \left(1 + \text{repo rate} \times \frac{\text{days}}{\text{year}}\right)$$

$$- \text{coupon received} \times \left(1 + \text{repo rate} \times \frac{\text{days from coupon to repo maturity}}{\text{year}}\right)$$

Example 5.10

Currency: DEM

Deal date: July 15, 1996

Settlement date: July 17, 1996

Term: 28 days (August 14, 1996)

Repo rate: 4.0% (ACT/360 basis)

Collateral: DEM 60,000,000 nominal 8.5% bond with maturity July 29, 2004 and annual coupons (30(E)/360 basis)

Clean bond price: 108.95

Clean price of bond for value July 17, 1996 is 108.95

Accrued coupon on bond on July 17, 1996 $= \dfrac{348}{360} \times 8.5 = 8.21666667$

Total purchase price = 117.16666667

**Flows on July 17, 1996**

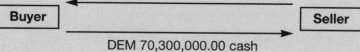

DEM 60,000,000 bond

**Buyer**        **Seller**

DEM 70,300,000.00 cash

On maturity of the repo, the seller owes the cash with interest calculated at 4.0%:

Principal = DEM 70,300,000.00

Interest = DEM 70,300,000.00 $\times$ 0.04 $\times \dfrac{28}{360}$ = DEM 218,711.11

Total due = DEM 70,518,711.11

However, the buyer has had the benefit of a coupon paid on July 29, 1996 which amounted to:

DEM 60,000,000 $\times$ 8.5% = DEM 5,100,000

The buyer has also earned interest on this – say at the repo rate of 4% from July 29 to August 14 – to give a total of:

$$DEM\ 5,100,000 \times \left(1 + 0.04 \times \frac{16}{360}\right) = DEM\ 5,109,066.67$$

**5.10 Cont'd**

This will therefore be deducted from the amount due at maturity of the repo, to give:

DEM 70,518,711.11 − DEM 5,109,066.67 = DEM 65,409,644.44

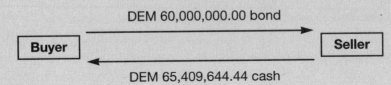

**Flows on August 14, 1996**

DEM 60,000,000.00 bond

Buyer ───────────────────────────► Seller

◄───────────────────────────

DEM 65,409,644.44 cash

If there are any other payments due on the bond during the repo, such as partial redemptions, these need to be taken into account in the same way. If the seller omits to take any such payments into account in calculating the forward price, the buyer is not legally obliged to compensate the seller. On the other hand, there would generally be a "gentlemen's understanding" that compensation should be made.

**Calculation summary**

## The cashflows in a buy/sell-back with a coupon payment

**Cash paid at the beginning**

= nominal bond amount × (clean price + accrued coupon)/100

**Value of intervening coupon**

= nominal bond amount × coupon ×

$$\left(1 + \text{repo rate} \times \frac{\text{days from coupon payment to end of repo}}{\text{year}}\right)$$

(Use $\frac{1}{2}$ × coupon rate if coupons are semi-annual)

**Total cash repaid at the end**

$$= \text{cash paid at the beginning} \times \left(1 + \text{repo rate} \times \frac{\text{repo days}}{\text{year}}\right) - \text{value of intervening coupon}$$

**Forward price (clean price) = forward dirty price − accrued coupon at end**

$$= \frac{\text{total cash repaid at the end}}{\text{nominal bond amount}} \times 100 - \text{accrued coupon at end}$$

# Initial margin

A haircut can be included for a buy/sell-back in the same way as for a classic repo. The initial collateral amount is increased by the amount of the haircut – or the cash amount reduced – and the forward price is then calculated as before.

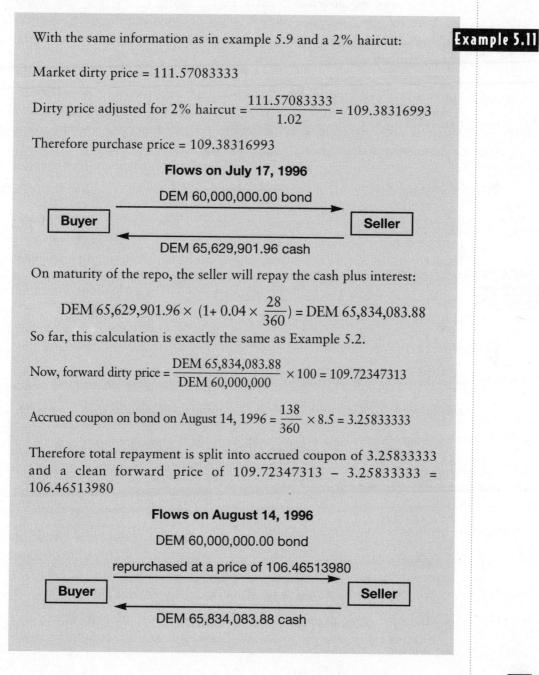

**Example 5.11**

With the same information as in example 5.9 and a 2% haircut:

Market dirty price = 111.57083333

Dirty price adjusted for 2% haircut $= \dfrac{111.57083333}{1.02} = 109.38316993$

Therefore purchase price = 109.38316993

**Flows on July 17, 1996**

DEM 60,000,000.00 bond

Buyer ────────────────────────────► Seller

◄────────────────────────────

DEM 65,629,901.96 cash

On maturity of the repo, the seller will repay the cash plus interest:

$$\text{DEM } 65,629,901.96 \times (1+ 0.04 \times \frac{28}{360}) = \text{DEM } 65,834,083.88$$

So far, this calculation is exactly the same as Example 5.2.

Now, forward dirty price $= \dfrac{\text{DEM } 65,834,083.88}{\text{DEM } 60,000,000} \times 100 = 109.72347313$

Accrued coupon on bond on August 14, 1996 $= \dfrac{138}{360} \times 8.5 = 3.25833333$

Therefore total repayment is split into accrued coupon of 3.25833333 and a clean forward price of 109.72347313 – 3.25833333 = 106.46513980

**Flows on August 14, 1996**

DEM 60,000,000.00 bond

repurchased at a price of 106.46513980

Buyer ────────────────────────────► Seller

◄────────────────────────────

DEM 65,834,083.88 cash

## Variation margin

If there is no legal agreement tying the two legs of the buy/sell-back together, there is no rationale for recording the security as "collateral" for the cash. There is therefore no procedure for marking to market, other than by an informal understanding between the two parties that the deal may be closed out early and re-established at a new bond price, in the same way as a classic repo. The practice regarding margin calls on a buy/sell-back therefore varies, but when it is done, it is to close out and reprice (as in Methods 3 and 4 for classic repos, *see* pages 86–91). Under the revised PSA/ISMA documentation, close out and repricing of buy/sell-backs is specifically included as a possibility.

In this case, the original buy/sell-back deal is closed out, and a new buy/sell-back established based on the original repo rate and the original maturity date, in exactly the same way as with a repo.

## Substitution

As the two legs of the transaction are separate, there is no possibility of substituting one security for another. As with margin calls, the only possibility is for the two parties to agree to close out the existing buy/sell-back and establish a new deal based on the same repo rate and maturity, but a different collateral.

## Maturity

As the second leg of the buy/sell-back has been agreed and dealt at a specific price, it is necessary to have a specific date – equivalent to a term repo. There is no means of transacting an "open" buy/sell-back.

## Comparison between classic repo and buy/sell-back

The following points summarize the pros and cons of the buy/sell back:

### Disadvantages

- Traditionally, buy/sell-backs have no special contractual close-out rights in the case of a default, since there is no legal documentation to specify events of default. The inclusion of buy/sell-backs in the revised PSA/ISMA documentation, however, allows for this.
- Buy/sell-backs have no margining rights, although in practice an initial margin may be taken and variation margin can be achieved

through closing out and repricing the transaction and is now covered under the PSA/ISMA agreement.

- In buy/sell-backs, the seller of a security has no right to the return of any coupon, and so must factor the expected coupon into the buy-back price. In practice, there may be an understanding that the buyer will compensate the seller if a payment is received which, through oversight, has not been factored into the forward price.

- There are no rights of substitution in buy/sell-backs, although a buyer may be prepared to accept this in practice through close-out and repricing.

- The ability to net obligations, in the case of default, reduces counterparty risk. This is increasingly recognized by central banks in determining capital adequacy requirements, so that undocumented buy/sell-backs may imply higher capital requirements. Again, the revised PSA/ISMA documentation does allow netting and close out for buy/sell-backs.

### Advantages

- A buy/sell-back is easier to book than a classic repo, as it does not require systems for marking to market and margining.

- Counterparties may find it simpler to trade without documentation; legal costs are reduced and the approval process is shortened. In markets such as Italy and Spain, for example, where it is usual for deals to be executed as buy/sell-backs rather than classic repos, there is no need for a master agreement. Corporates in general are often reluctant to accept the administration and legal costs involved with classic repos, particularly if their volume of business is not great.

# SECURITIES LENDING

When a repo is driven by the need of one party to borrow a particular security because he or she is short of it, the repo is special. It may be, however, that the lender of the security does not wish to borrow cash in return; for an already cash-rich lender to borrow more cash than is needed to place on deposit would probably cost him or her the bid–offer spread. Nevertheless, the lender wishes to take advantage of the fact of owning a security in short supply. Such a lender simply lends the securities for a fee. However, because the lender wishes to be secured against default by the borrower, he or she also takes collateral from the borrower, also in the form of securities. The exchange therefore becomes a loan of special against a loan of general collateral, with the lender of the special earning a fee, and is known as "securities lending" or "stock lending."

**Key Point**     *Securities lending is the loan of a special against collateral*

The terminology in securities lending follows that in a classic repo, but it must be remembered that the transaction is driven by the *special*, not by the general collateral. The "lender" is therefore the party lending the special and the borrower is the party borrowing the special (*see* Figure 5.4).

**Fig 5.4**

## Securities lending

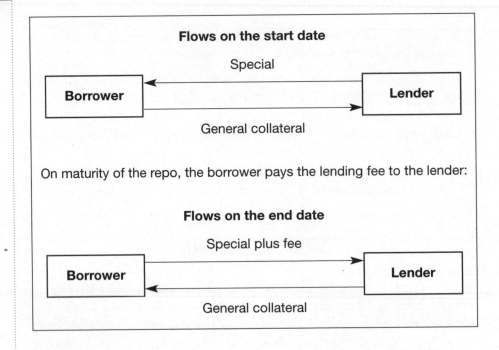

**Flows on the start date**

Special

Borrower → Lender

General collateral

On maturity of the repo, the borrower pays the lending fee to the lender:

**Flows on the end date**

Special plus fee

Borrower → Lender

General collateral

## Legal agreement

Securities lending is transacted under a single agreement, with provisions parallel to those in a classic repo agreement. The standard documentation generally used in the UK for international lending transactions is the December 1995 version of the Overseas Securities Lender's Agreement (OSLA) prepared by the International Securities Lenders' Association (ISLA), which is based on UK law. When the securities involved are equities, the documentation used is the Equity Stock Lending Agreement – recently revised in line with the latest versions of the GMRA (November 1995) and the UK's domestic Gilt Edged Stock Lending Agreement (April 1996). In the US the documentation used is the PSA's Master Securities Loan Agreement.

> *Securities lending is transacted under a single agreement – like a classic repo but unlike a traditional buy/sell-back*

**Key Point**

Classic repos and buy/sell-backs both involve an absolute transfer of legal title in the collateral from the borrower of the special to the lender for the period of the transaction. The situation with regard to securities lending depends on the documentation used. Under the OSLA, for example, ownership of the securities lent is transferred from lender to borrower as with a classic repo, and ownership of the collateral is transferred from borrower to lender. Under the PSA documentation, however, the transfer of collateral involves a pledge rather than an outright transfer of ownership.

## Collateral

The collateral used in securities lending may be general collateral of a similar nature to the special. There is, however, no need for the collateral to be similar, and in fact securities lending can be transacted against any collateral acceptable to the lender, such as Treasury bills, CDs, bankers' acceptances, or bank letters of credit. A letter of credit has the disadvantage that the bank providing it will charge the borrower for issuing it as a guarantee, but the borrower may still be willing to provide this collateral if no other is available. Cash can also be used as collateral; in that case the transaction is very similar in all respects to a classic repo for a special.

## Coupon payment and other rights

If a coupon, or other payment such as a partial redemption, is payable on the security lent during the transaction, the treatment is the same as in a classic repo, not as in a buy/sell-back – that is, the borrower is obliged to make a matching payment to the lender to compensate for the loss of the income. Similarly, if there is a payment on the collateral, the lender is obliged to make a matching payment to the borrower.

Depending on the nature of the security lent, there may also be other rights attached to ownership, such as voting rights, rights to convert the security to a different security (for example from a bond to equity), or rights to purchase more of the security (a "rights issue"). As far as the issuer of the security is concerned, it is the current registered owner of the security or, in the case of a bearer security, the current holder, who can exercise these rights – that is, the borrower. The treatment of such rights under the securities lending transaction varies according to the documentation used. In the OSLA and the Equities Stock Lending Agreement (ESLA), for example, the borrower is obliged to exercise voting rights in accordance with the lender's wishes, but only as long as the borrower does still own the security. In practice the borrower may well have either sold or on-lent the security and is therefore not in a position to exercise voting rights. If the borrower does still own the security, the lender must in any case give adequate notice of his or her wishes (and in the case of a rights issue, for example, pay the borrower the cash required for the new issue). In the PSA's documentation, the lender specifically waives the ability to exercise any control over voting.

> **Key Point**
>
> *Coupon payments on the security lent are received by the borrower, who must make matching payments to the lender*
>
> *Payments on the collateral, if ownership is transferred, are received by the lender, who must make matching payments to the borrower*
>
> *Voting rights depend on the agreement*

## Pricing

The lender in a securities lending transaction is paid a fee by the borrower. The fee is quoted in terms of basis points per annum and is generally paid on the market value of the securities lent and paid at the end of the transaction. The fee is equivalent in practice to the difference between the market classic repo rate for general collateral and the market classic repo rate for borrowing the security as a special.

If the collateral provided is cash, the lender (that is, the lender of the securities) pays the borrower interest on the collateral at an agreed rate. The fee is then deducted as a "rebate" off this interest.

> *The lender in securities lending is paid a fee based on the market value of the security*
>
> **Key Point**

## Settlement

The method of settlement in a securities lending transaction will depend on the nature of the collateral involved. Typically, as generally no cash is involved, the security and the collateral will each be delivered free at the beginning of the loan and at the end of the loan, with a separate payment of the fee at the end of the transaction. An alternative is for the security and the collateral each to be delivered by DVP, with the matching cash amounts offsetting.

In the case of a non-US government security lent under the PSA's documentation where the two parties have a series of transactions still outstanding under a master agreement, the lending fee is payable on the fifteenth of the month following the month in which the transaction ends.

## Margin

Initial margin may be demanded by the lender in the same way as in a classic repo or a buy/sell-back. In the case of securities lending, however, it is the lender who would request the initial margin, not the borrower as would normally be the case in a classic repo, because it is the securities being lent which are driving the deal. Variation margin may also be paid in the same way as in a classic repo, but again this is generally by adjusting the amount of collateral rather than the amount of the security lent, because the deal has been driven by the borrower's need for that particular amount of that security.

> *When initial margin is required, it is in favor of the lender, not the borrower*
>
> **Key Point**

# Other features

A securities lending transaction is similar to a classic repo in other respects such as:

- Substitution (the ability to substitute one acceptable form of collateral for another).
- Cross-currency lending (the ability to supply collateral in a different currency from the security lent, if acceptable to the lender).
- Maturity (open or fixed term).

**Example 5.12**

Deal date: July 15, 1996

Settlement date: July 17,1996

Term: 28 days (August 14, 1996)

Security: DEM 60,000,000 nominal 8.5% bond with maturity March 26, 2004 and annual coupons (30(E)/360 basis)

Lending fee: 50 basis points per annum (ACT/360 basis)

Clean bond price for security: 108.95

Collateral: DEM 60,000,000 nominal 6.5% bond with maturity September 20, 2001 and annual coupons (30(E)/360 basis)

Clean bond price for collateral: 99.26

Haircut: 2%

Clean price of security lent for value July 17, 1996 is 108.95

Accrued coupon on security lent on July 17, 1996 = $111/360 \times 8.5 = 2.62083333$

Market dirty price = 111.57083333

Value of security = DEM $60,000,000 \times \dfrac{111.57083333}{100}$ = DEM 66,942,500.00

Because the haircut of 2% is required by the *lender*, the value of the collateral must be 2% *greater* than this:

Clean price of collateral for value July 17, 1996 is 99.26

Accrued coupon on collateral on July 17, 1996 = $297/360 \times 6.5 = 5.3625$

Market dirty price = 104.6225

Therefore nominal amount of collateral required

$$= \frac{DEM\ 68,281,350.00}{104.6225/100} = DEM\ 65,264,498.55$$

Rounding up, the collateral passed would be, say DEM 65,265,000.

**Flows on July 17, 1996**

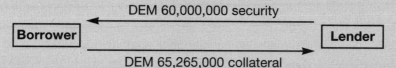

DEM 60,000,000 security

Borrower      Lender

DEM 65,265,000 collateral

On maturity of the loan, the security lent and the collateral are reversed. The fee paid to the lender is calculated on the value of the security lent, for the period of the loan, on a money market basis (ACT/360):

$$Fee = DEM\ 66,942,500.00 \times 0.005 \times \frac{28}{360} = DEM\ 26,033.19$$

**Flows on August 14, 1996**

DEM 60,000,000 security
plus DEM 26,033.19 fee

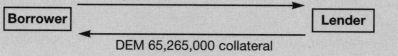

Borrower      Lender

DEM 65,265,000 collateral

Note that if the repo rate for general collateral was 4.0%, as in our earlier examples, the repo rate for this security as a special would be 50 basis points lower, at 3.50%

## Clearing organizations' lending facilities

As with classic repo, securities need to be borrowed when the trader is short, either because he has deliberately taken a short position or because a purchase trade has failed. An important facility offered by various securities clearing organizations is the automatic loan of securities under such circumstances. Thus for example, a securities firm which is a member of Cedel or Euroclear can set up a facility whereby if their account in a particular security is short at the end of the day, the clearing organization will automatically lend that security to it – particularly useful in the case of a failed trade.

This depends of course on the clearing organization being able to borrow that security from another member – either under a corresponding automatic lending arrangement with that member, or a "case-by-case" arrangement whereby the lender agrees each transaction separately. Lenders are selected from among members at random. As the clearing organization stands between the two sides of the transaction, the borrower and lender remain anonymous to each other. Such a facility can be used where the collateral for the transaction can be cleared through the organization (including cash, since member firms keep cash accounts with the clearers), but not where the collateral is say a letter of credit.

Cedel and Euroclear also offer triparty securities lending facilities, analogous to triparty repo. In this case, the clearing organization again has the following responsibilities:

- Arranging settlement at each end of the loan.
- Providing daily reports to both parties confirming the value of the collateral.
- Ensuring that the collateral is suitable.
- Marking to market daily to ensure that the collateral is adequate.
- Overseeing any substitutions.

As with triparty repo, such an arrangement requires a separate agreement between all three parties regarding the triparty arrangements, which is separate from and in addition to the securities lending agreement between the two parties.

## COMPARISON BETWEEN THE DIFFERENT TRANSACTIONS

Table 5.1 compares the classic repo, buy/sell-back, and securities lending.

## Comparison between the different transactions

Table 5.1

|  | Classic repo | Buy/sell-back | Securities lending |
|---|---|---|---|
| **Basis of transaction** | Cash v. securities | Cash v. securities | Securities v. other securities, letter of credit, cash, or any other acceptable collateral |
| **Documentation** | Single agreement such as the GMRA; full rights of offset in case of default | Two separate transactions with no specific rights of offset in case of default (although now also covered under the GMRA, which does include offset) | Single lending agreement such as the OSLA; full rights of offset in case of default |
| **Coupon payment** | Returned to seller | Kept by buyer | Returned to lender; other rights depend on documentation |
| **Fee/cost** | Quoted as repo rate; paid as interest rate on cash amount | Quoted as repo rate; paid through price differential between purchase price and forward repurchase price | Quoted as fee (% per annum on the cash value); paid at maturity. If collateral is cash, rebate is offset against interest paid on the cash |
| **Margin rights** | Initial margin and variation margin both possible; initial margin usually in favor of borrower | Initial margin possible, usually in favor of borrower. Variation margin possible only through close out and repricing | Initial margin and variation margin both possible; initial margin in favor of lender |
| **Substitution** | Lender can substitute collateral | Possible only through close out and repricing | Borrower can substitute collateral |
| **Maturity** | Fixed-term or open | Fixed-term only | Fixed-term or open |

# EXERCISES

**23.** A dealer repos out USD 10 million of US T-bills as follows:

| | |
|---|---|
| Settlement date: | March 4 |
| Maturity date of T-bills: | May 25 |
| Discount rate quoted on T-bills in the market: | 6.2% |
| Repo rate: | 6.4% |
| Term of repo: | 1 week |
| No haircut | |

   **a.** How much cash does the dealer receive?

   **b.** The next day, the discount rate quoted on the T-bills falls to 6.0%. What face value of T-bills will be transferred and to whom?

**24.** A dealer repos BEF 1000 million T-bills and demands a 2% haircut from the buyer, as follows:

| | |
|---|---|
| Remaining maturity of T-bills: | 91 days |
| Yield on T-bills: | 4.8% |
| Repo rate: | 4.9% |
| Repo term: | 7 days |

How much cash does the dealer receive?

**25.** For settlement on August 18, 1997, a dealer borrows DEM 100 million from a money market fund at 3.25% through a one-week repo, against a $7\frac{1}{2}$% Bund. The last coupon was June 15. The current price of the bond is 105.80. Assuming a haircut of 2% and minimum denominations for the bond of DEM 1000, draw a diagram showing all the flows involved.

**26.** A dealer needs to borrow DEM 50 million and uses an OBL as collateral as follows:

| | |
|---|---|
| Collateral: | 5.9% OBL March 26, 2001 |
| Price: | 101.49 |
| Start date of repo: | November 12, 1997 |
| Term of repo: | 30 days |
| Repo rate: | 3.76% |
| Haircut: | 2.5% |

**a.** How much collateral does the dealer transfer, assuming minimum denominations of DEM 1000?

**b.** On November 26, the price of the OBL has risen to 102.59. What nominal amount of the securities will be transferred, and to whom?

**c.** On December 3, the dealer wishes to make a substitution, using the following security instead:

Collateral:          6.1% OBL April 14, 2000
Price:             102.44

What nominal amount of this collateral does the dealer use to replace the original collateral?

**27.** A treasurer wants to borrow USD for two months using his holding of DEM 20 million Bunds in a cross-currency repo as follows:

| | |
|---|---|
| Clean price of Bunds: | 98.00 |
| Term: | July 5 (spot) to September 5 |
| Previous coupon date on Bund: | 21 March |
| Coupon rate on Bund: | 5% |
| Spot USD/DEM: | 1.4735 |
| 2-month USD repo rate: | 4.80% |
| Haircut: | 5% |

How many dollars does the treasurer receive on July 5?

**28.** A dealer does the following buy/sell-back:

| | |
|---|---|
| Start date: | April 14, 1997 |
| Maturity date: | July 14,1997 |
| Repo rate: | 5.52% |
| Security: | FRF 200 million 8% coupon OAT |
| Previous coupon date: | June 2,1996 |
| Clean price of bond at start: | 103.42 |
| Haircut: | 2.5% |

What is the forward price?

**29.** During the buy/sell-back in the previous question, the market clean price of the bond rises to 106.28 on May 14. The seller asks to close out and reprice the deal, and the buyer agrees. Assuming only a movement in securities rather than cash, what is the forward price of the new repriced deal? Assume a minimum denomination for the OAT of FRF 2000.

**30.** In the following securities lending transaction, what is the minimum face value of collateral required, and what is the amount of the lending fee?

| | |
|---|---|
| Start date: | April 14, 1997 |
| Maturity date: | July 14, 1997 |
| Lending fee: | 45 basis points per annum |
| Security lent: | DEM 50 million 6% coupon Bund |
| Previous coupon date: | June 2, 1996 |
| Clean price of bond at start: | 105.23 |
| Collateral: | Deutschmark CD with 4% coupon; issue date March 10, 1997; maturity date September 10, 1997; current market yield 5.85% |
| Initial margin: | 3.0% |

**31.** Discuss the differences between repo, buy/sell-back, and securities lending, comparing the advantages and disadvantages of each.

**32.** Discuss the advantages and disadvantages of triparty repos versus bilateral and HIC repos.

**33.** Discuss the factors which might affect the repo rate for a particular transaction.

■ ■ ■

*"A repo offers the unique credit enhancement provided by the double security of its structure – ... the credit standing of both the counter-party and the issuer of the collateral."*

# The Users and Applications of Repos

Although the concept of a repo is straightforward, there are various different situations which give rise to them. The examples discussed here have been categorized according to the type of market participant whose situation drives the deal. In practice, as there are always two parties involved, at least two of these situations arise.

# BOND DEALERS

## The need to fund a long position

There are two reasons why dealers may acquire a long position in a particular bond. First, they may buy it because they are bullish. Second, whether or not bullish, they may make a two-way price in the security and counterparties may deal on the bid price. Assuming that a dealer is starting from a square position, with no surplus funds, he or she needs to borrow cash to fund this position. In order to borrow the cash easily and cheaply, the dealer repos out the security being bought (or another already owned) as collateral against the cash, as shown in Figure 6.1.

**Fig 6.1**

### Funding a long position

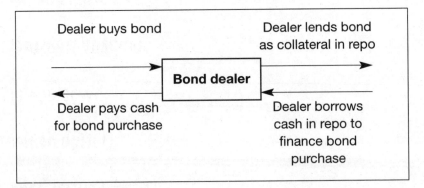

## The need to cover a short position

Conversely, bond dealers may acquire a short position in a particular security. First, they may sell it because they are bearish. Second, whether or not bearish, they may make a two-way price in the security and counterparties may deal on the offer price. Third, they may have a strategy to buy one bond and sell another because they anticipate a movement in one relative to the other; again this involves going short of a bond. A dealer who is not already long in that security cannot deliver on the sale. If the dealer does not deliver the security, however, the deal is not canceled and the dealer is still liable for delivery. Any delay can be very expensive for the defaulting dealer. Assuming that settlement is DVP, he or she will not receive the cash due until delivery, so that the counterparty continues to earn interest on the cash. On the other side, however, no adjustment will be made to the accrued coupon included in the sale price – when the security is finally delivered, the seller has not earned extra coupon on the security but has lost interest on the cash. In addition, dealers in some markets are charged a penalty for failed trades.

**Example 6.1**

Deal date: July 15, 1996

Settlement date: July 17, 1996

Dealer sells DEM 100,000,000 of 8.5% bond, maturity March 26, 2004

Clean bond price: 108.95

Day-to-day funding cost: 5.0%

Accrued coupon on bond on July 17, 1996 = 111/360 × 8.5 = 2.62083333

Total sale price = 111.57083333

Total sale consideration = DEM 111,570,833.33

If the dealer is unable to deliver the bond until July 18, he or she will still receive the same amount of cash, DEM 111,570,833.33, because he or she is entitled to accrued coupon only up to the agreed settlement date of July 17.

Because the dealer is receiving the cash a day late, however, he or she has effectively lost one day's interest on the cash, at 5.0%:

$$\text{DEM } 111{,}570{,}833.33 \times 0.05 \times \frac{1}{360} = \text{DEM } 15{,}495.95$$

The dealer must therefore borrow the security in order to deliver it on time. One possibility is to borrow the security from the exchange or clearing house through which it is settled (such as Cedel or Euroclear) if this facility is available. There are several disadvantages with this: first, the particular security may not be available, although this should not often be a problem as these clearing houses have access to large volumes of the security. Second, the cost is usually high. Third, the dealer does not know when the security borrowed will be demanded back by the seller.

An alternative is to reverse in the security against the cash which has been generated by the security sale. In this case the security is a special, because only that specific security, and no other, is of use to the dealer in this situation (*see* Figure 6.2).

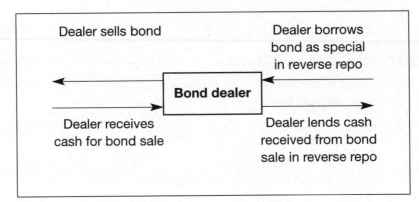

**Fig 6.2**

**Borrowing via reverse repo**

## Covering a failed purchase

Even a dealer who does not have a short position on his or her book, may still be short of a security on delivery because an offsetting purchase has failed on settlement. Suppose, for example, that a dealer has both bought and sold the same security; if the purchase settlement has failed, the dealer cannot deliver on the sale. Again, he can use a reverse repo to avoid default, as shown in Figure 6.3.

## Covering a failed purchase

Fig 6.3

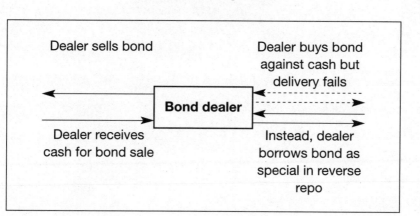

It may also be that a transfer of a security between a domestic clearing system and Euroclear or Cedel cannot take place on the same day, so that the dealer knows he or she will be short for a day or longer. It is therefore worthwhile borrowing the security to deliver on the sale, until such time as the purchase is delivered. As long as the dealer is earning some positive interest on the cash lent in the reverse repo, he or she is gaining.

---

**Example 6.2**

**Bond sale:**

Deal date: July 15, 1996

Settlement date: July 17, 1996

Dealer sells DEM 100,000,000 of 8.5% bond, maturity March 26, 2004

Clean bond price: 108.95

Accrued coupon on bond on July 17, 1996 = $111/360 \times 8.5 = 2.62083333$

Total sale price = 111.57083333

Total sale consideration = DEM 111,570,833.33

**Bond purchase:**

Deal date: July 15, 1996

Settlement date: July 18, 1996

**6.2 Cont'd**

Dealer buys DEM 100,000,000 of the same bond

Clean bond price: 108.90

Accrued coupon on bond on July18, 1996 = $\dfrac{112}{360} \times 8.5 = 2.64444444$

Total purchase price = 111.54444444

Total purchase consideration = DEM 111,544,444.44

**Reverse repo:**

Deal date:  July 15, 1996

Dealer reverses in the bond through a repo from July 17 to July 18

Overnight repo rate: 5.0%

Clean bond price: 108.95

Repo amount = DEM 111,570,833.33, as above (market clean price of the bond plus accrued coupon on July 17)

Total amount repaid on July 18:

$$\text{DEM } 111{,}570{,}833.33 \times \left(1 + 0.05 \times \frac{1}{360}\right) = \text{DEM } 111{,}586{,}329.28$$

**Resulting cashflows on July 18:**

The dealer pays DEM 111,544,444.44 for the bond purchase and receives DEM 111,586,329.28 on the second leg of the reverse repo – a net inflow of DEM 41,884.84.

In this case, the net amount is made up from the profit in the dealer's bond price spread (the difference between 108.90 and 108.95, worth DEM 50,000), the loss of a day's bond coupon between sale and purchase (1 day at 8.5%, worth DEM 23,611.11) and the gain of a day's repo interest (1 day at 5.0%, worth DEM 15,495.95).

## Hedging an overall long position

A dealer whose position is generally long of bonds may wish to hedge some part of that position. A reverse repo enables the dealer to establish a short hedge – by selling other bonds – not in his or her portfolio and which are seen as less attractive – and reversing them in. This short hedge can be taken as a short-term strategy and rolled over repeatedly as each reverse repo matures.

# INVESTORS

Investors with cash to deposit in the money market – that is, for a short-term investment – have a choice of instruments: a clean deposit, a certificate of deposit, a bill of exchange, a Treasury bill, commercial paper, or a repo. A repo offers the unique credit enhancement provided by the double security of its structure – investors can look to the credit standing of both the counterparty *and* the issuer of the collateral. It also has the advantage that investors can determine both the exact maturity and exact amount of the investment – features shared with a clean deposit but not with the other instruments. A repo also offers a range of risk/reward profiles. For example, a bilateral repo secured against government T-bills offers very little risk, and a correspondingly low return (often below LIBID, although if the seller is not of top creditworthiness the return will often be above LIBID and can be above LIBOR, particularly with a triparty or hold-in-custody (HIC) repo). A HIC repo, or a repo based on low quality collateral on the other hand, offers a higher return but higher risk – because of the possibility of default of either the counterparty or the collateral issuer, or both. Overall therefore, the repo market offers investors a liquid and flexible alternative to other money market instruments.

In general, investors using reverse repos gain from disintermediation – removal of the "middle man." If a weaker bank is looking for interbank cash, it will have to pay a first class bank more than LIBOR for the money. Instead it can go directly to an investor willing to lend cash against good quality collateral. This cuts out the bigger bank and gives the investor a better return and good security.

The collateralized nature of the investment has a further advantage if the investor is a bank. For cash placed on deposit, the bank must allocate part of its capital against the risk of default by the cash borrower. With a repo, the amount of capital to be allocated is significantly reduced and may be zero. This is discussed further in chapter 9.

A repo is essentially a short-term instrument, so that reverse repos provide rolling short-term investments. For investors wishing to fix their return long term, the reverse repos can be overlaid by FRAs or currency swaps. This will not fix the return precisely, because the differential between subsequent reverse repo rates and LIBOR (against which the FRAs or swaps would be settled) is unknown, but the investors would no longer be vulnerable to general movements in short-term interest rates.

# MATCHED BOOK DEALERS

"Matched book" dealers are not in fact dealers who always keep their trading book completely matched; but, rather, dealers who offer two-way prices, without necessarily matching the two sides of their trading at all.

## Taking a view on interest rates

A dealer who takes a view on interest rates – for example, that short-term rates will rise – can borrow cash through a longer-term repo and lend it through a shorter-term reverse. If correct, the dealer can then lend out the cash again through a new reverse repo when the first one matures. This is equivalent to selling short-term futures or buying an FRA. Having taken such a view, the position can in fact later be hedged through FRAs or futures if the dealer changes his or her mind.

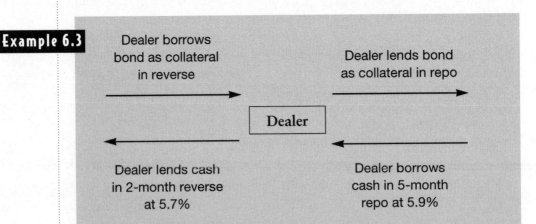

**Example 6.3**

Dealer borrows bond as collateral in reverse

Dealer lends bond as collateral in repo

Dealer

Dealer lends cash in 2-month reverse at 5.7%

Dealer borrows cash in 5-month repo at 5.9%

In this example, the dealer is hoping that interest rates will rise. If three-month rates rise by 0.4% after two months, for example, the dealer should be able to lend cash again for three months at 6.1%, using a new reverse repo, when the first reverse repo matures. The exact break-even rate (the rate at which the whole strategy gives neither profit nor loss) depends on compound interest, because the dealer will receive interest after two months, at the original two-month repo rate. This interest receipt will then be reinvested at the new three-month repo rate. This is exactly the same calculation as we did for a theoretical FRA rate in chapter 2.

If we assume a 360-day year basis, a two-month period of 61 days and a five-month period of 153 days, this gives as the break-even rate:

$$\left[ \frac{(1 + 0.059 \times \frac{153}{360})}{(1 + 0.057 \times \frac{61}{360})} - 1 \right] \times \frac{360}{92} = 5.97\%$$

If the dealer can roll over the reverse repo at higher than 5.97%, he or she will make a profit.

It may be that in the course of making two-way repo prices, the dealer becomes a seller in a five-month repo at 5.9 percent and a buyer in a two-month reverse repo at 5.7 percent, without actually wishing to take such a view. In this situation, the dealer can immediately hedge his or her position by selling an FRA or buying futures contracts, to protect against the risk that three-month interest rates may in fact fall (or at least, not rise as high as 5.97 percent). The forward-forward position (in this case a two-month v. five-month position) is known as a "tail." Figure 6.4 and Example 6.4 illustrate this.

## Hedging a tail

Fig 6.4

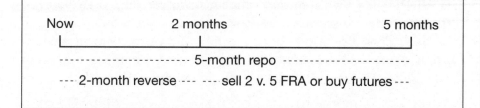

**Example 6.4**    Dealer does reverse now for two months (61 days) at 5.7% on US$1 million cash.

Dealer does repo now for 5 months (153 days) at 5.9% on US$ 1 million cash.

Dealer hedges the tail by selling 2 v. 5 FRA now at 6.15%.

What is the dealer's profit or loss?

The total proceeds received back by the dealer at the end of five months on the cash lent out now is given by:

$$\$1 \text{ million} \times (1 + 0.057 \times \tfrac{61}{360}) \times (1 + 0.0615 \times \tfrac{92}{360}) = \$1,025,526.80$$

The total payment he must make at the end of five months on the cash he has borrowed through the repo is given by:

$$\$1 \text{ million} \times (1 + 0.059 \times \tfrac{153}{360}) = \$1,025,075.00$$

The dealer therefore *appears* to have a fully hedged profit of $1,025,526.80 − $1,025,075.00 = $451.80

However, although the dealer is indeed approximately hedged against interest rate movements, this profit calculation takes no account of the differences between LIBOR (against which the FRA is settled) and the reverse repo rate. This is discussed further below.

There are several points to notice here:

1. Strictly, the amount of the FRA should be the same as the amount which needs to be rolled over with the new reverse repo after two months (the same as the maturing amount of the first reverse repo) – that is, not $1 million but:

$$\$1 \text{ million} \times (1 + 0.057 \times \tfrac{61}{360}) = \$1,009,658.33$$

2. If LIBOR after two months is higher or lower than 6.15 percent, there will be a discounted FRA settlement amount paid *after two months*. The calculation above assumes that the settlement amount can be reinvested at LIBOR until the end of five months. A different reinvestment rate would give a very slightly different result.

3. Much more importantly, the FRA is not in fact a complete hedge, because the FRA will be settled after two months against three-month LIBOR, but the new three-month reverse repo which the

dealer does after two months to replace the original one will be at a repo rate. This repo rate could be quite different from LIBOR, depending on the collateral and structure of the reverse repo.

Suppose, for example, that in Example 6.4 after two months, LIBOR is 5.85% and the dealer rolls over the reverse repo at 5.70%. Then:

Receipt on maturity of the original two-month reverse repo is $1,009,658.33

Settlement amount on FRA received by dealer

$$= \$1,009,658.33 \times \frac{(6.15\% - 5.85\%) \times \frac{92}{360}}{(1 + 5.85\% \times \frac{92}{360})} = \$762.67$$

Therefore amount to be rolled over in new reverse repo

$$= \$1,009,658.33 + \$762.67 = \$1,010,421.00$$

Total receipt from new reverse repo at end of 5 months

$$= \$1,010,421.00 \times (1 + 0.0570 \times \tfrac{92}{360}) = \$1,025,139.47$$

Therefore net result is: (final cash inflow from second reverse repo) − (final cash outflow from original 5-month repo)

$$= \$1,025,139.47 - \$1,025,075.00 = \$64.47$$

## Taking a view on specials

A dealer may reverse in a bond which he or she believes will become special in due course, repoing out general collateral on the other side. If correct, the dealer will be able in the future to repo out the special at a lower cost than he or she can reverse in general collateral – a "spread trade" – shown in Figure 6.5.

Fig 6.5

## Anticipating a bond going special

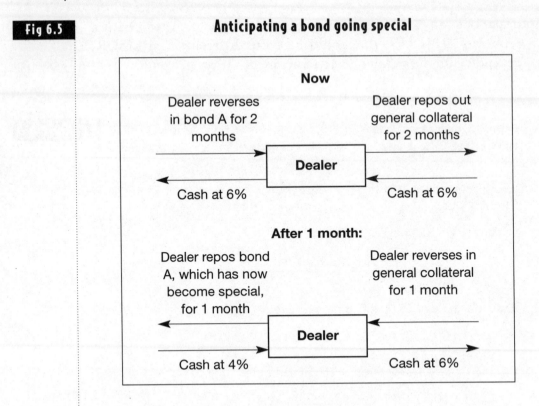

# FUND MANAGERS

## Yield enhancement

Fund managers who do not need funds, but own a security in demand, can use this special to repo in cash which they can then reverse out again against general collateral. Because the general collateral can be of the same creditworthiness as the special, they are using their existing portfolios to make an extra yield without sacrificing anything with regard to credit risk. The profit made is simply the difference between the two repo rates, for the period of the repos. Figure 6.6 illustrates this: if the transactions are for, say, 45 days on a 360-day year basis, the profit would be:

$$\text{Cash amount of transaction} \times 0.01 \times \frac{45}{360}$$

## Yield enhancement

Fig 6.6

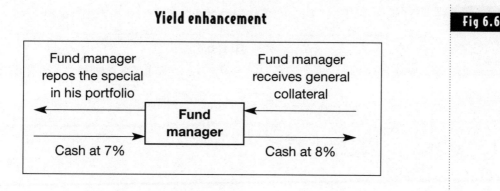

## Leverage

Managers of "hedge funds" (generally leveraged funds) can leverage their portfolios through repo, by using their existing holdings as collateral to repo in more cash, which they then invest in new securities. The process can be repeated to leverage as far as prudence and margin requirements allow, as shown in Figure 6.7. Similarly, they can short securities in a leveraged way by reversing them in against cash, selling them, and then repeating the cycle.

# FUTURES DEALERS

## Implied repo rate

When we constructed a theoretical bond futures price in chapter 3, we did so by considering how sellers of bond futures contracts could hedge themselves. This was by borrowing cash, using the cash to buy the bond, and holding the bond until the futures contract matures and the bond is delivered against it. If the actual futures price is the same as the theoretical price, this "round trip" should give a zero result – no profit and no loss.

The same calculation can be considered in reverse: assuming that we already know the current futures price and the current bond price, what is the interest rate at which it is necessary to borrow the cash to ensure a zero result?

Fig 6.7

## Leverage

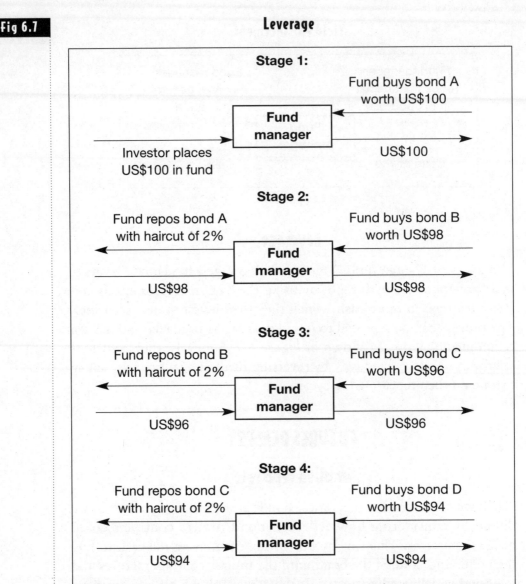

At this stage, the fund has purchased a total of US$388 worth of bonds, based on an original investment in the fund of only US$100. In theory, this chain can be repeated until the fund has no further ability to borrow. In the case of a series of 2 percent haircuts, the fund could theoretically invest in as much as 50 times the original investment. Clearly, if the bond market collapses, the fund is heavily exposed, and margin calls will be made in each repo along the chain, requiring the fund to sell the bonds in order to realize the collateral.

Taking our earlier formula and reversing it, we get interest rate

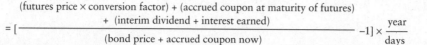

$$= [\frac{\text{(futures price} \times \text{conversion factor)} + \text{(accrued coupon at maturity of futures)} + \text{(interim dividend + interest earned)}}{\text{(bond price + accrued coupon now)}} - 1] \times \frac{\text{year}}{\text{days}}$$

This interest rate is called the "implied repo rate" and is the break-even rate at which the futures sale can be hedged. The reason for the name "implied repo rate" is that in order to borrow the money to buy the bond, the dealer can repo the bond out. It is thus the "repo borrowing rate implied by the current futures price." The "cheapest to deliver" bond will be the one with the highest implied repo rate (because any other deliverable bond will require a lower repo rate to break even).

## Cash-and-carry arbitrage

If in fact the current futures price, bond price, and actual repo rate are not all in line, an arbitrage opportunity will be available. Thus, if the actual repo rate is less than the implied repo rate, it will be possible to finance the hedge cheaply – that is, to buy the bond, repo it, sell the futures contract, and deliver the bond at maturity of the futures contract, all at a locked-in profit.

**Such a round trip is called "cash-and-carry arbitrage."**

If the actual repo rate is higher than the implied repo rate, it is possible to effect a cash-and-carry arbitrage in reverse – that is, borrow a bond through a reverse repo, sell the bond, buy the futures contract, and take delivery of a bond at maturity of the futures contract. A problem arises, however, that the buyer of the futures contract has no control over which bond will be delivered. If the "cheapest to deliver" bond at maturity is not the same as the bond the buyer has borrowed, arbitrage will not be complete; the buyer must then sell the bond which has been delivered and buy the bond he or she has borrowed.

**The difference between the current cash price for a bond and the futures price (adjusted by multiplying by the conversion factor) is known as the "basis."**

**Buying a bond and selling a futures contract is known as "buying the basis."**

**Similarly, selling a bond and buying a futures contract is "selling the basis."**

**Example 6.6**

| | |
|---|---|
| CTD bond $8\frac{7}{8}\%$ February 22, 2005 price: | 105.24 |
| Accrued coupon: | 1.922917 |
| Bond futures price: | 93.75 |
| Conversion factor for CTD: | 1.118073 |
| Repo rate: | 3.29% |
| Days to futures delivery date: | 31 |
| Futures contract amount: | DEM 250,000.00 |
| Accrued coupon on CTD at futures delivery date: | 2.6625 |

Depending on whether the implied repo rate (= the break-even funding rate implied by the current bond futures price and the current cash price of the "cheapest to deliver" bond) is higher or lower than the actual current repo rate, the cash-and-carry arbitrage is:

*Either* (A)

● Buy the cash CTD bond now.

● Fund this purchase by repoing the bond.

● Sell the bond futures contract.

● Deliver the bond at maturity of the futures contract.

*or* (B) the opposite:

● Sell the cash CTD bond now.

● Borrow this bond (to deliver it now) through a reverse repo, using the cash raised by the bond sale.

● Buy the futures contract.

● Take delivery of the futures contract at maturity and use the bond to deliver on the second leg of the reverse repo.

(In practice, rather than deliver or take delivery of the bond at maturity of the futures contract, the cash bond purchase or sale, and the futures contract, can both be reversed at maturity. In (B) particularly there would be no certainty that the bond delivered to us by the futures seller would match the bond we are obliged to return under the reverse repo.)

Assume for the moment that the profitable arbitrage is (A) (if in fact the result is negative, the profitable arbitrage is (B) instead):

Cost of buying CTD bond per DEM 100 nominal is (clean price + accrued coupon) = DEM (105.24 + 1.922917)

= DEM 107.162917

Total borrowing (principal + interest) to be repaid at the end

$$= \text{DEM } 107.162917 \times (1 + 0.0329 \times \frac{31}{360}) = \text{DEM } 107.466516$$

Anticipated receipt from selling futures contract and delivering bond per DEM 100 nominal = (futures price × conversion factor) + accrued coupon

$$= \text{DEM } (93.75 \times 1.118073) + 2.6625 = \text{DEM } 107.481844$$

Profit = DEM (107.481844 − 107.466516) = 0.015328 per DEM 100 nominal.

Size of DEM bond futures contract is DEM 250,000 nominal.

Therefore profit per futures contract = DEM 0.015328 × 250,000/100 = DEM 38.32

To calculate profit as a rate of return on the cash invested:

Cost of buying DEM 100 nominal is DEM 107.162917.

Profit from buying DEM 100 nominal is DEM 0.015328 over 31 days.

Therefore arbitrage is worth:

$$\frac{0.015328}{107.162917} \times \frac{360}{31} = 0.17\% \text{ per annum or 17 basis points}$$

In practice, the profit in Example 6.6 cannot be calculated precisely for several reasons:

- The CTD bond may not be the same at maturity of the futures contract as it is when the arbitrage is established.
- The futures price and the CTD bond cash price may not converge exactly by maturity of the futures contract (that is, the basis may not move exactly to zero).

● The profit or loss on the futures contract is realized through variation margin payments; because the timing of these payments is unknown in advance, it is impossible to calculate their exact value.

Calculation summary

### Cash-and-carry arbitrage

**Assume the arbitrage is achieved by buying the cash bond and selling the futures:**

**Cash cost at start**

= nominal bond amount × (cash bond price + accrued coupon at start)/100

**Total payments**

$$= \text{(cash cost at start)} \times \left(1 + \text{repo rate} \times \frac{\text{days to futures maturity}}{\text{year}}\right)$$

**Total receipts**

= nominal bond amount × (futures price × conversion factor + accrued coupon at maturity of futures)/100

**Profit** = Total receipts − total payments

**Expressed as interest rate**

$$= \frac{\text{receipts} - \text{payments}}{\text{cash at start}} \times \frac{\text{year}}{\text{days to future maturity}}$$

# COMPANY TREASURERS

## Borrowing

Company treasurers who need funds but also have investments may find that they have in their investment portfolios a security which is in short supply in the market. By repoing this out as a "special," they can reduce their cost of funds. This is particularly useful when a company has seasonal borrowing requirements. Rather than sell the investments to realize cash for only a short period, the treasurer can leave the investments undisturbed and use them to raise finance more cheaply: *see* Figure 6.8.

## Reducing the cost of borrowing

Fig 6.8

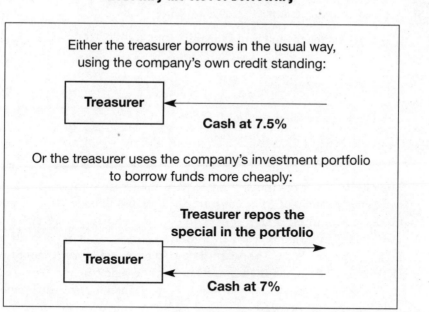

## Cross-currency repo

A treasurer may have assets in one currency but wish to borrow in another. One approach would be to transact a cross-currency repo, by using the securities in the first currency as collateral for a loan in the second currency. It may be, however, that the rate quoted for the cross-currency repo is not as attractive as the rate would be for a single currency repo. In that case, the treasurer could consider constructing a loan in the currency needed, from a single currency repo in the currency of the asset, combined with a forward foreign exchange swap.

Treasurer needs to borrow US$10 million for three months from November 13, 1996 to February 13, 1997 (92 days)

Example 6.7

Deal date: November 11, 1996

Collateral available: $7\frac{3}{4}$% Bund 2005

Clean Bund price: 107.42

**6.7 Cont'd**

Accrued coupon at start: 153 days (30(E)/360 basis)

US$ cross-currency repo rate available: 6.49% (ACT/360 basis)

DEM repo rate available: 4.05% (ACT/360 basis)

Haircut: 2%

US$/DEM spot exchange rate: 1.5240

3-month forward FX swap: 91/86 points (that is, − 0.0091/ − 0.0086)

The mechanics of the transaction are that the treasurer repos the Bund to borrow enough DEM to convert into US$10 million spot; then sells these DEM and buys US$ spot, and simultaneously buys DEM and sells US$ 3 months forward (a 3-month FX swap). The amount of DEM purchased for the forward date is determined by the amount of DEM needed to repay the repo, including the repo interest. The treasurer's all-in cost of borrowing US$ will then be the difference between the US$ forward cost of these DEM, and the US$10 million raised at the beginning.

**Repo structure:**

Spot equivalent of US$10 million to be borrowed through the repo is:

US$10 million × 1.5240 = DEM 15,240,000.00.

Therefore borrow DEM 15,240,000.00 through repo at 4.05% for 3 months.

On February 13, 1997 repay repo cash plus interest:

$$\text{DEM } 15,240,000.00 \times (1 + 0.0405 \times \frac{92}{360}) = \text{DEM } 15,397,734.00$$

**Repo details:**

Dirty price of Bund is 107.42 + accrued coupon

$$= 107.42 + 7.75 \times \frac{153}{360} = 110.71375$$

Nominal amount of Bund required to borrow DEM 15,240,000.00, allowing for a 2% haircut, is therefore:

$$\frac{\text{DEM } 15,240,000.00}{110.71375/100} \times 1.02 = \text{DEM } 14,040,532.45$$

or, rounded up: DEM 14,041,000

**FX swap:**

Value November 13, 1996, buy US$10,000,000.00 against DEM 15,240,000.00 (spot exchange rate 1.5240).

Value February 13, 1997, buy DEM 15,397,734.00 against US$10,164,191.70 (forward exchange rate 1.5240 – 0.0091 = 1.5149, assuming that this price is acceptable for a swap where the currency amounts on the two legs of the FX deal are slightly mismatched).

**All-in cost**

All-in cost of US$ borrowing is:

$$\left( \frac{10,164,191.70}{10,000,000.00} - 1 \right) \times \frac{360}{92} = 6.425\%$$

This is cheaper than the alternative cost of 6.49% for a straightforward cross-currency repo.

# SWAP DEALERS

## Hedging a swap

A swap dealer who establishes a position because a counterparty deals on his or her price is immediately vulnerable to a change in long-term interest rates. Suppose, for example, the swap dealer is paying fixed interest and receiving floating interest in the swap. If swap rates – that is, long-term interest rates – fall by the time the dealer does another swap the other way round, he or she will make a loss, as illustrated in Figure 6.9.

### An unhedged swap

Fig 6.9

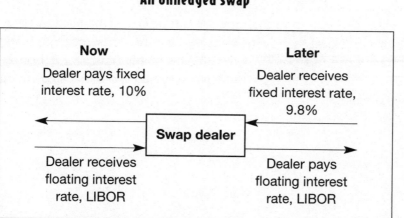

In order to avoid this risk, the swap dealer can immediately offset or hedge his or her position in various ways:

● *Deal a swap which exactly offsets the existing position*: in our example in Figure 6.9, the dealer would deal another swap in which he or she receives fixed and pays floating. It may, however, not be possible to deal at an attractive price at the time and the dealer chooses therefore to wait until it is.

● *Deal futures*: in our example, the dealer would buy bond futures contracts. A disadvantage could be that the maturity (or duration) of the bond futures does not match that of the swap, so that the hedge does not respond to yield changes in the same way as the swap.

● *Deal in options*: in our example, the dealer would buy a bond call option. Assuming that he or she is dealing in options based on bond futures, this might have the same drawback as dealing in futures themselves.

● *Buy a bond with similar maturity (and/or duration) to the swap*: this will give the dealer a fixed interest rate income offsetting the fixed interest rate he or she is paying out in the swap. This is not a perfect hedge, because swap rates are not the same as bond yields. However, swap interest rates do generally move in line with government bond yields of similar maturity, particularly over short periods – that is, the spread (the difference between their yields) will remain approximately the same for short periods. The dealer will therefore hope that if interest rates do fall, the loss he or she makes on the swap will be matched by a corresponding profit on the bond purchase. In order to finance the bond purchase, the dealer can then repo the bond to borrow the necessary cash. When the dealer does subsequently close out the swap position with an offsetting swap, he or she can sell the bond and close out the repo (*see* Figure 6.10).

The strategy shown in Figure 6.10 can of course be used in reverse. If the original deal is a swap whereby the dealer is receiving the fixed interest rate and paying floating, he or she can sell a bond, then borrow the bond against the cash received from the sale through a reverse repo.

### Hedging a swap with a bond purchase and repo

Fig 6.10

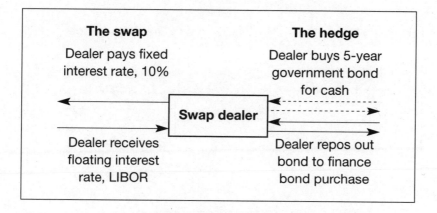

# OPTION DEALERS

## Hedging an option

A bond option dealer who sells bond call options, for example, is exposed immediately to the risk that the price of the underlying bond will rise. As in the case of the swap dealer in the previous section, the dealer has various choices regarding how to protect against this:

● Deal an option which exactly offsets the existing position: our dealer in the example above would buy a matching call option on the same bond. As with the swap, this offers little scope for dealing profit, assuming that the dealer must deal on another's price in order to achieve the hedge.

● Delta hedge with futures: in our example, the dealer would buy bond futures contracts. A disadvantage could be that the maturity (or duration) of the bond futures does not match that of the bond underlying the option, so that the hedge does not respond to yield changes in the same way as the option.

● Delta hedge by buying the bond underlying the option contract: the cost of these bonds is likely to be far greater than the net premium taken for the option the dealer has sold. In order to buy the bonds, therefore, the dealer can again raise the cash necessary by repoing them out (see Figure 6.11). The net cost of this hedge – considering both the cost of funds and the bond coupon – will affect the option pricing. Similarly, if the dealer needs to go short of the bonds for the delta hedge, he or she can reverse them in to sell them.

Fig 6.11

## Delta hedging

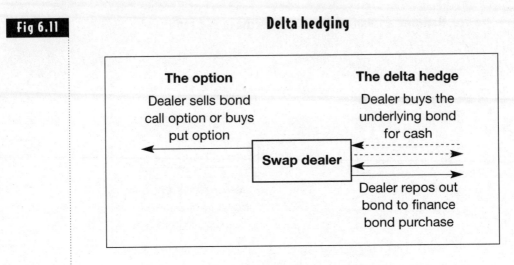

# CENTRAL BANKS

The development of a healthy domestic repo market is important to central banks for a variety of reasons.

## Liquidity management

When there is a shortage of liquidity in the market due to temporary cashflow fluctuations, a central bank can add cash to the banking system by reversing securities in from the banks, and when it wishes to drain liquidity from the banking system it can repo them out. It is important to be careful about the terminology here, however, as these operations are viewed from the commercial banking system's viewpoint rather than the central bank's. Thus, when the Bundesbank does "repos," it is in fact the banking system that is doing repos and the Bundesbank that is doing reverse repos – and thereby putting liquidity *into* the market. Similarly, central bank "reverse repos" *drain* liquidity from the system. In the US in particular, even more care is needed because "reverse repos" are also called "matched sale-purchases" (MSPs) where the terminology views the transaction from the *Federal Reserve's* point of view. When the Fed undertakes such repos or MSPs, they are called "system" repos or MSPs if they are for the purpose of deliberate adjustment to the banking system. The Fed also undertakes "customer" repos on behalf of clients – generally major foreign central banks and supranational bodies investing surplus funds – and normally announces the size of these transactions in advance in order not to disturb the market.

## Interest rate policy

Many central banks also use repos as the mechanism through which changes in interest rate levels are signaled to the market. For example, the Bundesbank will indicate a major change in interest rates by announcing a change in the discount or Lombard rate, but uses weekly repo tenders to fine-tune changes. Not all central banks use the repo market in this way, however. When the UK gilt repo market was opened to all market participants in January 1996, the Bank of England made it clear that it would continue to use the outright purchase and sale of bills as its customary method of operating in the market, rather than the repo market. On the other hand, it is widely expected that this policy will change in the future, to bring the Bank of England into line with other major central banks. Some individual central banks' use of repos is discussed further in chapter 8.

## Market development

As demonstrated throughout this chapter, repos are used in a wide range of circumstances linked to the bond and derivative markets. In particular, the existence of a strong repo market helps to provide liquidity and depth to markets by allowing dealers to take short positions. It is therefore in a central bank's interest to encourage and support a domestic repo market in order to foster the domestic bond and derivative markets, which in turn enhances the local financial center's reputation.

## Government borrowing costs

A more efficient and liquid bond market in turn helps to facilitate the government's issuance of bonds when it needs to borrow, and should also reduce the government's cost of borrowing slightly, as a greater demand for the bonds should tend to lower yields.

## Systemic risk

The ability to take a short position in a security has more implications than just market development. The financial markets generally continue both to grow in size and to become increasingly interlinked globally. This gives rise to greater concern over systemic risk – that is, the risk that a default in one deal leading to the bankruptcy of one particular institution will have a knock-on effect leading to a chain of defaults and bankruptcies throughout the global financial system. Any improvement in the ability of an institution to hedge a position quickly and efficiently clearly reduces risk. The repo market does just that, by facilitating short positions in specific securities to hedge specific positions, in both the cash markets and the derivatives markets. The alternative would be to sell futures, which is less precise as a hedge.

From the more straightforward viewpoint of cash lending, encouragement of repos as collateralized lending equally helps to prevent a single default from spreading to a chain of defaults. Assuming the cash lender is adequately secured by the collateral, there is no knock-on effect. Central banks therefore have an interest in replacing clean money market loans by repos. This has been reflected in the favorable capital treatment allowed to repos under the Capital Adequacy Directive (CAD).

# SYNTHETIC REPOS

**A synthetic repo is a strategy whereby a dealer puts a series of deals in place which together have the same economic effect as a repo.**

We know that a reverse repo is the simultaneous purchase of a security spot and sale of the same security for a forward date. One type of synthetic reverse repo is therefore the sale of a bond futures contract and simultaneous purchase of a deliverable bond in the cash market. This is exactly what is done in a cash-and-carry arbitrage; the arbitrage is completed by doing a repo at a cheaper rate than the implied repo rate of the synthetic reverse repo.

We also know from chapter 4 that the simultaneous purchase of a call option and sale of a put option on the same underlying security at the same strike is equivalent to a forward purchase of that security. Combining these two structures, therefore, we know that a repo can be economically replicated by the following simultaneous trades:

- Sell a bond in the cash market.
- Buy a call option on the bond.
- Sell a put option on the bond.

Again, one reason for such a strategy would be if dealers could then reverse in the bond they have sold in the cash market, at a higher rate than the repo rate implied in the synthetic structure.

Example 6.8

Transact a 3-month (91-day) reverse repo at 5.1%, receiving DEM 10 million 6% coupon bond (annual, 30(E)/360) as collateral (no haircut).

Sell the bond at a clean price of 102.57 with 78 days' accrued coupon.

Buy a 3-month call option on the bond at a strike price of 102 for a premium of 1.91 %.

Sell a 3-month put option on the bond at a strike price of 102 for a premium of 1.53%

*Cashflows now*:

From sale of bond, receive:

$$\text{DEM 10 million} \times \left(102.57 + 6 \times \frac{78}{360}\right)/100 = \text{DEM } 10,387,000.00$$

From sale of put, receive:

$$\text{DEM 10 million} \times 1.53\% = \text{DEM } 153,000.00$$

From reverse repo, pay DEM 10,387,000.00

From purchase of call, pay:

$$\text{DEM 10 million} \times 1.91\% = \text{DEM } 191,000.00$$

Net cashflow now: DEM 38,000 out

*Cashflows after 3 months*:

One of the two options will be exercised, so that we will buy the bond at 102 with accrued coupon of 168 days, for a total cost of:

$$\text{DEM 10 million} \times \left(102 + 6 \times \frac{168}{360}\right)/100 = \text{DEM } 10,480,000.00$$

Receive cash from reverse repo including interest (91 days):

$$\text{DEM } 10,387,000 \times \left(1 + 0.051 \times \frac{91}{360}\right) = \text{DEM } 10,520,905.74$$

**6.8 Cont'd** Net cashflow: DEM 40,905.74 in

*Result*:

After funding the net DEM 38,000 outflow for 91 days (assuming a cost of 5.1%), this round trip shows a profit of

$$\text{DEM } 40,905.74 - \text{DEM } 38,000 \times \left(1 + 0.051 \times \frac{91}{360}\right) = \text{DEM } 2,415.86$$

A reverse repo can be replicated similarly by buying a bond, buying a put option, and selling a call option.

The synthetic structure could be taken a step further, by, replacing the initial bond purchase in a reverse repo by a synthetic bond purchase – for example, by buying a floating rate note (FRN) and undertaking an interest rate swap to pay floating and receive fixed interest. The synthetic reverse repo could then be:

- Buy an FRN in the cash market.
- Pay floating/receive fixed interest in a swap.
- Sell a bond call option.
- Buy a bond put option.

As with any instrument, the financial engineering built around a repo can be made increasingly complicated, using more complex underlying assets, more complex swaps and more complex options. Such structures stray, however, from the subject of this book, which is essentially repos themselves. We have, therefore, left further details of these more involved structures to another book.

# EXERCISES

**34.** A matched book trader takes a view on the likely movement in interest rates by doing the following two trades for a cash consideration of DEM 10 million:

Repo out Bunds for one month (May 14 to June 14) at 4.1%
Reverse in Bunds for three months (May 14 to August 14) at 4.3%

**a.** What effective forward-forward interest rate has he achieved?

**b.** Is he expecting interest rates to rise or fall?

**c.** If he changes his mind, and he decides to hedge his position by using FRAs or futures, should he buy or sell an FRA; should he buy or sell futures?

**d.** If he is able to close out his position after 1 month at 4.3%, how much profit or loss will he make?

**35.** A fund manager owns BEF 500 million nominal of a 9% coupon bond which is currently on special. He can repo this at 2.15% for 30 days and invest in BEF Treasury bills at a yield of 4.1%. The bond currently has a clean price of 110.54 and 45 days' accrued coupon.

Assuming no haircut, how much profit can he make?

**36.** With the same details as in question 22 (chapter 3) but supposing that the actual futures price is 93.10, what is the implied repo rate?

**37.** Given the following information, there is a cash-and-carry arbitrage opportunity. What trades are necessary to exploit it and how much profit can be made?

| | |
|---|---|
| CTD Bund $8\frac{7}{8}$% December 20, 2000 price: | 102.71 |
| Accrued coupon: | 3.599 |
| Bund futures price: | 85.31 |
| Conversion factor for CTD: | 1.203046 |
| Repo rate: | 6.80% |
| Days to futures delivery date: | 24 |
| Futures contract amount: | DEM 250,000.00 |
| Accrued coupon on CTD at futures delivery date: | 4.191 |

**38.** Summarize the ways in which different market participants might use repos.

**39.** Discuss the various ways in which central banks are concerned with the repo markets.

■ ■ ■

*"From the point of view of repo as a collateralized loan, it is open to the same financial engineering possibilities as any other loan."*

# Market Developments

# HISTORY

**The repo market began in the US where it has grown into by far the largest domestic repo market in the world.**

The US Federal Reserve Bank began dealing in repos in 1918 in bankers' acceptances (BAs), in order to encourage the development of the BA market. In 1923, the Fed also began repos of government securities as a method of controlling bank reserves.

The interbank market in repos was stimulated by the Glass–Steagall Act in 1933, which forbade US investment banks from taking in customer deposits to fund their investment portfolios. These investment banks had to find new sources of borrowing in addition to their existing lines of credit from commercial banks. The repo market was an ideal source of such funding, as they could use their investment portfolios to collateralize the borrowing used for the investments in the first place. This therefore created a large supply of natural sellers for the repo market. On the other side of the market a supply of buyers of repos arose partly because of a series of bank defaults. Those money market funds which had been placing money in clean bank deposits and CDs wished to diversify their risk into other instruments. Repos provided just such an instrument, because of their "double indemnity" status – secured against both the seller's creditworthiness and that of the collateral, which diversified the risk away from bank credit. As trading in bonds increased in volume, so the need also grew for bond dealers to borrow bonds to cover short positions, establishing the market in specials alongside the GC market.

Most of the activity in the US market is domestic. The European repo market has, however, grown up since the mid-1980s, when international securities trading began to develop significantly. As a result, the European repo market has naturally developed with a greater international flavor.

The volume of repo trading worldwide has grown dramatically since the early 1990s, but the figures are rather uncertain. The US repo market, which still accounts for over half the total market, probably turns over more than US$1000 billion per day, with the European domestic and international markets rapidly catching up this total. The rapid growth in the market has been fueled by a series of factors, already mentioned in various contexts throughout this book, including:

- The growth in the securities markets, creating the need for dealers to use repo to fund their positions.

- The growing need to be able to take and hedge short positions in the capital and derivative markets.

- Growing concern over counterparty credit risk among both banks and investors.

- Investors' search for greater yields and a wider choice of risk/ return profiles.

- The favorable capital adequacy treatment given to repos – which is also encouraging the acceptance of properly documented classic repos over buy/sell-backs.

- Investors' growing awareness of the opportunities offered by the specials markets.

The biggest users of the repo markets are still the commercial and investment banks. The use of triparty repos is increasing, particularly for non-bank users of the market, for whom the administrative complications of repo – particularly classic repo with daily marking to market – may make bilateral repos less attractive. For reasons of both liquidity and security, government bonds are still the most widely used for repo collateral. This is particularly so in the international and European repo markets, which do not generally repo the same breadth of securities as the US market. As investors increase their awareness and seek higher returns, however, so the market's breadth continues to grow. Although there are wide variations from country to country, more business is transacted through classic repo than through buy/sell-back, for the various reasons discussed elsewhere in the book – the ability to margin, set-off provisions in the event of default, and capital adequacy requirements – and this trend is likely to continue for the same considerations.

As in all markets, problems do arise. One of the major ones arose in 1981–82 at Drysdale Government Securities in New York, out of the practice (common at that time) not to include accrued coupon when valuing securities in a repo. Drysdale sold securities short which had a large element of accrued coupon and then reversed them in. The reverse repo valued the securities at their clean price only, so that the cash lent by Drysdale through the reverse was rather less than the cash raised through the short sale of the securities. This cash difference was then available to Drysdale to finance further trading. Drysdale had effectively taken a large haircut on the reverse –

although neither party viewed it as such – and used the haircut to leverage its business rather than as collateral not to be touched. The difficulty came when Drysdale made losses on its dealing (compounded by inattention to the firm's cost of carry, which was nothing to do with its use of the repo market). When it came to pay the manufactured dividends to the reverse repo counterparties, there was a cash shortage which could be funded only by repeating the operation – reversing in increasing volumes of securities in the same way. Eventually, Drysdale was forced to default on a US$160 million payment. A systematic collapse of banks dealing in securities was uncomfortably close and the affair led to the inclusion of accrued coupon in marking to market as standard practice subsequently.

A more recent crisis was the bankruptcy of Orange County in California at the end of 1994. The county lost US$1.7 billion through leveraged financial investments which were financed through the repo market. The problem of course lay in the unfortunate investment decisions and the leveraging, rather than in any risk inherent in the use of repos; almost any financial instrument can be used for speculation as well as hedging or investment. On the other hand, repos can facilitate leveraging, and the knock-on effect of the bankruptcy has been that the use of repos has subsequently been restricted in some US local authorities.

# EMERGING MARKETS

In the international repo market there has been considerable growth in repos of US dollar Brady bonds. This is because of the good opportunities which have been available for investors and because of the funding ability this has given to institutions which would otherwise find it very difficult to finance themselves. Brady bonds were originally issued as part of the debt rescheduling exercise for developing countries which began in 1989, particularly in Latin American countries, and collateralized by US Treasury bonds – although the term Brady bonds is now sometimes used more widely. This gives the bonds good credit backing and has encouraged a liquid cash market in them, both factors which have encouraged a strong repo market.

Much of the emerging market repo business has been based on the Brady bonds of Latin American governments – particularly Mexico, Brazil, and Argentina. The seller end of this market is provided by the Latin American banks, which wish to borrow against their portfolio of Brady bonds at interest rates which can be much lower than the cost of funds to those banks in unsecured bank loans.

Despite the collateralization the repo rates have, however, still been relatively high compared with international rates. The buyer end of the market has therefore been supported by investors who are keen for the more attractive yields than would be available against the collateral of, say, a US Treasury bond. Because of the poor creditworthiness of the cash borrowers, haircuts are regularly 10 percent and can be rather higher. International banks act as intermediaries in this flow of funds, reversing the bonds in from Latin American counterparties and repoing them out in turn to international investors, and able to take an attractive spread in the middle.

To some extent, matched book trading in emerging market bonds has a different tone from traditional matched book trading. In repo trading generally, it is very often the case that the collateral provided in the deal is of a higher credit standing than the borrower of cash – hence one of the important reasons for the attractiveness of repos as an instrument. With emerging market debt, this situation is sometimes reversed at the investor end of the chain. That is, the international bank acting effectively as an intermediary between the Latin American cash borrower and the international investor is sometimes seen by the investor as at least as good a credit as the collateral. The international bank is therefore to some extent involved in credit intermediation, with its repo desk standing in the middle between the two end users. Because of this approach, the repo rates in emerging market debt tend to vary more according to the credit perception of the counterparties than is the case in traditional repo. Dealers will also use the emerging market to put on profitable spread trades – for example, repoing out a US Treasury bond and investing the cash in a reverse against a Brady, or repoing out one emerging market security and reversing in one of lower perceived credit standing.

The advantage of the Latin American Brady bonds for the development of repo is that they provide a large, liquid underlying bond market. Repo of other emerging markets' debt has also been growing however, particularly Eastern Europe (especially Poland and Bulgaria). Issue sizes of Eastern European debt tend to be smaller than those of Latin American debt, which gives rise to more opportunities to repo specials. Repo in South East Asian debt, as well as Middle Eastern, South African, and Nigerian, is also active.

# EQUITY REPO

The concept of a repo is a spot purchase or sale, with a forward transaction to reverse it – or equivalently a loan of cash against collateral.

This concept can be extended in principle to any form of collateral, such as commodities or equities. Equity repo has in fact developed since the early 1990s, driven by the same forces that created the repo market in bonds: investment houses seeking funding for their equity portfolios use those portfolios as repo collateral, while cash investors seeking to diversify their own portfolio are willing to take the equity collateral.

Repo in equity has developed later than repo in bonds for various reasons related to the nature of equities as a financial instrument. In the first place, the cashflows and rights relating to equities are in general less certain than those relating to bonds. There may, for example, be a rights issue during a repo which affects the original seller's portfolio. Equity dividends are also generally paid net of withholding tax, with the result that equities sold through a repo are usually called back over a dividend date. There is currently no standard documentation for use with equity repos, since documentation such as the GMRA, which is designed for gross-paying securities, is inappropriate. The London Investment Bankers' Association is currently developing alternative suitable documentation.

Equity markets in general also carry the risk of greater volatility, and the market in an individual equity will often be less liquid than the market in a bond typically used for repo. Both of these factors tend to increase the size of haircuts demanded for equity repo. On the other side of the coin, the greater risks involved with equities from the buyer's point of view imply higher returns for the cash investor than are generally available in bond repos.

# FUTURE DEVELOPMENTS

The future growth of the market is likely to see increased development of more complex structures built around repos.

From the point of view of repo as a collateralized loan, it is open to the same financial engineering possibilities as any other loan. Floating-rate repos, for example, although traditionally less common except in the French market, can be provided to borrowers looking for floating-rate funds, and hedged by the dealer through an interest rate swap if necessary. In practice, floating-rate repos are usually rather longer term – generally over six months – than fixed-rate repos, which tend to have very short maturities. This enables dealers with a floating-rate funding base to secure their funding for a longer period. Dealers can also take positions on the spread between repo rates and floating-rate benchmarks such as LIBOR – for example, reversing in a security at a floating rate of say LIBOR –0.1 percent with the expectation of being able to repo it out later at LIBOR –0.2 percent.

An option structure such as a cap or a collar can also be added to a floating-rate repo, in the same way as to any other loan; for an investor, a floating-rate repo can be combined with a floor. Another variation, a flex repo, provides the ability to tailor the user's need to a changing cashflow profile. An investor seeking to buy a security with an amortizing principal, for example, could finance this purchase through a repo with a matching amortization. If the security has built-in call or put options, the repo could again be structured with built-in options to match the asset. The investor is seeking in this way to take a view on the credit risk of the asset he is buying, without being exposed to interest rate risks arising from his or her funding costs. The dealer wishes to be able to sell the asset, and being able to offer such a repo structure may facilitate this.

# EXERCISE

**40.** Discuss the factors which have encouraged growth of the repo market and indicate how you think the market will develop in the future.

# Market Details and Documentation

■ ■ ■

*"The US repo
market has the
longest history of any
in the world and is
the largest and most
liquid by far . . ."*

# An Overview of Domestic Repo Markets

# UNITED STATES

The US repo market has the longest history of any in the world and is the largest and most liquid by far, supported by the largest domestic bond market. The US market is based largely on screen dealing, although there are some telephone brokers. Although much of the market is in US government bills, notes, and bonds, there are also active markets in a wide range of securities including junk bonds and mortgage-backed securities. Triparty repo is used particularly with mortgage-backed securities, because of the administrative settlement complications with these securities.

The market is typically in classic repo – hence known as "US style repo" – and securities lending, rather than buy/sell-back. The documentation used for classic repos is the Master Repurchase Agreement developed by the Public Securities Association (PSA), which has recently been revised. Settlement is generally for same-day value and overnight repo makes up much the largest volume.

Since 1994 the US market in repos has been stimulated further by the Federal Reserve Bank's introduction of charges for daylight overdrafts to reduce systemic risk. These overdrafts are negative cash balances run during the day by banks, for which the Fed charges around 1 basis point per hour. These overdrafts arise, for example, when a dealer is asked in the morning to return the cash he or she has previously borrowed through a repo, but does not refinance his or her position until the afternoon. This has encouraged the use of third-party repos. It also encourages open repo, where there is less likelihood of a daylight overdraft because the security might not be called back, rather than overnight repo.

The Federal Reserve operates daily in the repo market for the purposes of short-term liquidity management and also when it wishes to signal a change in interest rate policy. Repos and reverses (the latter are also known as "matched sale-purchases") are dealt with primary dealers in government securities and are dealt in securities of the government and government agencies. System repos are repos dealt for the Fed's own purposes as described; customer repos are repos dealt on behalf of the Fed's own customers – foreign central banks and supranational bodies – which have left cash with the Fed.

# FRANCE

The French domestic interbank repo market is the second largest in the world after the US and forms an important part of banks' risk-taking dealing rather than providing merely a bond-lending facility. Significantly, the volume of business dealt domestically is greater than the volume of business in the international market centered on London. The market has been strongly supported by the Bank of France and benefits from specific legislation and official documentation – the Pension Livrée Agreement. This agreement is not based on the PSA/ISMA agreement, but it is broadly equivalent to it. There is a system of market makers ("SPVT" – Spécialiste en Pension de Valeurs du Trésor).

The French classic repo is now the *pension livrée*, which has replaced the *vente à réméré* (which involved an option to repurchase rather than absolute commitment). The market tends to be very short term, with a large proportion of overnight business.

An unusual feature of the French market is the large proportion of repos based on the floating rate "TMP" (*taux moyen pondéré*, a weighted average of overnight rates). TMP is important in the French money markets because it is used as a benchmark rate for investment funds; there is, for example, a major market in money market interest rate swaps into TMP. A repo based on a spread compared to the TMP is dealt for a fixed term, but the repo rate is not known finally as an absolute rate until the end of the repo. The proportion of repos based on the TMP is now falling, however, because the Bank of France encourages fixed-rate repos by requiring the SPVTs to quote screen-based two-way prices in fixed-rate repos for a range of maturities from tom/next to three months.

Repos are booked as such through the domestic bond settlement systems SICOVAM and SATURNE and deals are reversed automatically at maturity. Repos are normally dealt for value the next day but it is possible to deal for same day value until 2 pm. Settlement can also be made through Euroclear or Cedel (this usually takes one day longer).

The Bank of France holds repo tenders once or twice per week. The repos are usually for around one week. The repo rate (*taux d'intervention*) is the Bank's most important signal to the market for interest rate policy.

# UNITED KINGDOM

Securities lending has existed in the UK for many years but repos in UK gilts are more recent. Following sterling's ERM crisis in September 1992, there was a liquidity crisis in the UK banking system which the Bank of England relieved through repos. This repo facility was formalized in 1994 but the market in repos was still restricted to official gilt-edged market makers (GEMMs). In January 1996 the Bank of England opened the market, permitting all professional market participants to take short positions in gilts. The Bank's decision to open the market stems from the considerations discussed in chapter 6, including the wish to maintain London as Europe's premier financial center.

The market is based on the latest (November 1995) PSA/ISMA agreement, a document already well established in the London repo market for international business, to which an annex was added relating specifically to gilts (*see* Appendix 1). The Bank of England has also published a Code of Best Practice for the market. Gilt repos are settled through the Central Gilts Office (CGO), the electronic book entry system run by the Bank of England for gilt settlements. Cedel, Euroclear, and Bank of New York are now all direct members of CGO, enabling triparty and international clearing of gilt repos.

In order to facilitate the new market, the Bank of England made some changes to the administration of gilts. Ex-dividend dates were reduced from 37 days to seven days before the coupon date. This means that when a bond is sold more than seven days before the next coupon date, the buyer receives the coupon (while less than seven days before the coupon date, the seller will still receive the coupon). This seven-day cut-off is still rather a long delay by international standards, however, and, as it tends to complicate repo transactions, the time may be shortened further in the future. As withholding tax also complicates repo transactions, coupon payments on all gilts are now available without deduction of tax to professional participants, provided they hold their gilts in a special CGO "STAR" account and, if they are UK-based, account for tax quarterly.

Delivery-by-value (DBV), an overnight mechanism for borrowing from other CGO members, with collateral automatically assigned by the CGO, continues alongside the new market. Under this mechanism, the repo is based on a cash amount rather than a securities amount, with the securities selected from the seller's account automatically by the CGO. The cash and securities are reversed the next day without any repo interest; this is paid by the buyer to the seller separately.

The Bank of England's activity in the market is restricted at the moment to repo operations every two weeks to manage liquidity. Unlike other major central banks, it has said that it will not yet use repos to signal changes in interest rate policy, or even as its main day-to-day intervention tool. For the time being, it will continue to use outright purchase of eligible bills for daily market intervention. It seems likely that this will change in the future, as the gilt repo market becomes increasingly established and liquid, and in order to bring the Bank of England's practice into line with that of other European central banks and that of the proposed European Central Bank.

# GERMANY

Although the influential status of the Bund as a benchmark in European bond markets has given a similar importance to the German repo market, which has grown very rapidly, the market is traded mainly in London rather than in Germany. This is partly because the level of derivatives trading in London is much higher than within Germany, due to London's status as the leading international financial center in Europe. Another important reason, however, is the Bundesbank's minimum reserve requirements, which make it very expensive for German banks to offer repos at competitive rates. For each cash deposit placed with a German bank, the bank in turn is required to place 2 percent of the deposit with the Bundesbank, free of interest. This same penalty is imposed on repos undertaken by a bank, despite the fact that collateral is passed to the counterparty.

Until now, the domestic interbank market has therefore been largely in securities lending, which does not suffer from this because it does not entail a customer deposit, with less activity in buy/sell-backs. The market has generally been driven by the need to borrow particular securities as specials rather than the perception of a repo as a cash borrowing/lending instrument. Repos are dealt between the banks and the Bundesbank.

There is no repo legislation in force at present, and no standard documentation. However, standard documentation based on the PSA/ISMA agreement is under discussion and expected to be introduced during 1997. DKV (Deutsche Kassenverein, the German bond-settlement system) has also now introduced a "delivery-repo" service for booking repos as such, with automatic generation of the instructions for the second leg of the deal.

The Bundesbank holds an important weekly repo auction to set the tone for interest rates. The repo rate is sometimes "fixed" (that is, the Bundesbank sets the rate and invites tenders at that rate) and sometimes "variable" (the Bundesbank invites banks to bid at rates of their own choosing). The repos are generally for 14 days, although sometimes for seven days.

# BELGIUM

The large size of outstanding Belgian government debt, and the need for the very cash-rich Belgian savings banks wishing to invest, have created a liquid domestic repo market.

The market is largely very short term (mostly one to seven days). There are fewer specials than in some markets, as shortages of a bond do not arise so much because OLOs are issued as a series of fungible tranches, so that shortages of a particular issue are less likely to arise.

As in France, there is specific legislation for repos (since May 1995), which facilitates the selling of collateral by the buyer in the event of default by the seller, and an official agreement adapted for the local market from the PSA/ISMA agreement. Belgian and Luxembourg banks sign this agreement with the Belgian National Bank rather than bilaterally with one another, and any repo dealt between two banks is considered to be under this agreement. Indeed, a repo of any security settled through the National Bank's system is presumed to be covered by this agreement, unless a different master agreement has been concluded between the two parties.

The legal structure of repo transactions has been rather complicated, with "code 70" transactions largely for domestic repos (with the two legs of the transaction linked as in a classic repo, but with repricing for mark-to-market prohibited under Belgian law), "code 10" transactions (settled as buy/sell-backs, allowing close-out and repricing), and "code 75" transactions (code 70 transactions with an annex to allow repricing). Day-to-day repos are not recognized under Belgian law, and cross-currency repos against Belgian securities cannot be settled through the domestic system (which is compulsory for Belgian and Luxembourg banks).

The National Bank uses two- and three-day repos for daily fine-tuning of interest rates, rather than for giving policy signals.

# SPAIN

The market in Spain has grown rapidly over the last few years, but is based largely on buy/sell-backs rather than classic repos. This is partly because the Bank of Spain has until now recognized buy/sell-backs as transferring ownership, while the status of repos was less clear. Relatively few specials are traded in the market.

Importantly also, the market has been driven largely by retail investment. Savings banks offer savings account products where the retail customer's deposit is reinvested by the bank in buy/sell-backs.

There is no official repo documentation, although the PSA/ISMA documentation is used increasingly.

The Bank of Spain uses repos daily to manage market liquidity and its ten-day repo auctions are regarded as the benchmark for official rates.

# ITALY

The Italian market is well developed, on the back of Europe's largest domestic bond market. As in Spain, however, it is based largely on buy/sell-back rather than classic repo. There is little securities lending.

An important factor in the Italian market is the withholding tax structure on bond coupons, because of which repo rates are often quoted net of tax. Unusually, accrued coupon on bond transactions is settled net of tax. This gives rise to an arbitrage through the repo market, as follows:

- A company borrows cash from a bank through a buy/sell-back.
- The total cash repayment at maturity is determined by the repo rate.
- Settlement of the bank's purchase and subsequent sale of the bond is recorded to show the bank as having paid and received the accrued coupon net of tax. This gives the bank a synthetic tax credit to offset against profits.
- This synthetic tax gain can be shared with the cash borrower, enabling a lower repo rate.

From the beginning of 1997, non-residents in countries with an appropriate double-tax treaty with Italy will no longer suffer the withholding tax. This is likely to remove a part of the driving force behind the market – as bond investors overseas will no longer need repo as a method to pass the complications of seeking tax reimbursement to a domestic Italian counterparty. It is also likely to move a portion of the Italian repo business away from domestic institutions, for the same reason.

There is also a market in specials, arising from the expansion of the BTP futures market on LIFFE (and hence the need to be able to short bonds as a hedge), from settlement problems in the Italian market, and from the fact that failure to deliver is strongly disapproved of in the Italian market.

The Bank of Italy usually uses repos several times per week, but on an irregular schedule and normally for terms of less than two months, both for liquidity management and for setting the tone for interest rates. The Bank holds tenders for repos in Deutschmarks as well as in lire.

# JAPAN

Development of the Japanese domestic market has been hindered by the fact that Japanese Government Bonds (JGBs) are registered and incur a local transfer tax payable by the seller each time a change of ownership takes place – which occurs on each leg of a repo. To overcome the problem of transfer tax, a market has arisen in "clean" JGBs traded offshore, not requiring re-registration on transfer. In addition, settlement of bond transactions other than on the stock exchange takes place only on the 5th, 10th, 15th, 20th, 25th, and 30th of each month, restricting the scope for repo settlement.

Given the tax problem, the local market has been mostly in uncollateralized securities lending in return for a fee ("Taishaku"); because this involves no payment for the bond, the transfer tax is not payable. Buy/sell-backs ("Gensaki") are also used, but usually for general collateral only rather than specials, and these do suffer from the transfer tax. The market is now moving toward collateralized securities lending, with the introduction of a new legal agreement for this in 1996. This new agreement provides the full security of collateral but the market still does not have Western-style classic repo because under present rules that would involve the transfer tax.

The Bank of Japan uses Gensaki for liquidity management rather than for setting interest rate policy.

# EXERCISES

**41.** Compare the different characteristics of the different major domestic repo markets.

**42.** Discuss the conditions necessary or helpful to the development of a liquid repo market.

■ ■ ■

*". . . any organization using the repo market should ensure that it has the necessary controls and systems in place to manage the trades."*

# The Legal and Regulatory Framework

# DOCUMENTATION

## The PSA/ISMA agreement

The current version of the GMRA produced in November 1995 by the PSA and ISMA jointly is based on the PSA's own Master Repurchase Agreement. The GMRA is the standard documentation for the international market centered on London and also forms the basis for the standard documentation in various European countries' domestic markets. The major European domestic exception to this is France, where the standard documentation is not based on the GMRA.

The GMRA is intended for gross-paying securities only – that is, ones where there is no withholding tax on the coupons. It is also not intended for US government bonds (for which the PSA agreement is used) or equities.

In order to understand the GMRA, we consider below various parts of the agreement, in the order in which they appear in it; the numbered headings refer to the headings in the agreement. A word or expression in *italics* indicates that this is the expression used in the GMRA itself. Clearly, this book is not a legal textbook, and our explanations are not a comprehensive expert legal opinion on the GMRA, but, rather, an attempt to explain some key areas in non-legal language. We have also not mentioned those areas covered in the GMRA – such as substitution – which we feel do not require any particular explanation. For the interested reader, we have included the whole agreement, together with the annex to it used in the UK domestic gilt repo market, in Appendix 1.

### 1. Applicability

The GMRA covers both classic repos and buy/sell-backs. This is a change from the previous version, and therefore now provides a standard legal framework for buy/sell-backs. When it is used for buy/sell-backs, the definitions and explanations in Annex III are used.

The GMRA is a "master" agreement. This means that, once signed by two parties, it can be used for all subsequent transactions between those parties. The agreement can be tailored to the parties' particular requirements by completing the various annexes to the agreement; these are mentioned below. Thereafter, each deal transacted under the agreement requires only a simple confirmation set out as in Annex II.

## 2. Definitions

The following explain some of the important terms in the agreement:

- *Equivalent securities*: When collateral is returned, it does not need to be exactly the same piece of paper or exactly the same numbered holding as originally transferred. Rather, it should be *equivalent* in the sense that the issuer, issue, type, value, description, and amount should be the same.

- *Income* (or *Distributions*): Coupon payments and other income arising from a security paid during the transaction.

- *Margin Ratio*: As explained in chapter 5, this is suggested to be the market value of the securities divided by the cash loan (the *purchase price*), so that if the haircut is 2 percent, the margin ratio is 1.02. However, the agreement allows the two parties to define the margin ratio differently.

- *Margin Transfer*: The settlement of a margin call.

- *Market Value*: The value of the securities including accrued coupon.

- *Net Exposure*: The net total of: the transaction exposures on all outstanding deals, the net margin paid or received on all outstanding deals, and any manufactured payments which are due but not yet paid or received. This calculation gives the amount of margin transfer which may be called for.

- *Net Margin*: The amount of variation margin paid (including *margin securities*, *margin cash* and accrued interest on *margin cash*) from one party to the other, netted against the amount of variation margin paid or repaid in the other direction.

- *Price Differential*: The accrued interest on the cash loan so far, at any time during the transaction.

- *Pricing Rate*: The repo interest rate.

- *Purchase Price*: The original cash loan.

- *Repurchase Date*: The end date of the transaction.

- *Repurchase Price*: The current value of the cash loan – that is, the original cash loan plus accrued interest on it so far, at any time during the transaction (= *purchase price* + *price differential*).

- *Transaction Exposure*: The difference between the current value of the cash loan (including accrued interest) plus margin, and the current market value of the securities (including accrued coupon) for any particular transaction (= *repurchase price* × *margin ratio* –

*market value*). Note that the existence of a *transaction exposure* does not mean that there is a risk to be protected, because the definition of *transaction exposure* does not take into account the margin transfer which may already have been made to cover it.

## 4. Margin maintenance

Because the GMRA is a master agreement designed to cover all repo transactions between the parties, margin calls are made on the basis of the total net transaction exposure (the *net exposure*) over all outstanding transactions between them, rather than on just one transaction.

The two parties may, however, agree that margin payments for any particular transaction are treated separately from the other transactions outstanding between them.

If the party making a margin call has previously paid margin in cash or securities, it may insist on any margin transfer back being made first in cash or in these same securities. Apart from this, however, the party paying the margin call may choose in what form to make the transfer (within any criteria agreed between the parties).

A net exposure can be settled by close-out and repricing (see chapter 5), rather than by a margin transfer. The GMRA distinguishes between two methods of close-out:

- *Repricing of transactions*: this is Method 4 in chapter 5 (see pages 89–91), with the cash amount adjusted, rather than the securities amount. The new transaction is called a *repriced transaction*, beginning on the *repricing* date.

- *Adjustment of transactions*: This is Method 3 in chapter 5 (see pages 86–89), with the securities amount adjusted rather than the cash amount. The new transaction is called a *replacement transaction*, beginning on the *adjustment* date.

The agreement does not now refer to any threshold which must be reached before margin calls may be made. Any such threshold must therefore be agreed separately.

## 5. Income payments

Whenever any *income* is received on a security, the buyer must pay the same amount to the seller on the same date (a manufactured dividend). The seller must reimburse the buyer similarly for any *income* received on securities the seller is holding as margin.

These payments must be made in full, even if the issuer of the security has deducted withholding tax.

## 6. Payment and transfer

Settlement of the two legs of the transaction should be by DVP, unless otherwise agreed, in which case the parties may agree any other arrangement they choose.

In any transfer of securities – such as at the beginning of the transaction from seller to buyer, or when margin transfers are made – full legal title (that is, ownership) passes from one party to the other.

All payments of cash, or transfers of a particular security, on any one date are netted across all the transactions outstanding between the parties.

## 10. Events of default

If one party defaults, the other may require that all the outstanding transactions (rather than only one particular transaction) be terminated immediately and a net settlement paid from one party to the other. The settlement is paid in *cash*, rather than by delivering securities. It is calculated by valuing all the securities bought and sold and margin calls transferred subsequently (whether cash or securities) at current rates including accrued coupon and interest. An important part of this is that liabilities to deliver securities are converted into liabilities to pay their cash value, because it is generally not possible legally to net claims for cash against claims for delivery of securities. One possible problem with this, however, is that if the securities are in short supply it is not possible to insist that they be delivered.

An important feature of the GMRA is the full right of set-off – that is, the *non-defaulting party* is able to ensure, first, that the securities and cash owed in one direction are set off against any securities and cash owed in the other direction, and second, that this offsetting is done across all the transactions outstanding. This is important because it avoids the possibility that an insolvent organization could agree to settle only the transactions currently in its favor and refuse to settle the others.

A party can claim that there has been an *event of default* if the other party does any of various things, including the following:

- Fails to pay the cash amount on either leg of a transaction.
- Fails to pay a margin call.
- Fails to pay a manufactured payment (see section 5, above).
- Becomes insolvent.

- Makes false statements about its own authorization to enter such transactions.
- Is suspended from membership of any securities exchange, association or self-regulating organization.

Note that failure to deliver the securities at the beginning or the end of the transaction is not an *event of default*, although the other party may terminate the transaction or demand repayment of the cash.

Except for some cases of insolvency, the *non-defaulting party* must give notice to the other party that it is claiming a default.

## 11. Tax event

If there are changes in a tax regime during a transaction which significantly affect the transaction for one of the parties, it may terminate the transaction unless the other party agrees to compensate it for the new tax effect.

## 13. Single agreement

All transactions outstanding between the two parties under the GMRA are considered together as a single contract. This feature is sometimes important in establishing the full right of set-off discussed above. Under the law in some countries (France, Spain, Belgium, and possibly Italy, for example), set-off on insolvency is not generally allowed – although France and Belgium have introduced legislation specifically permitting netting of repos. This *single agreement* clause attempts to overcome this problem.

## 17. Governing law

The agreement as published by PSA/ISMA is governed by English law, although local domestic variations of it will of course adjust this.

## 20. Recording

Under the agreement, each party is allowed to make recordings of telephone conversations.

## Annex I

This enables the two parties to tailor the agreement in various ways, including the following:

- Whether buy/sell-backs are included.
- What the *base currency* should be for margin calculations and settlements when there is a default, and what benchmark source should be used for spot exchange rates – this is not the same as the *contractual currency* of each transaction, which may be different for each one depending on the transaction.
- If transactions are to include Italian government securities (which are *net-paying securities* – coupons are paid net of withholding tax), all *income payments* will be treated as if they were paid gross.
- The interest rate to be paid on cash margin.
- The delivery period after which margin calls must be transferred.

## Annex II

This is the form of confirmation to be used under the agreement, giving the individual details for each transaction – dates, prices, securities, buyer, seller, contractual currency, bank accounts, whether the deal is a buy/sell-back, etc.

## Annex III – buy/sell-backs

This annex applies if the two parties have agreed that buy/sell-backs are included under the master agreement. In this case, the following apply:

- *Accrued interest* is the accrued coupon on the securities.
- *Sell back differential* at any time during the transaction is the accrued interest on the cash loan (equivalent to *price differential* in a classic repo).
- Buy/sell-backs cannot be open (*terminable on demand*).
- The *purchase price* and *sell back price* are quoted as clean prices when the deal is first transacted (unlike the *purchase price* and *repurchase price* for a classic repo).
- But *sell back price* at any time during the transaction other than the original repurchase date is an all-in price:

(purchase price + accrued interest + sell back differential)
    – (income payments plus reinvestment)

*Income payments* are assumed to be reinvested at the original repo rate (*pricing rate*).

- Buy/sell-backs may be *repriced* or *adjusted*.

● The original holder of securities is not compensated for *income payments* (coupon payments, etc. during the transaction).

# The gilt annex

For repos of UK government ("gilt-edged") securities, there is a second part to the GMRA's Annex I, which is also included in full in Appendix 1. The following are some of the important points in it.

## 3. CGO service

This section covers the arrangements particular to the CGO (Central Gilts Office), which is the Bank of England's settlement mechanism. In particular, it allows for DBV ("delivery-by-value") transactions, which are overnight repos. With a DBV transaction:

● The repo is based on a cash amount rather than a securities amount.
● The securities are selected from the seller's account automatically by the CGO.
● The cash and securities are reversed the next day *without* any repo interest; this is paid by the buyer to the seller separately.

## 5. Exercise of rights of conversion

If the holder of the gilt has a right to convert the gilt from one security to another during the transaction, the buyer must exercise this right on his or her behalf if the seller so requests. Note that this is not covered at all in the GMRA.

## 7. Dividend entitlements

In the gilt market, securities usually become "ex-dividend" seven days before a coupon date. This means that if a gilt transaction is settled less than seven days before the coupon date the original owner receives the coupon instead of the new owner. This section takes account of the effect of this on margin calls. If the first leg of a repo is ex-dividend, for example, the seller will receive the coupon during the transaction and this is treated as being cash margin paid by the buyer. Similarly, if the second leg of the repo is ex-dividend, the buyer will receive the coupon after the transaction is finished and so this is treated as cash margin paid by the seller.

# MANAGEMENT

As with any area of financial trading, any organization using the repo market should ensure that it has the necessary controls and systems in place to manage the trades. The following areas should be covered.

## Credit risk

Although the repo market is collateralized, this does not remove credit risk entirely. Rather, each transaction gives the buyer two credit risks to consider – the counterparty and the issuer of the security. Clearly, the chance of both defaulting together is less, but the risks must still be considered, credit analysis performed, and limits set both for the counterparties and for the total amount of any one issuer's collateral acceptable across all transactions. It should be possible to identify in particular the credit exposure to HIC repos where the credit risk may be seen as greater.

The seller similarly should monitor the credit risk on any securities held as variation margin.

## Margin maintenance

The organization must ensure that it has systems in place to do the following:

- Mark-to-market each transaction.
- Calculate margin calls under each agreement it has in place, taking any margin thresholds into account.
- Check that margin calls made by a counterparty are correct.
- Call promptly for margin transfers when appropriate.
- Check that transfers each way have been paid and received promptly.

## Settlement procedures

Whenever possible, settlement should be DVP for repos and buy/sell-backs, as in other securities transactions. The organization should check that it has the necessary mechanisms for DVP settlement. Care should be taken that non-DVP margin transfers are properly authorized.

Systems should be in place to ensure that any securities sold through HIC repos are held separately in custody for the buyer.

The organization must monitor all income payments due on securities sold and purchased and check that correct manufactured payments are received and paid on the due dates.

## Position management

On the cash side, the organization must ensure that its cash management systems give an accurate picture of the cash requirement now and in the future. On the securities side, the systems must show which securities are available for repoing out and in which securities the position is short.

For matched book trading, the organization must be able to identify any unmatched positions, and to measure its interest rate risk position and set trading limits for various time buckets, in the same way as for interest rate risk management elsewhere in its trading activities. Moreover, these positions should be integrated across the different trading activities.

Systems should be in place to monitor continually whether any securities in the organization's portfolio have become special, to ensure that advantage is taken of this.

## Legal/documentation risks

The collateralized nature of repo transactions is an advantage only to the extent that the legal position allows it to be. The organization should ensure that documentation such as the GMRA is in place to allow set-off of claims in the event of default. Clearly, the legal situation may vary from country to country and counterparty to counterparty.

## CAPITAL ADEQUACY REQUIREMENTS

When a bank or other financial institution lends money or deals in financial instruments, it is clearly taking risks. The major risks fall into two categories:

- *Credit risk* – the risk that the borrower, or the counterparty to the deal, will default on repayment or not deliver its side of the deal.
- *Market risk* – the risk that the value of the bank's deal falls; for example, the bank buys a security whose price subsequently falls.

In order to prevent banks from taking excessive risks (and hence protect the banking system as a whole), the European Union (EU) and the Basle Committee have established guideline limits to the risks which each bank may take. In turn, each country's central bank enforces these limits, or stronger ones if it prefers, on the banks under its control. The details of these guidelines are very complex, and the following remarks are necessarily a simplification of them.

The risk limits are defined in terms of the size of each bank's own funds (roughly equivalent to the value of its shareholders' equity in the bank plus reserves and certain other funding raised by the bank). Each loan or transaction undertaken by the bank is measured in terms of risk according to certain rules. The bank's own funds must always be equal to at least 8 percent of the total of all these risks. The concept is that if some of the risks are realized, the bank should still have adequate capital to remain in business – hence the term "capital adequacy." The various directives from the EU which together set out the risk measurement rules are known as the "Capital Adequacy Directive" (CAD). Each central bank may impose a higher requirement than 8 percent on any particular bank under its control if it so chooses.

The effect of the CAD is to limit the amount, and type, of business which a bank does. If the types of deal undertaken by a particular bank are measured as mostly having a low risk, it can do more of them than if they are measured as having a high risk. The significance of the CAD for repos lies in how the measurement of risk for repo transactions compares with the measurement of risk for other transactions. The situation can be summarized by saying that repos with careful legal documentation such as the PSA/ISMA agreement are generally measured as being of low risk, because of the collateralization and the legal right to net obligations in the event of default (the right of set-off).

For much of a bank's business, the capital requirement is 8 percent of the *total* of the following:

- *Position risk* on trading activities.
- *Settlement and counterparty risk* on trading activities.
- *Counterparty risk* on general banking business.
- *Currency risk* on all business.
- *Large exposure risk* on all business.

# Trading book or general banking book?

From the above it can be seen that a bank's business is split into two areas – the "trading book" and the rest of the "banking book." Although the trading book requires extra capital for the position risk, repos and similar transactions have special lower counterparty risk capital requirements when they are in the trading book than when they are in the banking book. The significance for the repo market is that most of a bank's repos, if properly documented, are in fact considered to be in the trading book.

**Essentially, a transaction is in the banking book if it is a cash loan made by the bank or a long-term investment. A transaction is in the trading book if it involves trading in financial instruments for the purpose of making trading profits – largely the type of activity undertaken by a bank's dealing rooms rather than by its lending departments.**

In particular, a repo is normally included in the trading book if it relates to securities which are in the trading book; a reverse repo is in the trading book if the local banking authorities approve, the deal is not "artificial", *and* the deal satisfies one of the following criteria:

- The deal is done with another financial institution (although some countries' banks are excluded); *or*

- The exposures are marked to market daily *and* margin calls are made *and* the documentation used has automatic and immediate set-off if the counterparty defaults.

According to these rules, repo business transacted by banks with other banks will generally be included in the trading book. This includes buy/sell-backs and securities lending, as it is the nature of the deal rather than what it is called that is important. The local banking authorities may well not approve, however, of including in the trading book a reverse repo with a corporate customer of the bank. Although the definitions in the CAD itself may imply that such a reverse could be included in the trading book if it is dealt under careful documentation and properly marked to market, individual central banks may well prefer to consider such business as general banking business. This is likely to be a matter where each central bank will take its own view, and will depend on the exact circumstances involved.

# Counterparty risk

The counterparty risk for any transaction takes account of two aspects: the creditworthiness of the counterparty and the nature of the transaction. For example, a USD 1 million FRA dealt with a particular counterparty does not expose the bank to the same potential loss as a USD 1 million loan made to the same counterparty. With the FRA, if the counterparty defaults, the bank can lose only the difference between two interest rates. With a loan, the bank can lose the entire principal amount as well as the interest on it. Counterparty risk is therefore measured as:

risk weighting for the counterparty × factor depending on the transaction

Examples of measures for some different risk weightings and transactions are given in Table 9.1.

## Risk weightings and transaction factors

Table 9.1

| Counterparties | Weighting |
|---|---|
| Government | 0% |
| Bank in "Zone A" (mostly OECD countries) | 20% |
| Corporate (for derivative transactions) | 50% |
| Corporate (other transactions) | 100% |
| *Transaction type* | *Factor* |
| Loan, or bond purchase | 100% of amount |
| Interest rate-related derivative transactions (such as an FRA or IRS) with maturity up to 1 year | Mark-to-market profit |
| Interest rate-related derivative transactions (such as an FRA or IRS) with maturity more than 1 year | Mark-to-market profit plus (0.5% of amount of deal) |
| Repos, buy/sell-backs, and securities lending *in the trading book* | Any amount of *under-collateralization* |

Thus, for example:

- The risk for a USD 1 million loan to a corporate is:

  100% × USD 1 million × 100% = USD 1 million

- The risk for a USD 1 million FRA 15 v. 18 dealt with a Zone A bank is:

  20% × [(the current mark-to-market profit on the deal) + (0.5% × USD 1 million)]

In the case of the FRA, if the deal is currently running at a loss, there is clearly no mark-to-market exposure if the counterparty defaults. The "add-on" of 0.5 percent is to allow for the possibility of the deal moving into profit before a mark-to-market calculation is next made.

- For a reverse repo of USD 1 million with a Zone A bank where our bank has taken a haircut of 2 percent, the risk is:

  20% × zero = zero

- For a reverse repo where the other bank has taken the haircut of 2 percent, the risk is:

  20% × (USD 1.02 million – USD 1 million) = USD 4,000

In calculating the degree of under-collateralization, both accrued coupon (on the bond) and accrued interest (on the cash) are taken into account, in the same way as when a repo is marked to market for the purpose of making margin calls. It is not clear from the CAD itself whether individual countries' authorities may allow the risk for repos to be measured across all the current repo transactions with a counterparty – so that, if there are several repos and reverse repos outstanding with a particular counterparty, the risk would be only the net under-collateralization of all the deals together.

Clearly, the advantage to a bank in dealing a reverse repo compared to making a straightforward loan is that the capital requirement is much less, as long as the deal can be considered as in the trading book. The favorable treatment given to repos has enabled the market to grow without significant capital adequacy constraint, and encourages the use of proper documentation and margining

When a reverse repo is included in the general banking book, the treatment is much harsher, as it treats the reverse in the same way as a collateralized loan, on which the full 100 percent capital requirement may be imposed, depending on the nature of the collateral.

## Other risks

The three other risks to be calculated in assessing capital adequacy requirements are:

- *Position risk*: exposure to changes in interest rates and security prices.
- *Currency risk*: net exposure to foreign currencies.
- *Large exposure risk*: total exposure to any one counterparty.

These three risks are very important to the bank's capital adequacy calculation, but less significant to the question of comparing repos with other instruments, because they apply similarly to positions and exposures whether established through repos or otherwise. Position risk in particular, which applies only to the trading book, involves rather complex calculations which are not necessary for the understanding of the repo market.

# ACCOUNTING AND TAX REGIMES

## Accounting

Although many countries may not have accounting rules which deal specifically with repos, the general principle of international accounting standards is to consider the "substance" of a transaction as more important than its "appearance." Although a repo *appears* to be a sale of a security and a subsequent purchase of a security, the substance of the transaction is, however, a collateralized loan. Ideally, therefore, the accounting treatment should reflect this.

The treatment of a repo under these principles – which is, for example, in accordance with the European Union Bank Accounting Directive – is therefore as follows:

### For the buyer

- The security purchased is not included on the balance sheet.
- The cash consideration is recorded as an asset in the same way as any money market loan, possibly under a separate heading indicating that it arises from a reverse repo.

### For the seller

- The security sold remains on the balance sheet, with a note in the accounts to say that it has been repoed out.
- The cash consideration is recorded as a liability in the same way as a cash borrowing, possibly under a separate heading indicating that it arises from a repo.

Some other points worth considering are as follows:

- An important principle in the PSA/ISMA agreement is that, when two parties undertake a series of repos and reverse repos, all obligations can be netted against one another in the event of default. Accounting treatment cannot generally apply the same principle, because the transactions will have a series of different maturity dates and, assuming no default, each repo will in any case be settled gross rather than net because the final payments are made against collateral under DVP. Although this is a general principle, some accounting regimes do nevertheless allow repos and reverses between two parties to be netted on the balance sheet provided there is an agreement, such as the GMRA, allowing for set-off.
- When securities are transferred to satisfy margin calls, the same treatment can be applied as for the original repo – the securities remain on the balance sheet of the party originally owning them. Where margin calls are settled in cash, however, the amount may be treated differently: for example, the bank receiving the cash collateral could include it as a liability to reflect the fact that it is due to be returned. If the cash collateral is legally able to be netted against the repo cash consideration, however, the bank could adjust the existing asset/liability (the cash lent in the repo) by the same amount.
- It is possible for repos not to require the return of the original security – as, for example, in a dollar repo. The practice in the US, where such repos are probably more frequent than in Europe, is to use the same accounting treatment as described above, provided that the security returned is "substantially the same." Again, the important issue is whether this type of repo is still essentially a collateralized loan.
- In the case of a "repo to maturity," where the term of the repo is the same as the maturity of the collateral, the "substance" of the repo is slightly different. In this case the security is not sold back to the original seller because it is redeemed. The substance of such a

transaction may therefore be better reflected by recording the transaction as an outright sale of the security (from the seller's point of view) or purchase (from the buyer's point of view), as the second leg does not in practice take place because the security is redeemed.

# Tax

Tax treatment of financial transactions varies significantly of course between countries, between organizations, and between transactions. It is therefore impossible (and unwise!) to be specific about the taxation of repos, and the few remarks here are aimed only at indicating some of the areas of concern particular to these instruments.

As with accounting, the ideal tax treatment for a repo might be to consider it as a collateralized loan, so that the effect of the taxation is the same as income tax on loan interest. Because of the structure of a repo, however, there are several areas where a country's taxation rules may conflict with this.

## Price differential

The loan interest is essentially the difference between the price of the security on the first leg of the transaction and the price on the second leg. With a straightforward security sale or purchase, such a price differential would normally be taxed as a capital gain in countries where there is a difference between the rate of tax on income and the rate of tax on capital gains. If the repo is to be treated as a loan, however, this differential needs to be taxed as income. There is less likely to be a difference in the two tax rates applied to a market trading organization, such as a bank, than to a corporate organization.

## Accrued coupon

The cash consideration paid on each leg includes, explicitly or implicitly, an amount of accrued coupon. In a straightforward security sale this accrual may again be taxed differently from the rest of the cash paid, because tax authorities wish to prevent the coupon income being "hidden" as a capital gain. Again, if a repo is to be treated as a loan this distinction should not be made.

## Manufactured dividend

When a coupon occurs during the term of a repo, the seller receives a manufactured dividend from the buyer as compensation – or, in a buy/sell-back, the same effect is achieved through an adjustment to the forward price. For the economic effect to be the same as with a cash loan, no withholding tax should be deducted from this explicit or implicit payment – assuming that no tax would be withheld on the coupon itself in the normal way. The actual situation with regard to withholding tax will depend not only on the tax regime in the dealer's own country but also on double taxation treaties with the counterparty's country.

# EXERCISES

**43.** Summarize the circumstances which give rise to a default under the PSA/ISMA agreement, and how the non-defaulting party is protected.

**44.** What are the internal controls and systems you would wish to see put in place before your bank started dealing in repos?

**45.** Discuss how the Capital Adequacy Directive relates to repos and how it affects the market's development.

# Part 4

# Practice ACI Exam, Hints, and Answers

# A Complete Practice ACI Exam

*The following pages contain a full exam, laid out in the same format as the repos exam currently set as part of the ACI series of exams leading to fellowship of the ACI*

*If you are serious about taking the ACI's exam, we recommend that you work through this practice version, and would like to make the following suggestions.*

*Familiarize yourself with the material throughout this book first – particularly chapters 5 to 9 and the appendices – and work through the examples and worked answers to the exercises.*

*Try to work through the practice exam under "exam conditions." The typical exam instructions (repeated at the beginning of the exam itself on the next page) are as follows:*

**The following exam should last two hours. It consists of:**

- **50 multiple choice questions**
- **4 calculation questions**
- **1 essay to be chosen from two subjects**

**Each section is allocated one third of the total marks available, and you are advised to spend approximately 40 minutes on each.**

*Chapter 11 includes answers to the first two parts of the exam.*

*Good luck!*

# REPOS EXAMINATION

The following exam should last two hours. It consists of:

- 50 multiple choice questions

- 4 calculation questions

- 1 essay to be chosen from two subjects

Each section is allocated one third of the total marks available, and you are advised to spend approximately 40 minutes on each.

## MULTIPLE CHOICE QUESTIONS

**Please answer ALL the following 50 questions. In each case, indicate which is the correct answer.**

1.  If the Fed wishes to add liquidity it will:

    a.  do customer repos
    b.  do system repos
    c.  do reverse repos
    d.  do matched sale-purchases

2.  In a USD repo collateralized by Treasury bonds,

    a.  the repo rate should generally be less than LIBOR and less than T-bill rates
    b.  the repo rate should generally be more than LIBOR and more than T bill rates
    c.  the repo rate should generally be more than LIBOR and less than T-bill rates
    d.  the repo rate should generally be less than LIBOR and more than T-bill rates

3.  The implied repo rate is:

    a.  the rate at which commercial banks can deal repos with the central bank
    b.  the repo rate applicable to collateral of the highest creditworthiness
    c.  the lowest rate at which it is possible to borrow in the repo market
    d.  the break-even repo rate at which it is possible to buy a bond, repo it out, and sell a futures contract

4. Under the CAD, "own funds" as a proportion of the relevant weighted assets of a bank must be at least:

   a. 8.0%
   b. 8.5%
   c. 7.5%
   d. 12.5%

5. Substitution is when:

   a. the seller substitutes one type of collateral for another
   b. the seller assigns his repo contract to another party
   c. the buyer assigns his repo contract to another party
   d. any of the above

6. The bid rate in the repo market is:

   a. the rate at which a dealer is prepared to lend cash and borrow securities
   b. the rate at which a dealer is prepared to borrow cash and lend securities
   c. neither of the above

7. When a repo is dealt on a flat basis:

   a. the collateral must be a zero-coupon bond
   b. there is no interest charged on the cash loan involved
   c. there is no margin
   d. the parties agree not to mark-to-market

8. If as a repo buyer you are required to return "equivalent securities" at maturity, you can deliver:

   a. any security of the same creditworthiness
   b. a larger amount of any security
   c. any government security
   d. the same security as you took originally

9. If you deal a single-currency repo in which the collateral is a BTP, then you have dealt in:

   a. French francs
   b. Italian lire
   c. Spanish pesetas
   d. Japanese yen

**10.** The latest version of the GMRA does the following for buy/sell-backs:

a. nothing
b. makes them exactly the same as a classic repo
c. provides them with a legal framework
d. prohibits them

**11.** Bundesbank reserve requirements on domestic repos are:

a. zero
b. the same as for deposits
c. 8%
d. less than for deposits

**12.** Coupon payments made during a buy/sell-back are:

a. paid to the original owner of the bond
b. paid to the original owner of the bond but then passed to the new owner
c. paid to the new owner of the bond
d. paid to the new owner of the bond but then passed to the original owner

**13.** An open repo is the same as:

a. a day-to-day repo
b. a hold-in-custody repo
c. a repo where the seller can substitute the collateral

**14.** Under PSA/ISMA documentation, which of the following would give rise to an event of default?

a. suspension from membership of a securities exchange
b. failure to make a margin transfer
c. untrue statements regarding authorization to deal
d. all of the above

**15.** GEMM is:

a. a quotation system for repo prices
b. the domestic settlement system for Spanish bonds
c. a professional association for dealers in government bonds
d. a dealer in UK government securities

**16.** A classic repo provides the cash lender with more safety than a straightforward loan or deposit because of:

    a. stricter market supervision

    b. the counterparty's obligation to buy back the collateral

    c. the creditworthiness of the issuer of the collateral

    d. the counterparty's obligation to pass back coupons paid on the collateral

**17.** The repurchase price in a repo (as defined in the GMRA) is:

    a. the price at which the collateral will be repurchased at maturity

    b. the current market value of the collateral

    c. the amount of cash lent plus accrued interest

    d. the current market value of the collateral plus accrued coupon

**18.** The purchase price in a repo (as defined in the GMRA) is:

    a. the cash lent by the buyer originally

    b. the cash lent by the buyer originally, adjusted by subsequent transfers of cash as variation margin

    c. the price at which the collateral can be purchased in the market

    d. the price at which the collateral is repurchased at maturity

**19.** The rebate in a securities lending transaction is:

    a. the lending fee deducted from interest paid on cash collateral

    b. additional security which the borrower gives to the lender at maturity

    c. a reduction in the fee level allowed to borrowers who do frequent business

    d. none of the above

**20.** Central banks might use a domestic repo market to:

    a. signal changes in interest rate policy

    b. fine-tune liquidity in the money market

    c. encourage the development of a strong bond market

    d. all the above

**21.** A securities lending transaction is different from a classic repo because:

   a.  securities lending is never documented

   b.  the lender always keeps legal title to the securities in securities lending, but not in a repo

   c.  equities can be lent but not repoed

   d.  securities lending can use a letter of credit as collateral

**22.** A cross-currency repo is one in which:

   a.  the cash is repaid in a different currency from that in which it is originally borrowed

   b.  the repo is in a non-dollar currency

   c.  the cash loan and collateral are in different currencies

**23.** The lender in a repo is the same as:

   a.  the seller

   b.  the investor

   c.  the buyer

   d.  none of the above

**24.** In the basket of bonds deliverable into a futures contract, the "cheapest to deliver" is the one which produces:

   a.  the lowest implied repo rate

   b.  the highest implied repo rate

   c.  the implied repo rate is the same for all deliverable bonds

   d.  the implied repo rate is irrelevant

**25.** Double-dipping is:

   a.  a repo where the seller is allowed to substitute the collateral twice

   b.  a repo involving two lenders of collateral

   c.  using the same collateral for two repo deals

   d.  lowering the interest rate on a cash loan for particularly good collateral

**26.** A manufactured dividend is:

   a.  a coupon payment repaid by the repo buyer to the repo seller

   b.  an artificial payment made to the repo buyer in compensation for a low repo interest rate

   c.  an arbitrage profit made by transacting a repo and a reverse repo at different rates

   d.  the dividend on an equity issued by a manufacturing company

**27.** Cash-and-carry arbitrage is:

a. borrow a bond through a reverse repo and then sell the bond in the cash market
b. buy a bond in the cash market and then lend it through a reverse repo
c. buy a bond in the cash market, fund it through a repo, and sell bond futures
d. buy a bond in the cash market, fund it through a repo, and buy bond futures

**28.** A synthetic repo can be created by:

a. selling a bond, selling a put, and selling a call
b. selling a bond, selling a put, and buying a call
c. selling a bond, buying a put, and buying a call
d. selling a bond, buying a put, and selling a call
e. none of the above

**29.** The international professional body governing securities and repo dealing is:

a. AIBD
b. PSA
c. ISMA
d. ISRA

**30.** Under the Capital Adequacy Directive, the risk weighting for a repo with another bank is:

a. lower for bilateral than for triparty repos
b. higher for bilateral than for triparty repos
c. zero for both
d. the same for both but not necessarily zero

**31.** Variation margin is:

a. extra collateral demanded at the beginning of a repo to protect against variations in the collateral value
b. extra collateral demanded in compensation for allowing the seller to substitute the collateral during the term of a repo
c. change required in the nominal amount of the collateral or the cash because of a change in market value

**32.** Basis is:

   a. the difference between the theoretical futures market price and the current cash market price
   b. the difference between the actual futures market price and the theoretical futures market price
   c. the difference between the actual futures market price and the current cash market price
   d. none of the above

**33.** A special is:

   a. a repo for an unusual period
   b. a bond in particular demand by borrowers
   c. repo of a junk bond
   d. a repo under non-standard documentation

**34.** The forward price in a sell/buy-back is lower than the start price:

   a. generally if the coupon is higher than the repo rate
   b. generally if the coupon is lower than the repo rate
   c. always
   d. never

**35.** A term repo is:

   a. a repo lasting until the maturity date of the collateral
   b. a repo with a fixed maturity date
   c. a repo lasting for a standard market period (30 days, 60 days, etc.)
   d. none of the above

**36.** Accrued coupon on OATs is calculated on the following basis:

   a. ACT/360
   b. 30/360
   c. ACT/ACT
   d. ACT/365

**37.** A repo where the collateral returned at maturity can be different, within agreed limits, from the collateral delivered originally is:

   a. a classic repo
   b. a US-style repo
   c. a dollar repo
   d. a variable repo

**38.** Under a flex repo:

    a. the seller may substitute different collateral during the repo

    b. the buyer may demand different collateral during the repo

    c. the repo rate changes during the repo

    d. the cash is repaid to the buyer in stages during the repo

**39.** If you need to borrow a bond through a reverse repo, which is more suitable?

    a. a triparty repo

    b. a bilateral repo

    c. an HIC repo

    d. all are equally suitable

**40.** A special is repoed at 2.80% at a time when a repo for GC would be 4.35%. If the seller had instead lent the special through a securities lending transaction, he might have asked for a fee of approximately:

    a. 7.15%

    b. 1.55%

    c. 2.80%

    d. 0.775%

**41.** Who generally pays for most of the costs of a triparty agent in a repo?

    a. the buyer

    b. the seller

    c. the costs are shared equally

    d. the buyer pays all the initial costs and the seller pays the costs for all substitutions

**42.** The clean price of a bond is:

    a. bond price excluding accrued coupon

    b. bond price including accrued coupon

    c. the net present value of the bond's cashflows

    d. the value of the bond at maturity

**43.** When a repo is marked to market, the calculation takes account of:

    a. accrued coupon on the collateral

    b. accrued interest on the cash loan

    c. neither of the above

    d. both of the above

**44.** Legal title to collateral passes from lender to borrower.

    a. in a repo but not in a buy/sell-back or in a securities lending transaction

    b. in a repo and in a securities lending transaction but not in a buy/sell-back

    c. in a repo and in a buy/sell-back and sometimes in a securities lending transaction

    d. in none of the three transactions

    e. always in all three transactions

**45.** The repo rate is generally:

    a. higher with special collateral than general collateral

    b. lower with special collateral than general collateral

    c. the same in both

**46.** The collateral in a repo under the PSA/ISMA agreement:

    a. must be government bonds

    b. must be government bonds or Treasury bills

    c. must be AAA-rated

    d. can be anything if agreed between the two parties

**47.** Interest on a ITL repo is calculated on the following basis:

    a. ACT/365

    b. ACT/360

    c. 30/360

    d. 30/365

**48.** Matched book trading means that:

    a. the dealer is not exposed to bond price movements

    b. the dealer is not exposed to interest rate risk

    c. the dealer's book is always balanced

    d. the dealer makes two-way prices for repos

**49.** Given the same term and collateral:

    a. the rate for a bilateral repo should generally lie between the rates for an HIC and a triparty repo

    b. the rate for an HIC repo should generally lie between the rates for a triparty and a bilateral repo

    c. the rate for a triparty repo should generally lie between the rates for an HIC and a bilateral repo

    d. there is no way of knowing

**50.** Gensaki is:

    a. rice wine
    b. an honorary title for the Japanese prime minister
    c. a Japanese official interest rate
    d. none of the above

## CALCULATION QUESTIONS

### Please answer ALL the following 4 questions

**1.** A dealer repos FRF Treasury bills as follows:

| | |
|---|---|
| Face value of bills: | FRF 100 million |
| Current yield on bills: | 6.78% |
| Term to maturity of bills: | 182 days |
| Term of repo: | 30 days |
| Repo rate: | 5.18% |
| No haircut | |

    (a) How much cash does the dealer borrow?
    (b) How much cash does the dealer repay at maturity?
    (c) After 14 days, the T-bill yield has risen to 7.5%. What margin call can in theory be made, and by whom?

**2.** A dealer does the following repo:

| | |
|---|---|
| Nominal amount of collateral: | £10,000,000 |
| Security: | Treasury 6% 2009 |
| Last coupon: | April 12 |
| Term: | 30 days, June 5 – July 5 |
| Market clean price at start: | 95.00 |
| Repo rate: | 5.28125% |
| Haircut: | 2.5% |

The next day, the market clean price of the collateral has risen to 98.00. What nominal amount of Treasury 6% 2009 needs to be transferred as margin call and who transfers it to whom? All-in prices are rounded to two decimal places in the repo and the marking-to-market.

**3.** A dealer wants to borrow US$20 million through a cross-currency repo, using UK gilts as collateral:

| | |
|---|---|
| Start date: | May 21, 1997 |
| Maturity date of repo: | August 21, 1997 |
| Repo rate: | 5.72% |

| | |
|---|---|
| Collateral: | UK 7¾% Treasury January 14, 2004 |
| Price: | 101.95 |
| Haircut: | 5% |
| Spot exchange rate £/US$: | 1.5145 |

(a) How much collateral is transferred (UK gilts can be transferred in denominations of £0.01)? All-in prices are rounded to six decimal places.

After 21 days, the dealer wishes to make a substitution, using a US government security instead of the UK gilt. The buyer agrees to reduce the haircut to 2%.

| | |
|---|---|
| New collateral: | US 6¾% Treasury August 13, 2001 |
| Price: | 98.42 |

(b) What nominal amount of the new collateral is required (assuming minimum denominations of US$1000)?

4. What is the forward price, if a bank buys FRF 150,000,000.00 of 8¼% OAT March 20, 2000 in a buy/sell-back?

| | |
|---|---|
| Start date: | February 13, 1997 |
| Maturity: | May 13, 1997 |
| Repo rate: | 5.82% |
| Start price: | 104.63 |
| Haircut: | 2% |

## ESSAY QUESTIONS

### Please write on ONE of the following subjects

1. Summarize the different ways in which a dealer might use a repo.

2. Summarize the major aspects of a repo which are covered in the PSA/ISMA agreement with a brief explanation of their relevance.

# Hints and Answers to Exercises and Practice Exam

# HINTS ON EXERCISES

1. Future value = Present value $\times \left( 1 + \text{yield} \times \dfrac{\text{days}}{\text{year}} \right)$

2. Present value = $\dfrac{\text{Future value}}{\left( 1 + \text{yield} \times \frac{\text{days}}{\text{year}} \right)}$

3. Yield = $\left( \dfrac{\text{Future value}}{\text{Present value}} - 1 \right) \times \dfrac{\text{year}}{\text{days}}$

4. Future value = Present value $\times (1 + \text{yield})^{N}$

5. Future value = Present value $\times (1 + \text{yield})^{N}$

   Interest = Future value − Principal

6. Present value = $\dfrac{\text{Future value}}{(1 + \text{yield})^{N}}$

7. First known rate + difference between known rates $\times \dfrac{\text{days to interpolated rate}}{\text{days between known rates}}$

8. Proceeds = Face value $\times \left( 1 + \text{coupon rate} \times \dfrac{\text{days}}{\text{year}} \right)$

9. Price = Present value = $\dfrac{\text{Future value}}{\left( 1 + \text{yield} \times \frac{\text{days}}{\text{year}} \right)}$

10. Yield = $\left( \dfrac{\text{Future cashflow}}{\text{Present cashflow}} - 1 \right) \times \dfrac{\text{year}}{\text{days held}}$

11. What is the day/year count?

    Price = Present value = $\dfrac{\text{Future value}}{\left( 1 + \text{yield} \times \frac{\text{days}}{\text{year}} \right)}$

12. Discount rate = $\dfrac{\text{Rate of true yield}}{\left(1 + \text{yield} \times \dfrac{\text{days}}{\text{year}}\right)}$

   Discount amount = Principal $\times$ discount rate $\times \dfrac{\text{days}}{\text{year}}$

13. Rate of true yield = $\dfrac{\text{discount rate}}{\left(1 - \text{discount rate} \times \dfrac{\text{days}}{\text{year}}\right)}$

   Amount paid = Principal − Discount amount

14. Discount amount = Face value − Amount paid

   Discount rate = $\dfrac{\text{Discount amount}}{\text{Face value}} \times \dfrac{\text{year}}{\text{days}}$

15. What is the day/year count?

   a. Amount paid = Principal $\times \left(1 - \text{discount rate} \times \dfrac{\text{days}}{\text{year}}\right)$

   b. Rate of true yield = $\dfrac{\text{discount rate}}{\left(1 - \text{discount rate} \times \dfrac{\text{days}}{\text{year}}\right)}$

16. Yield = $\left(\dfrac{\text{Future cashflow}}{\text{Present cashflow}} - 1\right) \times \dfrac{\text{year}}{\text{days held}}$

17. What is the day/year count in each case?
   Is the quote a yield or a discount rate in each case?

18. Convert all rates to the same basis in order to compare them – for example, true yield, on a 365-day basis.

19. Forward-forward rate = $\left[\dfrac{\left(1 + \text{longer rate} \times \dfrac{\text{days}}{\text{year}}\right)}{\left(1 + \text{shorter rate} \times \dfrac{\text{days}}{\text{year}}\right)} - 1\right] \times \left(\dfrac{\text{year}}{\text{days difference}}\right)$

   If the above is based on middle rates, add $\frac{1}{16}\%$ to benchmark against LIBOR.

20. What are all the cashflows from the bond?

   Clean price = NPV using the yield.

   Clean price = dirty price because there is no accrued coupon.

**21.** For each one:

- Are coupons paid annually or semi-annually?
- What was the last coupon date?
- What is the day/year basis?

**22.** Either build up the price from the arbitrage mechanism:

- Buy the bond
- Borrow to finance the bond purchase
- At maturity of the futures contract, repay the financing plus interest and
- Deliver the bond in return for payment plus accrued

Or,

Theoretical futures price =

$$\frac{\left([\text{Bond price} + \text{Accrued coupon now}] \times \left[1 + i \times \dfrac{\text{days}}{\text{year}}\right]\right) - (\text{Accrued coupon at maturity of futures})}{\text{Conversion factor}}$$

**23. a.** Price of T-bill = ?
Cash raised = value of T-bills.

   **b.** Remaining maturity of T-bill is?
Price of T-bill = ?
Collateral required = cash loan plus one day's accrued interest.
Face value of T-bills now required = ?
Therefore dealer receives back how much face value, assuming minimum denomination of US$1000?

**24.** Value of T-bills = ?
Who takes the haircut from whom?
Cash amount = value adjusted for haircut.

**25.** What are the day/year count bases for the collateral, and for the repo rate?

**Flows on August 18, 1997:**
Accrued coupon = ?
Dirty price of the bond = ?
Value of collateral needed, including haircut = ?
Nominal amount of the bond required as collateral = ?
Amount of collateral, assuming minimum denomination of DEM 1000 = ?

**Flows on August 25, 1997:**
Repayment of loan principal and interest = ?

26. What are the day/year count bases for the collateral, and for the repo rate?
    Are the bond coupons annual or semi-annual?

    a.  Accrued coupon = ?
        Dirty price of OBL = ?
        With haircut of 2.5%, value of collateral required = ?
        Nominal amount of OBL required = ?
        Assuming minimum denomination of DEM 1000, nominal amount = ?

    b.  Accrued coupon = ?
        Dirty price of OBL = ?
        Current value of cash including accrued interest = ?
        With haircut of 2.5%, value of collateral required = ?
        Nominal amount of OBL now required = ?
        Assuming minimum denomination of DEM 1000, nominal amount = ?
        Margin transfer therefore = ?

    c.  Accrued coupon = ?
        Dirty price of new collateral = ?
        Current value of cash including accrued interest = ?
        With haircut of 2.5%, value of collateral required = ?
        Nominal amount of new OBL required = ?
        Assuming minimum denomination of DEM 1000, nominal amount = ?

27. Accrued coupon on Bund = ?
    Dirty price of Bund = ?
    Adjusted price of Bund allowing for haircut = ?
    Amount of cash loan in DEM = ?
    Converted at spot rate into US$ = ?

28. What are the day/year count bases for the collateral, and for the repo rate?
    Are the bond coupons annual or semi-annual?
    Accrued coupon = ?
    Dirty price = ?
    Dirty price adjusted for haircut = ?
    Cash consideration at start = ?
    Cash plus interest at maturity = ?
    Coupon received by buyer during the buy/sell-back = ?
    Reinvested, the value of this coupon at maturity = ?
    Therefore forward dirty value of bond = ?
    Therefore forward dirty price = ?
    Accrued coupon at maturity = ?
    Clean forward price = ?

29. Accrued interest due on closed-out original deal = ?
    Establish new repo for this same amount for remaining period.
    Accrued coupon = ?
    Dirty price = ?
    Dirty price adjusted for haircut = ?
    Nominal amount of collateral required for new repriced deal = ?
    Rounding up, new nominal = ?
    Nominal transferred = ?
    Cash amount due at maturity of the repriced deal = ?
    Value at maturity of coupon received by buyer and reinvested = ?
    Therefore cash repaid at maturity = ?
    Forward dirty price = ?
    Accrued coupon at maturity = ?
    Clean forward price = ?

30. What are the day/year count bases for the security lent, for the collateral, and for the lending fee? Are the bond coupons annual or semi-annual?

    Accrued coupon on security lent = ?
    Market dirty price = ?
    Value of security = ?
    Does the initial margin requirement increase or decrease the amount of collateral required?
    The value of the collateral taking into account this margin = ?
    What are the original maturity and remaining maturity of the CD?
    Therefore price of each DEM 1 of CD = ?
    Therefore face value of CD required as collateral = ?
    Lending fee is based on the market value of the security loaned.

34.
    a. Forward-forward rate $= \left[ \dfrac{\left(1+ \text{longer rate } \times \dfrac{\text{days}}{\text{year}}\right)}{\left(1+ \text{shorter rate } \times \dfrac{\text{days}}{\text{year}}\right)} -1\right] \times \left(\dfrac{\text{year}}{\text{days difference}}\right)$

    b. When he rolls the deal over after a month, what deal will he be doing? Does he want rates higher or lower?

    c. Is an FRA based on a borrowing or a deposit?
       Is a futures contract based on a borrowing or a deposit?

    d. *Compound* the two repos to give the total cash amount paid at the end. Compare with the total cash amount received from the reverse repo.

**35.** What are the day/year count bases for the bond, the T-bill, and the repo?

> Accrued coupon = ?
>
> Dirty price of bond = ?
>
> Cash consideration = ?
>
> Compare the cost of the repo with the yield on the T-bill.

**36.** Implied repo rate =

$$\left[\frac{(\text{Futures price} \times \text{Conversion factor}) + (\text{Accrued coupon at maturity of futures})}{(\text{Bond price} + \text{Accrued coupon now})} - 1\right] \times \frac{\text{year}}{\text{days}}$$

**37.** Assume the cash-and-carry arbitrage is:

- Buy the cash CTD bond now.
- Fund this purchase by repoing the bond.
- Sell the bond futures contract.
- Deliver the bond at maturity of the futures contract.

Accrued coupon for CTD bond = ?

Cost of buying CTD bond per DEM 100 nominal = ?

Total borrowing (principal + interest) to be repaid at the end = ?

Anticipated receipt from selling futures contract and delivering bond per DEM 100 nominal = ?

Profit per DEM 100 nominal = ?

Size of DEM bond futures contract = ?

Therefore profit per futures contract = ?

*Profit as a rate of return on the cash invested:*

Cost of buying DEM 100 nominal = ?

Profit from buying DEM 100 nominal = ?

Annualized return = ?

# ANSWERS TO EXERCISES

1. Future value $= £43 \times \left(1 + 0.075 \times \dfrac{120}{365}\right) = £44.06$

2. Present value $= \dfrac{£89}{\left(1 + 0.101 \times \frac{93}{365}\right)} = £86.77$

3. Yield $= \left(\dfrac{83.64}{83.00} - 1\right) \times \dfrac{365}{28} = 0.1005 = 10.05\%$

4. $36 \times (1 + 0.09)^{10} = 85.23$

5. $342 \times (1 + 0.06)^5 = 457.67$

    $457.67 - 342 = 115.67$

6. DEM $\dfrac{98}{(1 + 0.11)^5} = $ DEM 58.16

7. $5.2\% + (5.4\% - 5.2\%) \times \dfrac{(41 - 30)}{(60 - 30)} = 5.2733\%$

8. $£1,000,000 \times \left(1 + 0.11 \times \dfrac{181}{365}\right) = £1,054,547.95$

9. $\dfrac{£1,000,000 \times (1 + 0.11 \times \frac{181}{365})}{(1 + 1.10 \times \frac{134}{365})} = £1,017,204.02$

10. $\left[\dfrac{(1 + 0.10 \times \frac{134}{365})}{(1 + 0.095 \times \frac{71}{365})} - 1\right] \times \dfrac{365}{63} = 10.37\%$

11. Day/year count is ACT/365 basis – that is, $\dfrac{62}{365}$ in this case.

    Purchase price $= \dfrac{2,000,000}{(1 + 0.082 \times \frac{62}{365})} = £1,972,525.16$

12. $\dfrac{9.5\%}{(1 + 0.095 \times \frac{60}{365})} = 9.35\%$

    $1,000,000 \times 9.35\% \times \dfrac{60}{365} = 15,369.86$

    (The answer is 15,376.32 if you do this calculation without any rounding.)

13. $\dfrac{9.5\%}{(1 - 0.095 \times \frac{60}{365})} = \mathbf{9.65\%}$

$1,000,000 \times 9.5\% \times \dfrac{60}{365} = \mathbf{15,616.44}$

Amount paid $= 1,000,000 - 15,616.44 = \mathbf{984,383.56}$

14. $\left( \dfrac{1,000,000 - 975,000}{1,000,000} \right) \times \dfrac{365}{60} = \mathbf{15.21\%}$

15. **a.** Amount paid $= \$1,000,000 \times \left(1 - 0.065 \times \dfrac{91}{360}\right) = \mathbf{\$983,569.44}$

  **b.** Yield $= \dfrac{6.5\%}{(1 - 0.065 \times \frac{91}{360})} = \mathbf{6.6086\%}$

16. $\left[ \dfrac{(1 - 0.067 \times \frac{112}{360})}{(1 - 0.070 \times \frac{176}{360})} - 1 \right] \times \frac{365}{64} = \mathbf{7.90\%}$

17. *US*

  $US\$1,000,000 \times \left(1 - 0.05 \times \dfrac{91}{360}\right) = \mathbf{US\$987,361.11}$

  *UK*

  $£1,000,000 \times \left(1 - 0.05 \times \dfrac{91}{365}\right) = \mathbf{£987,534.25}$

  *Belgium*

  $\dfrac{BEF\ 1,000,000}{(1 + 0.05 \times \frac{91}{365})} = \mathbf{BEF\ 987,687.73}$

  *France*

  $\dfrac{FRF\ 1,000,000}{(1 + 0.05 \times \frac{91}{360})} = \mathbf{FRF\ 987,518.86}$

18. Convert all rates to true yield on a 365-day basis to compare:

  *30-day T-bill (£)* $8\frac{1}{4}\%$ discount rate

  Yield $= \dfrac{8.25\%}{\left[1 - \left(\dfrac{0.0825 \times 30}{365}\right)\right]} = \mathbf{8.3063\%}$

  *30-day UK CP (£)* **8.1875%** yield

*30-day ECP (£)* **8.125%** yield

*30-day US T-bill* 8.3125% discount rate

$$\text{Yield} = \frac{8.3125\%}{\left[1-\left(\frac{0.083125 \times 30}{360}\right)\right]} = 8.3705\% \text{ on 360-day basis}$$

$$= 8.3705\% \times \frac{365}{360} = \textbf{8.4867\%} \text{ on 365-day basis}$$

*30-day interbank deposit (£)* **8.25%** yield

*30-day USCP* 8.5% discount rate on 360-day basis

$$\text{Yield} = \frac{8.5\%}{\left[1-\left(\frac{0.085 \times 30}{360}\right)\right]} = 8.5606\% \text{ on 360-day basis}$$

$$= 8.5606\% \times \frac{365}{360} = \textbf{8.6795\%} \text{ on 365-day basis}$$

*30-day US$ CD* 8.625% yield on ACT/360 basis

$$= 8.625\% \times \frac{365}{360} = \textbf{8.7448\%} \text{ on 365-day basis}$$

*30-day French T-bill* 8.5% yield on ACT/360 basis

$$= 8.5\% \times \frac{365}{360} = \textbf{8.6181\%} \text{ on 365-day basis}$$

**Therefore in descending order:**

| | |
|---|---|
| US$ CD | 8.7448% |
| USCP | 8.6795% |
| French T-bill | 8.6181% |
| US T-bill | 8.4867% |
| UK T-bill (£) | 8.3063% |
| Interbank deposit (£) | 8.25% |
| UK CP | 8.1875% |
| ECP (£) | 8.125% |

**19.** $\left( \dfrac{1 + 0.1006 \times \frac{273}{360}}{1 + 0.09935 \times \frac{91}{360}} - 1 \right) \times \dfrac{360}{(273 - 91)} = 9.87\%$

$9.87\% + \dfrac{1}{16}\% = \textbf{9.93\% middle FRA}$

**20.** Cashflows remaining are FRF 8 million after 1 year, FRF 8 million after 2 years and FRF 108 million after 3 years. Discount to NPV at 7.0%:

Clean price = FRF $\dfrac{8,000,000}{(1 + 0.07)} + \dfrac{8,000,000}{(1 + 0.07)^2} + \dfrac{108,000,000}{(1 + 0.07)^3}$

$= \textbf{FRF 102,624,316.04}$

**21. a.** Last coupon June 7, 1997

    ACT/365 basis: $\dfrac{51}{365} \times 7.5 = \textbf{1.047945}$

**b.** Last coupon February 15, 1997
Next coupon August 15, 1997 (181-day coupon period)

    ACT/ACT basis: $\dfrac{163}{362} \times 5.625 = \textbf{2.532804}$

**c.** Last coupon October 26, 1996

    30/360 basis: $\dfrac{272}{360} \times 6.25 = \textbf{4.722222}$

**d.** Last coupon October 25, 1996

    ACT/ACT basis: $\dfrac{276}{365} \times 7.25 = \textbf{5.482192}$

**e.** Last coupon March 20, 1997

    ACT/365 basis: $\dfrac{130}{365} \times 3.00 = \textbf{1.068493}$

**f.** Last coupon November 15, 1996

    30/360 basis: $\dfrac{253}{360} \times 7.00 = \textbf{4.919444}$

**g.** Last coupon October 28, 1996

    ACT/ACT basis: $\dfrac{273}{365} \times 8.80 = \textbf{6.581918}$

**h.** Last coupon February 1, 1997

30/360 basis plus 1 extra day: $\frac{178}{360} \times 9.50 =$ **4.697222**

**22.** Payment for the bond purchased by the futures seller to hedge himself or herself is made on April 25. Coupon on the purchase of the bond is accrued for 112 days. Therefore:

Accrued coupon now = $7.375 \times 112/360 = 2.294444$

Delivery of the bond to the futures buyer would require payment to the futures seller on September 10. The futures seller must therefore fund his or her position from April 25 to September 10 (138 actual days) and coupon on the bond on September 10 will be accrued for 247 days. Therefore:

Accrued coupon then = $7.375 \times \frac{247}{360} = 5.060069$

Theoretical futures price =

$$\frac{\left([\text{Bond price} + \text{Accrued coupon now}] \times \left[1 + i \times \frac{\text{days}}{\text{year}}\right]\right) - (\text{Accrued coupon at maturity of futures})}{\text{Conversion factor}}$$

$$= \frac{(106.13 + 2.294444) \times (1 + 0.0335 \times \frac{138}{360}) - 5.060069}{1.1247} = \textbf{93.14}$$

**23. a.** Remaining maturity of T-bill is 82 days

Price of T-bill is $\left(1 - 0.062 \times \frac{82}{360}\right) = 0.985877778$

Therefore cash raised = value of T-bills = **US\$9,858,777.78**

**b.** Remaining maturity of T-bill is 81 days

Price of T-bill is $\left(1 - 0.060 \times \frac{81}{360}\right) = 0.986500000$

Collateral required = cash loan plus one day's accrued interest

$= 9,858,777.78 \times (1 + 0.064 \times \frac{1}{360}) = \text{US\$9,860,530.45}$

Face value required $= \frac{\text{US\$9,860,530.45}}{0.9865} = \text{US\$9,995,469.29}$

Therefore dealer receives back US\$10,000,000 − US\$9,995,469.29 = US\$4,530.71 face value

Assuming minimum multiples of US$1000, the dealer would receive back **US$4,000 face value**

24. Value of T-bills is $\dfrac{BEF\ 1,000,000,000.00}{(1+0.048 \times \frac{91}{365})}$ = BEF 988,174,395.18

In this case, the 2% haircut is demanded by the *seller* not the buyer as is usual, so the seller receives:

BEF 998,174,395.18 × 1.02 = **BEF 1,007,937,883.08**

25. **Flows on August 18, 1997:**

Accrued coupon (30/360 basis) is $7.5 \times \dfrac{63}{360}$ = 1.312500

The dirty price of the bond is (clean price + accrued coupon)

= 105.80 + 1.312500 = 107.1125

The amount to be secured is the loan plus haircut = DEM 102 million.

Therefore the nominal amount of the bond required as collateral =

DEM $\dfrac{102,000,000.00}{107.1125/100}$ = DEM 95,226,980.98

As the minimum nominal denomination available for the bond is DEM 1000, the amount of collateral which must be placed is DEM 95,227,000.

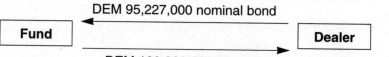

DEM 95,227,000 nominal bond

Fund ← → Dealer

DEM 100,000,000.00 cash

**Flows on August 25, 1997:**
Repayment of loan principal and interest (ACT/360 basis) is:

DEM $100,000,000.00 \times \left(1+0.0325 \times \dfrac{7}{360}\right)$

= DEM 100,063,194.44

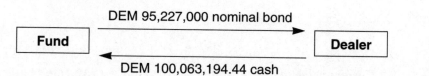

DEM 95,227,000 nominal bond

Fund → Dealer

DEM 100,063,194.44 cash

**26. a.** Last coupon date (annual) was March 26, 1997.
Accrued coupon (30/360 basis) is:

$$5.9 \times \frac{226}{360} = 3.703889$$

Dirty price of OBL = 101.49 + 3.703889 = 105.193889

Dealer wishes to borrow DEM 50 million.
With haircut of 2.5%, collateral must therefore be worth:
DEM 50,000,000.00 × 1.025 = DEM 51,250,000.00

Therefore nominal amount of OBL =

$$\frac{\text{DEM } 51,250,000.00}{105.193889/100} = \text{DEM } 48,719,560.13$$

Dealer transfers **DEM 48,720,000 nominal collateral**

**b.** Accrued coupon is:

$$5.9 \times \frac{240}{360} = 3.933333$$

Dirty price of OBL is 102.59 + 3.933333 = 106.523333

Current value of cash including accrued interest (ACT/360 basis) is:

$$\text{DEM } 50,000,000.00 \times \left(1 + 0.0376 \times \frac{14}{360}\right) = \text{DEM } 50,073,111.11$$

With haircut of 2.5%, collateral must now be worth:
DEM 50,073,111.11 × 1.025 = DEM 51,324,938.89

Therefore nominal amount of OBL required now is:

$$\frac{\text{DEM } 51,324,938.89}{106.523333/100} = \text{DEM } 48,181,874.75$$

Rounding up, this needs to be DEM 48,182,000 nominal. Buyer
already has DEM 48,720,000 nominal. Therefore buyer returns the
difference to the seller: **nominal DEM 538,000.**

**c.** Last coupon date (annual) was April 14, 1997.

Accrued coupon (30/360 basis) is:

$$6.1 \times \frac{229}{360} = 3.880278$$

Dirty price of new collateral = 102.44 + 3.880278 = 106.320278

Current value of cash including accrued interest (ACT/360 basis) is:

$$\text{DEM } 50,000,000 \times (1 + 0.0376 \times \frac{21}{360}) = \text{DEM } 50,109,666.67$$

With haircut of 2.5%, collateral must be worth:

$$\text{DEM } 50,109,666.67 \times 1.025 = \text{DEM } 51,362,408.33$$

Therefore nominal amount of new collateral required is:

$$\frac{\text{DEM } 51,362,408.33}{106.320278/100} = \text{DEM } 48,309,136.60$$

Rounding up, the dealer will transfer **DEM 48,310,000** of the new collateral to replace the original.

**27.** Accrued coupon on Bunds $\quad = 5.0 \times \dfrac{104}{360} = 1.444444$

Dirty price of Bund $\quad = 98.00 + 1.444444 = 99.444444$

Adjusted price allowing for haircut $\quad = \dfrac{99.444444}{1.05}$

$\quad = 94.708994$

Cash loan $\quad = \text{DEM } 20 \text{ million} \times 94.708994/100$

$\quad = \text{DEM } 18,941,798.80$

Converted at 1.4735: $\quad$ **US\$12,854,970.34**

**28.** Accrued coupon (ACT/ACT basis) at start $= 8.0 \times \dfrac{316}{365} = 6.926027$

Market dirty price at start $\quad = 103.42 + \text{accrued coupon}$

$\quad = 110.346027$

Dirty price adjusted for haircut $\quad = \dfrac{110.346027}{1.025} = 107.654661$

Cash consideration at start $\quad = \text{FRF } 200 \text{ million} \times \text{dirty price}/100$

$\quad = \text{FRF } 215,309,321.75$

Cash principal plus interest at maturity $=$

$$\text{FRF } 215,309,321.75 \times (1 + 0.0552 \times \tfrac{91}{360}) = \text{FRF } 218,313,604.49$$

The coupon received by the buyer during the buy/sell-back is FRF 16,000,000 on June 2, 1997.

Reinvest this coupon at 5.52% to give total proceeds on July 14, 1997 of:

FRF 16,000,000 × (1 + 0.0552 × $\frac{42}{360}$) = FRF16,103,040.00

Therefore forward dirty value of bond is (total final amount – reinvested coupon received)

= FRF 218,313,604.49 – 16,103,040.00 = FRF 202,210,564.49

Therefore forward dirty price = $\frac{202,210,564.49}{200,000,000}$ × 100 = 101.105282245

Accrued coupon at maturity = 8.0 × $\frac{42}{365}$ = 0.920547945

Clean forward price = dirty price – accrued coupon = **100.184734300**

Note that the early stages of this calculation do not require a specific level of accuracy in prices; if the prices are less accurate, the result will be only that the cash loan amount will be slightly different. The final calculations of the accrued coupon and clean forward price however must be carried out to enough decimal places to ensure that the total cash repaid at the end is exactly the correct amount due to repay the cash loan plus interest.

29. Accrued interest (ACT/360 basis) due on May 14 for the closed-out original deal is:

FRF 215,309,321.75 × 0.0552 × $\frac{30}{360}$ = FRF 990,422.88

New repo is established for the original amount of FRF 215,309,321.75, also at 5.52% for remaining period May 14 to July 14.

Accrued coupon (ACT/ACT basis) on May 14 = 8.0 × $\frac{346}{365}$ = 7.583562

Therefore market dirty price on May 14 = 106.28 + 7.583562 = 113.863562

Dirty price adjusted for haircut = $\frac{113.863562}{1.025}$ = 111.086402

Therefore nominal amount of collateral required for new repriced deal is:

$\frac{FRF\ 215,309,321.75}{111.086402/100}$ = FRF 193,821,491.99

Rounding up, the collateral will be FRF 193,822,000 nominal.

Therefore a net FRF 200,000,000 (original collateral) – FRF 193,822,000 = FRF 6,178,000 nominal will be transferred from buyer to seller.

Cash amount due at maturity of the repriced deal is:

$$\text{FRF } 215{,}309{,}321.75 \times \left(1 + 0.0552 \times \frac{61}{360}\right) = \text{FRF } 217{,}323{,}181.60$$

But, coupon received by buyer on June 2, 1997 and reinvested at 5.52% is worth at maturity:

$$\text{FRF } 193{,}822{,}000 \times 0.08 \times \left(1 + 0.0552 \times \frac{42}{360}\right) = \text{FRF } 15{,}605{,}617.09$$

Therefore cash repaid at maturity = FRF 217,323,181.60 – FRF 15,605,617.09

= FRF 201,717,564.51

Therefore forward dirty price $= \dfrac{\text{cash repaid}}{\text{new nominal}} \times 100 = \dfrac{201{,}717{,}564{,}51}{193{,}822{,}000} \times 100$

= 104.073616261

Accrued coupon at maturity $= 8.0 \times \dfrac{42}{365} = 0.920547945$

Clean forward price = dirty price – accrued coupon = **103.153068316**

Note that early payment of the accrued interest amount FRF 990,422.88 (which must itself be funded by the seller) alters the economics of the deal slightly. To avoid this, payment of this amount could be deferred until 14 July. In this case, the buyer should require collateral to cover this amount also. This would increase the nominal collateral amount required to FRF 194,713,070.85 – rounded up to FRF 194,714,000 – and increase the cash repaid at maturity to FRF 202,636,167.83. The forward clean price would then be 103.148069530.

**30.** Accrued coupon on security lent (30/360 basis) $= \dfrac{312}{360} \times 6.0 = 5.2$

Market dirty price = 105.23 + 5.2 = 110.43

Value of security = DEM 50,000,000 × 110.43/100 = DEM 55,215,000.00

Because the initial margin of 3% is required by the *lender*, the value of the collateral must be 3% *greater* than this:

DEM 55,215,000.00 × 1.03 = DEM 56,871,450.00

Original maturity of CD is 184 days; remaining maturity is 149 days

Therefore price of each DEM 1 of CD is:

$$\frac{1 + 0.04 \times \frac{184}{360}}{1 + 0.0585 \times \frac{149}{360}} = 0.99632102$$

Therefore face value of CD required as collateral is:

$$\frac{DEM\ 56,871,450.00}{0.99632102} = \textbf{DEM 57,081,451.44} \text{ (rounded up as appropriate)}$$

Period of loan (ACT/360 basis) is 91 days. Therefore lending fee is:

$$DEM\ 55,215,000.00 \times 0.0045 \times \frac{91}{360} = \textbf{DEM 62,807.06}$$

34. a. $\left[\dfrac{(1 + 0.043 \times \frac{92}{360})}{(1 + 0.041 \times \frac{31}{360})} - 1\right] \times \dfrac{360}{61} = \textbf{4.3862\%}$

   b. He will need to roll over the repo after one month, so he is expecting that, after one month, two-month rates will be lower than 4.3862%

   c. **Sell an FRA 1 v. 3 or buy futures.**

   d. If he rolls over the repo at 4.3%, the all-in cash amount he repays at the end of 3 months will be:

   $DEM\ 10$ million $\times (1 + 0.041 \times \frac{31}{360}) \times (1 + 0.043 \times \frac{61}{360})$

   $= \ DEM\ 10,108,423.91$

   The all-in amount he receives back on the reverse repo at the end of 3 months will be:

   $DEM\ 10$ million $\times (1 + 0.043 \times \frac{92}{360}) = DEM\ 10,109,888.89$

   Profit = DEM $(10,109,888.89 - 10,108,423.91) = $ **DEM 1,464.98**

35. Accrued coupon $\quad = 9.0 \times \dfrac{45}{360} = 1.125$

   Dirty price of bond $\ = 111.665$

   Cash consideration $\ = $ BEF 500 million $\times$ dirty price/100

   $\qquad\qquad\qquad\quad = $ BEF 558,325,000.00

   Profit = BEF 558,325,000.00 $\times (0.041 - 0.0215) \times \dfrac{30}{365}$

   $\qquad\quad = $ **BEF 894,849.66**

**36.** Implied repo rate =

$$\left[ \frac{(\text{Futures price} \times \text{Conversion factor}) + (\text{Accrued coupon at maturity of futures})}{(\text{Bond price} + \text{Accrued coupon now})} - 1 \right] \times \frac{\text{year}}{\text{days}}$$

$$= \left[ \frac{(93.10 \times 1.1247) + 5.060069}{(106.13 + 2.294444)} - 1 \right] \times \frac{360}{138} = 3.24\%$$

**37.** Assume to start with that the implied repo rate is higher than the actual current repo rate. The cash-and-carry arbitrage is then:

- Buy the cash CTD bond now
- Fund this purchase by repoing the bond
- Sell the bond futures contract
- Deliver the bond at maturity of the futures contract

Cost of buying CTD bond per DEM 100 nominal is (clean price + accrued coupon) = DEM (102.71 + 3.599) = DEM 106.309

Total borrowing (principal + interest) to be repaid at the end

$$= \text{DEM } 106.309 \times \left( 1 + 0.068 \times \frac{24}{360} \right) = \text{DEM } 106.790934$$

Anticipated receipt from selling futures contract and delivering bond per DEM 100 nominal = (futures price × conversion factor) + accrued coupon

$$= \text{DEM } (85.31 \times 1.203046) + 4.191 = \text{DEM } 106.822854$$

Profit = DEM (106.822854 − 106.790934) = 0.031920 per DEM 100 nominal

Size of DEM bond futures contract is DEM 250,000 nominal.

Therefore profit per futures contract = $\text{DEM } 0.031920 \times \dfrac{250,000}{100} = \text{DEM } 79.80$

To calculate profit as a rate of return on the cash invested:

Cost of buying DEM 100 nominal is DEM 106.309

Profit from buying DEM 100 nominal is DEM 0.031920 over 24 days

Therefore arbitrage is worth $\dfrac{0.031920}{106.309} \times \dfrac{360}{24}$

= **0.45% per annum or 45 basis points**

# ANSWERS TO PRACTICE EXAM

## Multiple choice answers

| | | | | | | | | | |
|---|---|---|---|---|---|---|---|---|---|
| 1. | b | 11. | b | 21. | d | 31. | c | 41. | b |
| 2. | d | 12. | c | 22. | c | 32. | c | 42. | a |
| 3. | d | 13. | a | 23. | a | 33. | b | 43. | d |
| 4. | a | 14. | d | 24. | b | 34. | a | 44. | c |
| 5. | a | 15. | d | 25. | c | 35. | b | 45. | b |
| 6. | a | 16. | c | 26. | a | 36. | c | 46. | d |
| 7. | c | 17. | c | 27. | c | 37. | c | 47. | a |
| 8. | d | 18. | a | 28. | b | 38. | d | 48. | d |
| 9. | b | 19. | a | 29. | c | 39. | b | 49. | c |
| 10. | c | 20. | d | 30. | d | 40. | b | 50. | d |

## Calculation answers

1. (a) Market value of bills $= \dfrac{\text{FRF } 100,000,000}{(1 + 0.0678 \times \frac{182}{360})} = $ **FRF 96,685,928.65**

   This is the amount the dealer can borrow.

   (b) At maturity, the dealer repays this cash plus interest at 5.18% for 30 days (ACT/360 basis):

   $$\text{FRF } 96,685,928.65 \times \left(1 + 0.0518 \times \frac{30}{360}\right) = \textbf{FRF } \textbf{97,103,289.58}$$

   (c) After 14 days, value of cash including accrued interest is:

   $$\text{FRF } 96,685,928.65 \times \left(1 + 0.0518 \times \frac{14}{360}\right) = \text{FRF } 96,880,697.08$$

   Collateral must therefore be worth this amount at the new T-bill yield. Therefore:

   $$\frac{\text{new face value of collateral}}{(1 + 0.075 \times \frac{168}{360})} = \text{FRF } 96,880,697.08$$

   Therefore face value of collateral

   $$= \text{FRF } 96,880,697.08 \times \left(1 + 0.075 \times \frac{168}{360}\right) = \text{FRF } 100,271,521.48$$

Buyer (borrower of T-bills) can therefore call for extra T-bills with face value of at least **FRF 271,521.48** or the cash equivalent, which would be the current market value of the extra collateral:

$$\frac{FRF\ 271,521.48}{(1 + 0.075 \times \frac{168}{360})} = \textbf{FRF 262,339.59 cash}$$

2. *June 5*

Accrued coupon (ACT/365 basis) at beginning of deal on June 5 is:

$$\frac{54}{365} \times 6.00 = 0.887671$$

Therefore market dirty price of collateral originally is 95.887671.

Therefore allowing for 2.5% haircut, the adjusted all-in price is $\dfrac{95.887671}{1.025}$

$= 93.55$

Therefore cash lent is £10,000,000 × 93.55/100 = £9,355,000.00

*June 6*

Accrued coupon on June 6 is $\dfrac{55}{365} \times 6.00$

$= 0.904110$

Therefore market dirty price of collateral on June 6 is 98.00 + 0.904110

$= 98.904110$

Therefore allowing for 2.5% haircut, the adjusted all-in price is $\dfrac{98.904110}{1.025}$

$= 96.49$

Accrued interest on cash lent on June 6 is

$$\frac{1}{365} \times 5.28125\% \times £9,355,000.00 = £\ 1,353.59$$

Therefore total value of cash loan $= £9,355,000.00 + £1,353.59$

$= £9,356,353.59$

Therefore nominal collateral now required $= \dfrac{9,356,353.59}{96.49/100}$

$= £9,696,708.04$

Therefore decrease in collateral required is:

£10,000,000.00 – £9,696,708.04 = **£303,291.96**

**The buyer (borrower) transfers securities to the seller (lender).**

3. (a) Last coupon on gilt (semi-annual) was January 14, 1997.

Accrued coupon (ACT/365 basis) is $7.75 \times \dfrac{127}{365} = 2.696575$

Dirty price of gilt is: $101.95 + 2.696575 = 104.646575$

Cash amount is US$20,000,000.00

Add haircut of 5%: US$20,000,000.00 × 1.05 = US$21,000,000.00

Convert to sterling at spot rate $= £\dfrac{21,000,000.00}{1.5145} = £13,865,962.36$

Collateral must therefore be worth this amount. Therefore nominal amount of gilt must be:

$$\frac{£13,865,962.36}{104.646575/100} = \textbf{£13,250,278.24}$$

(b) Last coupon on US Treasury (semi-annual) was February 13, 1997. Next coupon on US Treasury is August 13, 1997.

Coupon period is 181 days.

Accrued coupon (ACT/ACT basis) is $6.75 \times \dfrac{118}{362} = 2.200276$

Dirty price of Treasury is: $98.42 + 2.200276 = 100.620276$

Cash amount plus accrued interest (ACT/360 basis) is:

$$US\$20,000,000.00 \times \left(1 + 0.0572 \times \frac{21}{360}\right) = US\$20,066,733.33$$

Add haircut of 2%: US$20,066,733.33 × 1.02 = US$20,468,068.00

New collateral must therefore be worth this amount. Therefore nominal amount of US Treasury must be:

$$\frac{US\$20,468,068.00}{100.620276} = US\$20,341,892.13$$

Seller must therefore replace original UK gilt collateral by at least **US$20,342,000** of new US Treasury collateral.

4. Start price: 104.63 plus accrued coupon (ACT/ACT basis) at $8.25 \times \dfrac{330}{365}$

$= 112.08890411$ dirty price

Adjusted for 2% haircut, start cash amount

$$= \frac{\text{FRF } 150,000,000 \times 112.08890411/100}{1.02} = \text{FRF } 164,836,623.69$$

The repo rate is 5.82% based on ACT/360 for 89 days.

Therefore the total final amount is:

$$\text{FRF } 164,836,623.69 \times \left(1 + 0.0582 \times \frac{89}{360}\right) \text{FRF } 167,208,347.98$$

The coupon received by the buyer during the repo is 8.25% on March 20, 1997.

Reinvest this coupon at 5.82% (ACT/360 basis) for total proceeds on May 13, 1997 of:

$$\text{FRF } 150,000,000 \times 0.0825 \times \left(1 + 0.0582 \times \frac{54}{360}\right) = \text{FRF } 12,483,033.75$$

Therefore the cash amount at maturity is (total final amount − reinvested coupon already received):

FRF 167,208,347.98 − FRF 12,483,033.75 = FRF 154,725,314.23

Accrued coupon amount on May 13, 1997 (ACT/ACT basis) is:

$$\text{FRF } 150,000,000 \times 0.0825 \times \frac{54}{365} = \text{FRF } 1,830,821.92$$

Therefore clean amount to be paid for is:

FRF 154,725,314.23 − FRF 1,830,821.92 = FRF 152,894,492.31

Therefore clean price

$$= \frac{\text{clean cash amount}}{\text{nominal amount}} \times 100 = \frac{\text{FRF } 152,894,492.31}{\text{FRF } 150,000,000} \times 100$$

= 101.92966154

Note that the early stages of this calculation do not require that prices are quoted to eight decimal places as shown; if the prices are less accurate, the result will be only that the cash loan amount will be slightly different. The final calculation of the clean forward price however must be carried out to enough decimal places to ensure that the total cash repaid at the end is exactly the correct amount due to repay the cash loan plus interest.

# APPENDIX 1
# PSA/ISMA Documentation

# THE PSA/ISMA AGREEMENT

Public Securities Association
40 Broad Street, New York, NY 10004-2373

INTERNATIONAL SECURITIES MARKET ASSOCIATION

Rigistrasse 60, PO Box, CH-8033 Zürich

**VERSION 1**

**GROSS PAYING SECURITIES**

**GLOBAL MASTER REPURCHASE AGREEMENT**

**This agreement is to be used for repos or reverse repos and buy/sell backs of securities other than equities, US Treasury instruments and Net Paying Securities**

Dated as of _____

**Between:**

_____ ("Party A")

**and**

_____ ("Party B")

## 1. Applicability

**(a)** From time to time the parties hereto may enter into transactions in which one party, acting through a Designated Office, ("*Seller*") agrees to sell to the other, acting through a Designated Office, ("*Buyer*") securities and financial instruments ("*Securities*") (other than equities, US Treasury instruments and Net Paying Securities) against the payment of the purchase price by Buyer to Seller, with a simultaneous agreement by Buyer to sell to Seller Securities equivalent to such Securities at a date certain or on demand against the payment of the purchase price by Seller to Buyer.

**(b)** Each such transaction (which may be a repurchase transaction ("*Repurchase Transaction*") or a buy and sell back transaction ("*Buy/Sell Back Transaction*")) shall be referred to herein as a "*Transaction*" and shall be governed by this Agreement, including any supplemental terms or conditions contained in Annex I hereto, unless otherwise agreed in writing. If this Agreement may be applied to Buy/Sell Back Transactions, this shall be specified in Annex I, and the provisions of Annex III shall apply to such Buy/Sell Back Transactions. If Transactions are to be effected under this Agreement by either party as an

November 1995

agent, this shall be specified in Annex I, and the provisions of Annex IV shall apply to such Agency Transactions.

## 2. Definitions

**(a)** *"Act of Insolvency"* shall occur with respect to any party hereto upon:

**(i)** its making a general assignment for the benefit of, or entering into a reorganisation, arrangement, or composition with creditors; or

**(ii)** its admitting in writing that it is unable to pay its debts as they become due; or

**(iii)** its seeking, consenting to or acquiescing in the appointment of any trustee, administrator, receiver or liquidator or analogous officer of it or any material part of its property; or

**(iv)** the presentation or filing of a petition in respect of it (other than by the counterparty to this Agreement in respect of any obligation under this Agreement) in any court or before any agency alleging or for the bankruptcy, winding-up or insolvency of such party (or any analogous proceeding) or seeking any reorganisation, arrangement, composition, re-adjustment, administration, liquidation, dissolution or similar relief under any present or future statute, law or regulation, such petition (except in the case of a petition for winding-up or any analogous proceeding, in respect of which no such 30 day period shall apply) not having been stayed or dismissed within 30 days of its filing; or

**(v)** the appointment of a receiver, administrator, liquidator or trustee or analogous officer of such party or over all or any material part of such party's property; or

**(vi)** the convening of any meeting of its creditors for the purposes of considering a voluntary arrangement as referred to in section 3 of the Insolvency Act 1986 (or any analogous proceeding);

**(b)** *"Agency Transaction"*, the meaning specified in paragraph 1 of Annex IV hereto;

**(c)** *"Base Currency"*, the currency indicated in Annex I hereto;

**(d)** *"Business Day"*:

**(i)** in relation to the settlement of any Transaction which is to be settled through Cedel or Euroclear, a day on which Cedel or, as the case may be, Euroclear is open to settle business in the currency in which the Purchase Price and the Repurchase Price are denominated;

**(ii)** in relation to the settlement of any Transaction which is to be settled through a settlement system other than Cedel or Euroclear, a day on which that settlement system is open to settle such Transaction;

**(iii)** in relation to any delivery of Securities not falling within (i) or (ii) above, a day on which banks are open for business in the place where delivery of the relevant Securities is to be effected; and

**(iv)** in relation to any obligation to make a payment not falling within (i) or (ii) above, a day other than a Saturday or a Sunday on which banks are open for business in the principal financial centre of the country of which the currency in which the payment is denominated is the official currency and, if different, in the place where any account designated by the parties for the making or receipt of the payment is situated (or, in the case of ECU, a day on which ECU clearing operates);

**(e)** "*Cash Margin*", a cash sum paid to Buyer or Seller in accordance with paragraph 4;

**(f)** "*Cedel*", Cedel Bank, société anonyme;

**(g)** "*Confirmation*", the meaning specified in paragraph 3(b);

**(h)** "*Contractual Currency*", the meaning specified in paragraph 7(a);

**(i)** "*Defaulting Party*", the meaning specified in paragraph 10;

**(j)** "*Default Market Value*" with respect to any Securities on any date:

  **(i)** in the case of Securities to be delivered to the Defaulting Party,

  **(aa)** if the non-Defaulting Party has between the occurrence of the relevant Event of Default and the Default Valuation Time (as defined below) sold Securities forming part of the same issue and being of an identical type and description to those Securities and in substantially the same amount as those Securities, the net proceeds of sale (after deducting all reasonable costs, fees and expenses incurred in connection therewith) and

  **(bb)** failing such sale before the Default Valuation Time, the Market Value of such Securities at the Default Valuation Time;

  **(ii)** in the case of Securities to be delivered by the Defaulting Party,

  **(aa)** if the non-Defaulting Party has between the occurrence of the relevant Event of Default and the Default Valuation Time purchased Securities forming part of the same issue and being of an identical type and description to those Securities and in substantially the same amount as those Securities, the cost of such purchase (including all reasonable costs, fees and expenses incurred in connection therewith) and

  **(bb)** failing such purchase before the Default Valuation Time, the amount it would cost to buy such Securities at the Default Valuation Time at the best available offer price therefor (and where different offer prices are available for different delivery dates, such offer price in respect of the earliest available such delivery date) on the most appropriate market, together with all reasonable costs, fees and expenses that would be incurred in connection therewith (calculated on the assumption that the aggregate thereof is the least that could reasonably be expected to be paid in order to carry out the Transaction),

in each case as determined by the non-Defaulting Party; and for this purpose the "*Default Valuation Time*" means, with respect to any Securities

  **(A)** if the relevant Event of Default occurs during normal business hours on a day which is a dealing day in the most appropriate market for Securities of the relevant description (as determined by the non-Defaulting Party), the close of business in that market on the following dealing day;

  **(B)** in any other case, the close of business on the second dealing day in that market after the day on which the relevant Event of Default occurs;

Where the amount of any Securities sold or purchased as mentioned in (i)(aa) or (ii)(aa) above is not identical to that of the Securities to be valued for the purposes of this definition, the Default Market Value of those Securities shall be ascertained by dividing the net proceeds of sale or cost of purchase by the amount of the Securities sold or purchased so as to obtain a net unit price and multiplying that net unit price by the amount of the Securities to be valued;

**(k)** *"Default Notice"*, a written notice served by the non-Defaulting Party on the Defaulting Party under paragraph 10 stating that an event shall be treated as an Event of Default for the purposes of this Agreement;

**(l)** *"Designated Office"*, with respect to a party, a branch or office of that party which is specified as such in Annex I hereto or such other branch or office as may be agreed to by the Parties;

**(m)** *"Distributions"*, the meaning specified in sub-paragraph(s) below;

**(n)** *"Equivalent Margin Securities"*, Securities equivalent to Securities previously transferred as Margin Securities;

**(o)** *"Equivalent Securities"*, with respect to a Transaction, Securities equivalent to Purchased Securities under that Transaction. If and to the extent that such Purchased Securities have been redeemed the expression shall mean a sum of money equivalent to the proceeds of the redemption;

**(p)** Securities are *"equivalent to"* other Securities for the purposes of this Agreement if they are: (i) of the same issuer; (ii) part of the same issue; and (iii) of an identical type, nominal value, description and (except where otherwise stated) amount as those other Securities;

**(q)** *"Euroclear"*, Morgan Guaranty Trust Company of New York, Brussels office, as operator of the Euroclear System;

**(r)** *"Event of Default"*, the meaning specified in paragraph 10 hereof;

**(s)** *"Income"*, with respect to any Security at any time, all interest, dividends or other distributions thereon (*"Distributions"*);

**(t)** *"Income Payment Date"*, with respect to any Securities, the date on which Income is paid in respect of such Securities, or, in the case of registered Securities, the date by reference to which particular registered holders are identified as being entitled to payment of Income;

**(u)** *"LIBOR"*, in relation to any sum in any currency, the one-month London Inter Bank Offered Rate in respect of that currency as quoted on Page 3750 on the Telerate Service (or such other page as may replace Page 3750 on that service) as of 11:00 am, London time, on the date on which it is to be determined;

**(v)** *"Margin Ratio"*, with respect to a Transaction, the Market Value of the Purchased Securities at the time when the Transaction was entered into divided by the Purchase Price (and so that, where a Transaction relates to Securities of different descriptions and the Purchase Price is apportioned by the parties among Purchased Securities of each such description, a separate Margin Ratio shall apply in respect of Securities of each such description), or such other proportion as the parties may agree with respect to that Transaction;

**(w)** *"Margin Securities"*, in relation to a Margin Transfer, Securities reasonably acceptable to the party calling for such Margin Transfer;

**(x)** *"Margin Transfer"*, any, or any combination, of the payment or repayment of Cash Margin and the transfer of Margin Securities or Equivalent Margin Securities;

**(y)** *"Market Value"*, with respect to any Securities as of any time on any date, the price for such Securities at such time on such date obtained from a generally recognised source agreed to by the parties (and where different prices are obtained for different delivery dates, the price so obtainable for the earliest available such delivery date) (provided that the price of Securities that are suspended shall (for the purposes of paragraph 4) be nil unless the parties otherwise agree and (for all other purposes) shall be the price of those Securities as of close of business on the dealing day in the relevant market last preceding the date of suspension) plus the aggregate amount of Income which, as of such date, has accrued but not yet been paid in respect of the Securities to the extent not included in such price as of such date, and for these purposes any sum in a currency other than the Contractual Currency for the Transaction in question shall be converted into such Contractual Currency at the Spot Rate prevailing at the relevant time;

**(z)** "*Net Exposure*", the meaning specified in paragraph 4(c);

**(aa)** the "*Net Margin*" provided to a party at any time, the excess (if any) at that time of (i) the sum of the amount of Cash Margin paid to that party (including accrued interest on such Cash Margin which has not been paid to the other party) and the Market Value of Margin Securities transferred to that party under paragraph 4(a) (excluding any Cash Margin which has been repaid to the other party and any Margin Securities in respect of which Equivalent Margin Securities have been transferred to the other party) over (ii) the sum of the amount of Cash Margin paid to the other party (including accrued interest on such Cash Margin which has not been paid by the other party) and the Market Value of Margin Securities transferred to the other party under paragraph 4(a) (excluding any Cash Margin which has been repaid by the other party and any Margin Securities in respect of which Equivalent Margin Securities have been transferred by the other party) and for this purpose any amounts not denominated in the Base Currency shall be converted into the Base Currency at the Spot Rate prevailing at the relevant time;

**(bb)** "*Net Paying Securities*", Securities which are of a kind such that, were they to be the subject of a Transaction to which paragraph 5 applies, any payment made by Buyer under paragraph 5 would be one in respect of which either Buyer would or might be required to make a withholding or deduction for or on account of taxes or duties or Seller would or might be required to make or account for a payment for or on account of taxes or duties (in each case other than tax on overall net income) by reference to such payment;

**(cc)** "*New Purchased Securities*", the meaning specified in paragraph 8(a) of this Agreement;

**(dd)** "*Price Differential*", with respect to any Transaction as of any date, the aggregate amount obtained by daily application of the Pricing Rate for such Transaction to the Purchase Price for such Transaction (on a 360 day basis or 365 day basis in accordance with the applicable ISMA convention, unless otherwise agreed between the parties for the Transaction), for the actual number of days during the period commencing on (and including) the Purchase Date for such Transaction and ending on (but excluding) the date of calculation or, if earlier, the Repurchase Date;

**(ee)** "*Pricing Rate*", with respect to any Transaction, the per annum percentage rate for calculation of the Price Differential agreed to by Buyer and Seller in relation to that Transaction;

**(ff)** "*Purchase Date*", with respect to any Transaction, the date on which Purchased Securities are to be sold by Seller to Buyer in relation to that Transaction;

**(gg)** "*Purchase Price*", on the Purchase Date, the price at which Purchased Securities are sold or are to be sold by Seller to Buyer;

**(hh)** *"Purchased Securities"*, with respect to any Transaction, the Securities sold or to be sold by Seller to Buyer under that Transaction, and any New Purchased Securities transferred by Seller to Buyer under paragraph 8 of this Agreement in respect of that Transaction;

**(ii)** *"Repurchase Date"*, with respect to any Transaction, the date on which Buyer is to sell Equivalent Securities to Seller in relation to that Transaction;

**(jj)** *"Repurchase Price"*, with respect to any Transaction and as of any date, the sum of the Purchase Price and the Price Differential as of such date;

**(kk)** *"Spot Rate"*, where an amount in one currency is to be converted into a second currency on any date, unless the parties otherwise agree, the spot rate of exchange quoted by Barclays Bank PLC in the London inter bank market for the sale by it of such second currency against a purchase by it of such first currency;

**(ll)** *"Term"*, with respect to any Transaction, the interval of time commencing with the Purchase Date and ending with the Repurchase Date;

**(mm)** *"Termination"*, with respect to any Transaction, refers to the requirement with respect to such Transaction for Buyer to sell Equivalent Securities against payment by Seller of the Repurchase Price in accordance with paragraph 3(f), and references to a Transaction having a *"fixed term"* or being *"terminable upon demand"* shall be construed accordingly;

**(nn)** *"Transaction Exposure"*, with respect to any Transaction at any time during the period from the Purchase Date to the Repurchase Date (or, if later, the date on which Equivalent Securities are delivered to Seller or the Transaction is terminated under paragraph 10(e) or 10(f)), the difference between (i) the Repurchase Price at such time multiplied by the applicable Margin Ratio (or, where the Transaction relates to Securities of more than one description to which different Margin Ratios apply, the amount produced by multiplying the Repurchase Price attributable to Equivalent Securities of each such description by the applicable Margin Ratio and aggregating the resulting amounts, the Repurchase Price being for this purpose attributed to Equivalent Securities of each such description in the same proportions as those in which the Purchase Price was apportioned among the Purchased Securities) and (ii) the Market Value of Equivalent Securities at such time. If (i) is greater than (ii), Buyer has a Transaction Exposure for that Transaction equal to that excess. If (ii) is greater than (i), Seller has a Transaction Exposure for that Transaction equal to that excess; and

**(oo)** except in paragraphs 14(b)(i) and 18, references in this Agreement to *"written"* communications and communications *"in writing"* include communications made through any electronic system agreed between the parties which is capable of reproducing such communications in hard copy form.

## 3. Initiation; Confirmation; Termination

**(a)** A Transaction may be entered into orally or in writing at the initiation of either Buyer or Seller.

**(b)** Upon agreeing to enter into a Transaction hereunder Buyer or Seller (or both), as shall have been agreed, shall promptly deliver to the other party written confirmation of such Transaction (a *"Confirmation"*).

The Confirmation shall describe the Purchased Securities (including CUSIP or CINS or other identifying number or numbers, if any), identify Buyer and Seller and set forth:

**(i)**  the Purchase Date;

**(ii)**  the Purchase Price;

**(iii)**  the Repurchase Date, unless the Transaction is to be terminable on demand (in which case the Confirmation will state that it is terminable on demand);

**(iv)**  the Pricing Rate applicable to the Transaction;

**(v)**  in respect of each party the details of the bank account[s] to which payments to be made hereunder are to be credited;

**(vi)**  where Annex III applies, whether the Transaction is a Repurchase Transaction or a Buy/Sell Back Transaction;

**(vii)**  where Annex IV applies, whether the Transaction is an Agency Transaction and, if so, the identity of the party which is acting as agent and the name, code or identifier of the Principal; and

**(viii)**  any additional terms or conditions of the Transaction;

and may be in the form of Annex II hereto or may be in any other form which the parties agree.

The Confirmation relating to a Transaction shall, together with this Agreement, constitute prima facie evidence of the terms agreed between Buyer and Seller for that Transaction, unless objection is made with respect to the Confirmation promptly after receipt thereof. In the event of any conflict between the terms of such Confirmation and this Agreement, the Confirmation shall prevail in respect of that Transaction and those terms only.

**(c)**  On the Purchase Date for a Transaction, Seller shall transfer the Purchased Securities to Buyer or its agent against the payment of the Purchase Price by Buyer.

**(d)**  Termination of a Transaction will be effected, in the case of on demand Transactions, on the date specified for Termination in such demand, and, in the case of fixed term Transactions, on the date fixed for Termination.

**(e)**  In the case of on demand Transactions, demand for Termination shall be made by Buyer or Seller, by telephone or otherwise, and shall provide for Termination to occur after not less than the minimum period as is customarily required for the settlement or delivery of money or Equivalent Securities of the relevant kind.

**(f)**  On the Repurchase Date, Buyer shall transfer to Seller or its agent Equivalent Securities against the payment of the Repurchase Price by Seller (less any amount then payable and unpaid by Buyer to Seller pursuant to paragraph 5).

#### 4. Margin Maintenance

**(a)**  If at any time either party has a Net Exposure in respect of the other party it may by notice to the other party require the other party to make a Margin Transfer to it of an aggregate amount or value at least equal to that Net Exposure.

**(b)**  A notice under sub-paragraph (a) above may be given orally or in writing.

**(c)**  For the purposes of this Agreement a party has a Net Exposure in respect of the other party if the aggregate of all the first party's Transaction Exposures plus any amount payable to the first party under paragraph 5 but unpaid less the amount of any Net Margin provided to the first party exceeds the aggregate of all the other party's Transaction Exposures plus any amount payable to the other party under paragraph 5 but unpaid less the amount of any Net Margin provided to the other party; and the amount of the Net Exposure is the amount of the excess. For this purpose any amounts not denominated in the Base Currency shall be converted into the Base Currency at the Spot Rate prevailing at the relevant time.

**(d)** To the extent that a party calling for a Margin Transfer has previously paid Cash Margin which has not been repaid or delivered Margin Securities in respect of which Equivalent Margin Securities have not been delivered to it, that party shall be entitled to require that such Margin Transfer be satisfied first by the repayment of such Cash Margin or the delivery of Equivalent Margin Securities but, subject to this, the composition of a Margin Transfer shall be at the option of the party making such Margin Transfer.

**(e)** Any Cash Margin transferred shall be in the Base Currency or such other currency as the parties may agree.

**(f)** A payment of Cash Margin shall give rise to a debt owing from the party receiving such payment to the party making such payment. Such debt shall bear interest at such rate, payable at such times, as may be specified in Annex I in respect of the relevant currency or otherwise agreed between the parties, and shall be repayable subject to the terms of this Agreement.

**(g)** Where Seller or Buyer becomes obliged under sub-paragraph (a) above to make a Margin Transfer, it shall transfer Cash Margin or Margin Securities or Equivalent Margin Securities within the minimum period specified in Annex I or, if no period is there specified, such minimum period as is customarily required for the settlement or delivery of money, Margin Securities or Equivalent Margin Securities of the relevant kind.

**(h)** The parties may agree that, with respect to any Transaction, the provisions of sub-paragraphs (a) to (g) above shall not apply but instead that margin may be provided separately in respect of that Transaction in which case:

    **(i)** that Transaction shall not be taken into account when calculating whether either party has a Net Exposure;

    **(ii)** margin shall be provided in respect of that Transaction in such manner as the parties may agree; and

    **(iii)** margin provided in respect of that Transaction shall not be taken into account for the purposes of sub-paragraphs (a) to (g) above.

**(i)** The parties may agree that any Net Exposure which may arise shall be eliminated not by Margin Transfers under the preceding provisions of this paragraph but by the repricing of Transactions under sub-paragraph (j) below, the adjustment of Transactions under sub-paragraph (k) below or a combination of both these methods.

**(j)** Where the parties agree that a Transaction is to be repriced under this sub-paragraph, such repricing shall be effected as follows:

    **(i)** the Repurchase Date under the relevant Transaction (the "*Original Transaction*") shall be deemed to occur on the date on which the repricing is to be effected (the "*Repricing Date*");

    **(ii)** the parties shall be deemed to have entered into a new Transaction (the "*Repriced Transaction*") on the terms set out in (iii) to (vi) below;

    **(iii)** the Purchased Securities under the Repriced Transaction shall be Securities equivalent to the Purchased Securities under the Original Transaction;

**(iv)** the Purchase Date under the Repriced Transaction shall be the Repricing Date;

**(v)** the Purchase Price under the Repriced Transaction shall be such amount as shall, when multiplied by the Margin Ratio applicable to the Original Transaction, be equal to the Market Value of such Securities on the Repricing Date;

**(vi)** the Repurchase Date, the Pricing Rate, the Margin Ratio and, subject as aforesaid, the other terms of the Repriced Transaction shall be identical to those of the Original Transaction;

**(vii)** the obligations of the parties with respect to the delivery of the Purchased Securities and the payment of the Purchase Price under the Repriced Transaction shall be set off against their obligations with respect to the delivery of Equivalent Securities and payment of the Repurchase Price under the Original Transaction and accordingly only a net cash sum shall be paid by one party to the other. Such net cash sum shall be paid within the period specified in sub-paragraph (g) above.

**(k)** The adjustment of a Transaction (the "*Original Transaction*") under this sub-paragraph shall be effected by the parties agreeing that on the date on which the adjustment is to be made (the "*Adjustment Date*") the Original Transaction shall be terminated and they shall enter into a new Transaction (the "*Replacement Transaction*") in accordance with the following provisions:

**(i)** the Original Transaction shall be terminated on the Adjustment Date on such terms as the parties shall agree on or before the Adjustment Date;

**(ii)** the Purchased Securities under the Replacement Transaction shall be such Securities as the parties shall agree on or before the Adjustment Date (being Securities the aggregate Market Value of which at the Adjustment Date is substantially equal to the Repurchase Price under the Original Transaction at the Adjustment Date multiplied by the Margin Ratio applicable to the Original Transaction);

**(iii)** the Purchase Date under the Replacement Transaction shall be the Adjustment Date;

**(iv)** the other terms of the Replacement Transaction shall be such as the parties shall agree on or before the Adjustment Date; and

**(v)** the obligations of the parties with respect to payment and delivery of Securities on the Adjustment Date under the Original Transaction and the Replacement Transaction shall be settled in accordance with paragraph 6 within the minimum period specified in sub-paragraph (g) above.

### 5. Income Payments

Unless otherwise agreed:

**(i)** where the Term of a particular Transaction extends over an Income Payment Date in respect of any Securities subject to that Transaction, Buyer shall on the date such Income is paid by the issuer transfer to or credit to the account of Seller an amount equal to (and in the same currency as) the amount paid by the issuer;

**(ii)** where Margin Securities are transferred from one party ("the first party") to the other party ("the second party") and an Income Payment Date in respect of such Securities occurs before Equivalent Margin Securities are transferred by the second party to the first party, the second party shall on the date such Income is paid by the issuer transfer to or credit to the account of the first party an amount equal to (and in the same currency as) the amount paid by the issuer;

and for the avoidance of doubt references in this paragraph to the amount of any income paid by the issuer of any Securities shall be to an amount paid without any withholding or deduction for or on account of taxes or duties notwithstanding that a payment of such Income made in certain circumstances may be subject to such a withholding or deduction.

## 6. Payment and Transfer

**(a)** Unless otherwise agreed, all money paid hereunder shall be in immediately available, freely convertible funds of the relevant currency. All Securities to be transferred hereunder (i) shall be in suitable form for transfer and shall be accompanied by duly executed instruments of transfer or assignment in blank (where required for transfer) and such other documentation as the transferee may reasonably request, or (ii) shall be transferred through the book entry system of Euroclear or Cedel, or (iii) shall be transferred through any other agreed securities clearance system, or (iv) shall be transferred by any other method mutually acceptable to Seller and Buyer.

**(b)** Unless otherwise agreed, all money payable by one party to the other in respect of any Transaction shall be paid free and clear of, and without withholding or deduction for, any taxes or duties of whatsoever nature imposed, levied, collected, withheld or assessed by any authority having power to tax, unless the withholding or deduction of such taxes or duties is required by law. In that event, unless otherwise agreed, the paying party shall pay such additional amounts as will result in the net amounts receivable by the other party (after taking account of such withholding or deduction) being equal to such amounts as would have been received by it had no such taxes or duties been required to be withheld or deducted.

**(c)** Unless otherwise agreed in writing between the parties, under each Transaction transfer of Purchased Securities by Seller and payment of Purchase Price by Buyer against the transfer of such Purchased Securities shall be made simultaneously and transfer of Equivalent Securities by Buyer and payment of Repurchase Price payable by Seller against the transfer of such Equivalent Securities shall be made simultaneously.

**(d)** Subject to and without prejudice to the provisions of sub-paragraph 6(c), either party may from time to time in accordance with market practice and in recognition of the practical difficulties in arranging simultaneous delivery of Securities and money waive in relation to any Transaction its rights under this Agreement to receive simultaneous transfer and/or payment provided that transfer and/or payment shall, notwithstanding such waiver, be made on the same day and provided also that no such waiver in respect of one Transaction shall affect or bind it in respect of any other Transaction.

**(e)** The parties shall execute and deliver all necessary documents and take all necessary steps to procure that all right, title and interest in any Purchased Securities, any Equivalent Securities, any Margin Securities and any Equivalent Margin Securities shall pass to the party to which transfer is being made upon transfer of the same in accordance with this Agreement, free from all liens, claims, charges and encumbrances.

**(f)** Notwithstanding the use of expressions such as *"Repurchase Date"*, *"Repurchase Price"*, *"margin"*, *"Net Margin"*, *"Margin Ratio"* and *"substitution"* which are used to reflect terminology used in the market for transactions of the kind provided for in this Agreement, all right, title and interest in and to Securities and money transferred or paid under this Agreement shall pass to the transferee upon transfer or payment, the obligation of the party receiving Purchased Securities or Margin Securities being an obligation to transfer Equivalent Securities or Equivalent Margin Securities.

**(g)** Time shall be of the essence in this Agreement.

**(h)** Subject to paragraph 10, all amounts in the same currency payable by each party to the other under any Transaction or otherwise under this Agreement on the same date shall be combined in a single calculation of a net sum payable by one party to the other and the obligation to pay that sum shall be the only obligation of either party in respect of those amounts.

**(i)** Subject to paragraph 10, all Securities of the same issue, denomination, currency and series, transferable by each party to the other under any Transaction or hereunder on the same date shall be combined in a single calculation of a net quantity of Securities transferable by one party to the other and the obligation to transfer the net quantity of Securities shall be the only obligation of either party in respect of the Securities so transferable and receivable.

## 7. Contractual Currency

**(a)** All the payments made in respect of the Purchase Price or the Repurchase Price of any Transaction shall be made in the currency of the Purchase Price (the *"Contractual Currency"*) save as provided in paragraph 10(c)(ii). Notwithstanding the foregoing, the payee of any money may, at its option, accept tender thereof in any other currency, provided, however, that, to the extent permitted by applicable law, the obligation of the payer to pay such money will be discharged only to the extent of the amount of the Contractual Currency that such payee may, consistent with normal banking procedures, purchase with such other currency (after deduction of any premium and costs of exchange) for delivery within the customary delivery period for spot transactions in respect of the relevant currency.

**(b)** If for any reason the amount in the Contractual Currency received by a party, including amounts received after conversion of any recovery under any judgment or order expressed in a currency other than the Contractual Currency, falls short of the amount in the Contractual Currency due and payable, the party required to make the payment will, as a separate and independent obligation, to the extent permitted by applicable law, immediately transfer such additional amount in the Contractual Currency as may be necessary to compensate for the shortfall.

**(c)** If for any reason the amount in the Contractual Currency received by a party exceeds the amount of the Contractual Currency due and payable, the party receiving the transfer will refund promptly the amount of such excess.

## 8. Substitution

**(a)** A Transaction may at any time between the Purchase Date and the Repurchase Date, if Seller so requests and Buyer so agrees, be varied by the transfer by Buyer to Seller of Securities equivalent to the Purchased Securities, or to such of the Purchased Securities as shall be agreed, in exchange for the transfer by Seller to Buyer of other Securities of such amount and description as shall be agreed ("*New Purchased Securities*") (being Securities having a Market Value at the date of the variation at least equal to the Market Value of the Equivalent Securities transferred to Seller).

**(b)** Any variation under sub-paragraph (a) above shall be effected, subject to paragraph 6(d), by the simultaneous transfer of the Equivalent Securities and New Purchased Securities concerned.

**(c)** A Transaction which is varied under sub-paragraph (a) above shall thereafter continue in effect as though the Purchased Securities under that Transaction consisted of or included the New Purchased Securities instead of the Securities in respect of which Equivalent Securities have been transferred to Seller.

**(d)** Where either party has transferred Margin Securities to the other party it may at any time before Equivalent Margin Securities are transferred to it under paragraph 4 request the other party to transfer Equivalent Margin Securities to it in exchange for the transfer to the other party of new Margin Securities having a Market Value at the time of transfer at least equal to that of such Equivalent Margin Securities. If the other party agrees to the request, the exchange shall be effected, subject to paragraph 6(d), by the simultaneous transfer of the Equivalent Margin Securities and new Margin Securities concerned. Where either or both of such transfers is or are effected through a settlement system in circumstances which under the rules and procedures of that settlement system give rise to a payment by or for the account of one party to or for the account of the other party, the parties shall cause such payment or payments to be made outside that settlement system, for value the same day as the payments made through that settlement system, as shall ensure that the exchange of Equivalent Margin Securities and new Margin Securities effected under this sub-paragraph does not give rise to any net payment of cash by either party to the other.

## 9. Representations

Each party represents and warrants to the other that:

**(a)** it is duly authorised to execute and deliver this Agreement, to enter into the Transactions contemplated hereunder and to perform its obligations hereunder and thereunder and has taken all necessary action to authorise such execution, delivery and performance;

**(b)** it will engage in this Agreement and the Transactions contemplated hereunder (other than Agency Transactions) as principal;

**(c)** the person signing this Agreement on its behalf is, and any person representing it in entering into a Transaction will be, duly authorised to do so on its behalf;

**(d)** it has obtained all authorisations of any governmental or regulatory body required in connection with this Agreement and the Transactions contemplated hereunder and such authorisations are in full force and effect;

**(e)** the execution, delivery and performance of this Agreement and the Transactions contemplated hereunder will not violate any law, ordinance, charter, bye-law or rule applicable to it or any agreement by which it is bound or by which any of its assets are affected;

**(f)** it has satisfied itself and will continue to satisfy itself as to the tax implications of the Transactions contemplated hereunder;

**(g)** in connection with this Agreement and each Transaction:

    **(i)** unless there is a written agreement with the other party to the contrary, it is not relying on any advice (whether written or oral) of the other party, other than the representations expressly set out in this Agreement;

    **(ii)** it has made and will make its own decisions regarding the entering into of any Transaction based upon its own judgment and upon advice from such professional advisers as it has deemed it necessary to consult;

    **(iii)** it understands the terms, conditions and risks of each Transaction and is willing to assume (financially and otherwise) those risks;

**(h)** at the time of transfer to the other party of any Securities it will have the full and unqualified right to make such transfer and that upon such transfer of Securities the other party will receive all right, title and interest in and to those Securities free of any lien, claim, charge or encumbrance; and

**(i)** the paying and collecting arrangements applied in relation to any Securities prior to their transfer from that party to the other under this Agreement will not have resulted in the payment of any Income in respect of such Securities to the party transferring such Securities under deduction or withholding for or on account of UK tax.

On the date on which any Transaction is entered into pursuant hereto, and on each day on which Securities, Equivalent Securities, Margin Securities or Equivalent Margin Securities are to be transferred under any Transaction, Buyer and Seller shall each be deemed to repeat all the foregoing representations. For the avoidance of doubt and notwithstanding any arrangements which Seller or Buyer may have with any third party, each party will be liable as a principal for its obligations under this Agreement and each Transaction.

### 10. Events of Default

**(a)** If any of the following events (each an "*Event of Default*") occurs in relation to either party (the "*Defaulting Party*", the other party being the "*non-Defaulting Party*") whether acting as Seller or Buyer:

    **(i)** Buyer fails to pay the Purchase Price upon the applicable Purchase Date or Seller fails to pay the Repurchase Price upon the applicable Repurchase Date, and the non-Defaulting Party serves a Default Notice on the Defaulting Party; or

    **(ii)** Seller or Buyer fails to comply with paragraph 4 and the non-Defaulting Party serves a Default Notice on the Defaulting Party; or

    **(iii)** Seller or Buyer fails to comply with paragraph 5 and the non-Defaulting Party serves a Default Notice on the Defaulting Party; or

    **(iv)** an Act of Insolvency occurs with respect to Seller or Buyer and (except in the case of an Act of Insolvency which is the presentation of a petition for winding-up or any analogous proceeding or the appointment of a liquidator or analogous officer of the Defaulting Party in which case no such notice shall be required) the non-Defaulting Party serves a Default Notice on the Defaulting Party; or

    **(v)** any representations made by Seller or Buyer are incorrect or untrue in any material respect when made or repeated or deemed to have been made or repeated, and the non-Defaulting Party serves a Default Notice on the Defaulting Party; or

**(vi)** Seller or Buyer admits to the other that it is unable to, or intends not to, perform any of its obligations hereunder and/or in respect of any Transaction and the non-Defaulting Party serves a Default Notice on the Defaulting Party; or

**(vii)** Seller or Buyer is suspended or expelled from membership of or participation in any securities exchange or association or other self regulating organisation, or suspended from dealing in securities by any government agency, or any of the assets of either Seller or Buyer or the assets of investors held by, or to the order of, Seller or Buyer are transferred or ordered to be transferred to a trustee by a regulatory authority pursuant to any securities regulating legislation and the non-Defaulting Party serves a Default Notice on the Defaulting Party; or

**(viii)** Seller or Buyer fails to perform any other of its obligations hereunder and does not remedy such failure within 30 days after notice is given by the non-Defaulting Party requiring it to do so, and the non-Defaulting Party serves a Default Notice on the Defaulting Party;

then sub-paragraphs (b) to (d) below shall apply.

**(b)** The Repurchase Date for each Transaction hereunder shall be deemed immediately to occur and, subject to the following provisions, all Cash Margin (including interest accrued) shall be immediately repayable and Equivalent Margin Securities shall be immediately deliverable (and so that, where this sub-paragraph applies, performance of the respective obligations of the parties with respect to the delivery of Securities, the payment of the Repurchase Prices for any Equivalent Securities and the repayment of any Cash Margin shall be effected only in accordance with the provisions of sub-paragraph (c) below).

**(c) (i)** The Default Market Values of the Equivalent Securities and any Equivalent Margin Securities to be transferred, the amount of any Cash Margin (including the amount of interest accrued) to be transferred and the Repurchase Prices to be paid by each party shall be established by the non-Defaulting Party for all Transactions as at the Repurchase Date; and

**(ii)** on the basis of the sums so established, an account shall be taken (as at the Repurchase Date) of what is due from each party to the other under this Agreement (on the basis that each party's claim against the other in respect of the transfer to it of Equivalent Securities or Equivalent Margin Securities under this Agreement equals the Default Market Value therefor) and the sums due from one party shall be set off against the sums due from the other and only the balance of the account shall be payable (by the party having the claim valued at the lower amount pursuant to the foregoing) and such balance shall be due and payable on the next following Business Day. For the purposes of this calculation, all sums not denominated in the Base Currency shall be converted into the Base Currency on the relevant date at the Spot Rate prevailing at the relevant time.

**(d)** The Defaulting Party shall be liable to the non-Defaulting Party for the amount of all reasonable legal and other professional expenses incurred by the non-Defaulting Party in connection with or as a consequence of an Event of Default, together with interest thereon at LIBOR or, in the case of an expense attributable to a particular Transaction, the Pricing Rate for the relevant Transaction if that Pricing Rate is greater than LIBOR.

**(e)** If Seller fails to deliver Purchased Securities to Buyer on the applicable Purchase Date Buyer may:

**(i)** if it has paid the Purchase Price to Seller, require Seller immediately to repay the sum so paid;

**(ii)** if Buyer has a Transaction Exposure to Seller in respect of the relevant Transaction, require Seller from time to time to pay Cash Margin at least equal to such Transaction Exposure;

**(iii)** at any time while such failure continues, terminate the Transaction by giving written notice to Seller. On such termination the obligations of Seller and Buyer with respect to delivery of Purchased Securities and Equivalent Securities shall terminate and Seller shall pay to Buyer an amount equal to the excess of the Repurchase Price at the date of Termination over the Purchase Price.

**(f)** If Buyer fails to deliver Equivalent Securities to Seller on the applicable Repurchase Date Seller may:

**(i)** if it has paid the Repurchase Price to Buyer, require Buyer immediately to repay the sum so paid;

**(ii)** if Seller has a Transaction Exposure to Buyer in respect of the relevant Transaction, require Buyer from time to time to pay Cash Margin at least equal to such Transaction Exposure;

**(iii)** at any time while such failure continues, by written notice to Buyer declare that that Transaction (but only that Transaction) shall be terminated immediately in accordance with sub-paragraph (c) above (disregarding for this purpose references in that sub-paragraph to transfer of Cash Margin and delivery of Equivalent Margin Securities).

**(g)** The provisions of this Agreement constitute a complete statement of the remedies available to each party in respect of any Event of Default.

**(h)** Neither party may claim any sum by way of consequential loss or damage in the event of a failure by the other party to perform any of its obligations under this Agreement.

**(i)** Each party shall immediately notify the other if an Event of Default, or an event which, upon the serving of a Default Notice, would be an Event of Default, occurs in relation to it.

### 11. Tax Event

**(a)** This paragraph shall apply if either party notifies the other that:

**(i)** any action taken by a taxing authority or brought in a court of competent jurisdiction (regardless of whether such action is taken or brought with respect to a party to this Agreement); or

**(ii)** a change in the fiscal or regulatory regime (including, but not limited to, a change in law or in the general interpretation of law but excluding any change in any rate of tax) has or will, in the notifying party's reasonable opinion, have a material adverse effect on that party in the context of a Transaction.

**(b)** If so requested by the other party, the notifying party will furnish the other with an opinion of a suitably qualified adviser that an event referred to in sub-paragraph (a)(i) or (ii) above has occurred and affects the notifying party.

**(c)** Where this paragraph applies, the party giving the notice referred to in sub-paragraph (a) may, subject to sub-paragraph (d) below, terminate the Transaction with effect from a date specified in the notice, not being earlier (unless so agreed by the other party) than 30 days after the date of the notice, by nominating that date as the Repurchase Date.

**(d)** If the party receiving the notice referred to in sub-paragraph (a) so elects, it may override that notice by giving a counter-notice to the other party. If a counter-notice is given, the party which gives the counter-notice will be deemed to have agreed to indemnify the other party against the adverse effect referred to in sub-paragraph (a) so far as relates to the relevant Transaction and the original Repurchase Date will continue to apply.

**(e)** Where a Transaction is terminated as described in this paragraph, the party which has given the notice to terminate shall indemnify the other party against any reasonable legal and other professional expenses incurred by the other party by reason of the termination, but the other party may not claim any sum by way of consequential loss or damage in respect of a termination in accordance with this paragraph.

**(f)** This paragraph is without prejudice to paragraph 6(b) (obligation to pay additional amounts if withholding or deduction required); but an obligation to pay such additional amounts may, where appropriate, be a circumstance which causes this paragraph to apply.

## 12. Interest

To the extent permitted by applicable law, if any sum of money payable hereunder or under any Transaction is not paid when due, interest shall accrue on such unpaid sum as a separate debt at the greater of the Pricing Rate for the Transaction to which such sum relates (where such sum is referable to a Transaction) and LIBOR on a 360 day basis or 365 day basis in accordance with the applicable ISMA convention, for the actual number of days during the period from and including the date on which payment was due to, but excluding, the date of payment.

## 13. Single Agreement

Each party acknowledges that, and has entered into this Agreement and will enter into each Transaction hereunder in consideration of and in reliance upon the fact that, all Transactions hereunder constitute a single business and contractual relationship and are made in consideration of each other. Accordingly, each party agrees (i) to perform all of its obligations in respect of each Transaction hereunder, and that a default in the performance of any such obligations shall constitute a default by it in respect of all Transactions hereunder, and (ii) that payments, deliveries and other transfers made by either of them in respect of any Transaction shall be deemed to have been made in consideration of payments, deliveries and other transfers in respect of any other Transactions hereunder.

## 14. Notices and Other Communications

**(a)** Any notice or other communication to be given under this Agreement:

**(i)** shall be in the English language and, except where expressly otherwise provided in this Agreement, shall be in writing;

**(ii)** may be given in any manner described in sub-paragraph (b) below;

    **(iii)** shall be sent to the party to whom it is to be given at the address or number, or in accordance with the electronic messaging details, set out in Annex V.

**(b)** Any such notice or other communication shall be effective:

    **(i)** if in writing and delivered in person or by courier, at the time when it is delivered;

    **(ii)** if sent by telex, at the time when the recipient's answerback is received;

    **(iii)** if sent by facsimile transmission, at the time when the transmission is received by a responsible employee of the recipient in legible form (it being agreed that the burden of proving receipt will be on the sender and will not be met by a transmission report generated by the sender's facsimile machine);

    **(iv)** if sent by certified or registered mail (airmail, if overseas) or the equivalent (return receipt requested), at the time when that mail is delivered or its delivery is attempted;

    **(v)** if sent by electronic messaging system, at the time that electronic message is received;

except that any notice or communication which is received, or delivery of which is attempted, after close of business on the date of receipt or attempted delivery or on a day which is not a day on which commercial banks are open for business in the place where that notice or other communication is to be given shall be treated as given at the opening of business on the next following day which is such a day.

**(c)** Either party may by notice to the other change the address, telex or facsimile number or electronic messaging system details at which notices or other communications are to be given to it.

## 15. Entire Agreement; Severability

This Agreement shall supersede any existing agreements between the parties containing general terms and conditions for Transactions. Each provision and agreement herein shall be treated as separate from any other provision or agreement herein and shall be enforceable notwithstanding the unenforceability of any such other provision or agreement.

## 16. Non-assignability; Termination

**(a)** Subject to sub-paragraph (b) below, the rights and obligations of the parties under this Agreement and under any Transaction shall not be assigned, charged or otherwise dealt with by either party without the prior written consent of the other party. Subject to the foregoing, this Agreement and any Transactions shall be binding upon and shall inure to the benefit of the parties and their respective successors and assigns.

**(b)** Sub-paragraph (a) above shall not preclude a party from assigning, charging, or otherwise dealing with all or any part of its interest in any sum payable to it under paragraph 10(c) or (d) above.

**(c)** Either party may terminate this Agreement by giving written notice to the other, except that this Agreement shall, notwithstanding such notice, remain applicable to any transactions then outstanding.

**(d)** All remedies hereunder shall survive Termination in respect of the relevant Transaction and termination of this Agreement.

## 17. Governing Law

This Agreement shall be governed by and construed in accordance with the laws of England. Buyer and Seller hereby irrevocably submit for all purposes of or in connection with this Agreement and each Transaction to the jurisdiction of the Courts of England.

Party A hereby appoints the person identified in Annex VI hereto as its agent to receive on its behalf service of process in such courts. If such agent ceases to be its agent, Party A shall promptly appoint, and notify Party B of the identity of, a new agent in England.

Party B hereby appoints the person identified in Annex VII hereto as its agent to receive on its behalf service of process in such courts. If such agent ceases to be its agent, Party B shall promptly appoint, and notify Party A of the identity of, a new agent in England.

Nothing in this paragraph shall limit the right of any party to take proceedings in the courts of any other country of competent jurisdiction.

## 18. No Waivers, etc.

No express or implied waiver of any Event of Default by either party shall constitute a waiver of any other Event of Default and no exercise of any remedy hereunder by any party shall constitute a waiver of its right to exercise any other remedy hereunder. No modification or waiver of any provision of this Agreement and no consent by any party to a departure herefrom shall be effective unless and until such modification, waiver or consent shall be in writing and duly executed by both of the parties hereto. Without limitation on any of the foregoing, the failure to give a notice pursuant to sub-paragraph 4(a) hereof will not constitute a waiver of any right to do so at a later date.

## 19. Waiver of Immunity

Each party hereto hereby waives, to the fullest extent permitted by applicable law, all immunity (whether on the basis of sovereignty or otherwise) from jurisdiction, attachment (both before and after judgment) and execution to which it might otherwise be entitled in any action or proceeding in the Courts of England or of any other country or jurisdiction, relating in any way to this Agreement or any Transaction, and agrees that it will not raise, claim or cause to be pleaded any such immunity at or in respect of any such action or proceeding.

## 20. Recording

The parties agree that each may electronically record all telephone conversations between them.

[Name of Party]

By _____

Title _____

Date _____

[Name of Party]

By _____

Title _____

Date _____

# Annex I
## Supplemental Terms or Conditions

Paragraph references are to paragraphs in the Agreement.

1. The following elections shall apply:

[(a)    paragraph 1. Buy/Sell Back Transactions may be effected under this Agreement, and accordingly Annex III will apply.]*

[(b)    paragraph 1. Agency Transactions may be effected under this Agreement, and accordingly Annex IV will apply.]*

(c)    paragraph 2(c). The Base Currency shall be _____;

(d)    paragraph 2(l). [list Buyer's and Seller's Designated Offices]

[(e)    paragraph 2(s). For the avoidance of doubt, if Securities in any Transaction include Italian government bonds, the Income in respect of such Italian government bonds shall exclude any amount deducted for or on account of tax at source and any tax credits or refunds in respect of Distributions (if any) on such Italian government bonds.]*

(f)    paragraph 2(y). The pricing source for calculation of Market Value shall be: _____ .

(g)    paragraph 2(kk). Spot Rate to be: _____ .

(h)    paragraph 3(b). [Seller/Buyer/both Seller and Buyer]* to deliver Confirmation.

(i)    paragraph 4(f). Interest rate on Cash Margin to be  [  ]% for _____ currency

                                                          [  ]% for _____ currency

        Interest to be payable [payment intervals and dates]

(j)    paragraph 4(g). Delivery period for margin calls to be: _____ .

2.    The following Supplemental Terms and Conditions shall apply

---

* Delete as appropriate.

## Annex II
## Form of Confirmation

To: _____

From: _____

Date: _____

Subject: [Repurchase] [Buy/Sell]* Transaction
  (Reference Number:    )

Dear Sirs,

The purpose of this [letter]/[facsimile]/[telex] is to set forth the terms and conditions of the above repurchase transaction entered into between us on the Contract Date referred to below.

This confirmation supplements and forms part of, and is subject to, the Global Master Repurchase Agreement as entered into between us as of [ ] as the same may be amended from time to time (the *Agreement*). All provisions contained in the Agreement govern this confirmation except as expressly modified below. Words and phrases defined in the Agreement and used in this confirmation shall have the same meaning herein as in the Agreement.

1.  Contract Date:

2.  Purchased Securities [state type[s] and nominal value[s]]:

3.  CUSIP, CINS or other identifying number[s]:

4.  Buyer:

5.  Seller:

6.  Purchase Date:

7.  Purchase Price:

8.  Contractual Currency:

[9.  Repurchase Date]:*

[10. Terminable on demand]*

11. Pricing Rate:

[12. Sell Back Price:]

13. Buyer's Bank Account[s] Details:

14. Seller's Bank Account[s] Details:

[15. The Transaction is an Agency Transaction. [Name of Agent] is acting as agent for [name or identifier of Principal]]*

[16. Additional Terms]:

Yours faithfully,

_____

*Delete as appropriate.

# Annex III
# Buy/Sell Back Transactions

1.  In the event of any conflict between the terms of this Annex III and any other term of the Agreement, the terms in this Annex shall prevail.

2.  Each Transaction shall be identified at the time it is entered into and in the Confirmation relating to it as either a Repurchase Transaction or a Buy/Sell Back Transaction.

3.  In the case of a Buy/Sell Back Transaction the Confirmation delivered in accordance with paragraph 3 of the Agreement may consist of a single document in respect of both of the transactions which together form the Buy/Sell Back Transaction or separate Confirmations may be delivered in respect of each such transaction. Such Confirmations may be in the form of Annex II to the Agreement except that, subject to paragraph 5 below, such Confirmations shall not include the item specified in paragraph 10 of Annex II.

4.  The following definitions shall apply to Buy/Sell Back Transactions:

    (i) *"Accrued Interest"*, with respect to any Purchased Securities subject to a Buy/Sell Back Transaction, unpaid Income that has accrued during the period from (and including) the issue date or the last Income Payment Date (whichever is the later) in respect of such Purchased Securities to (but excluding) the date of calculation. For these purposes unpaid Income shall be deemed to accrue on a daily basis from (and including) the issue date or the last Income Payment Date (as the case may be) to (but excluding) the next Income Payment Date or the maturity date (whichever is the earlier);

    (ii) *"Sell Back Differential"*, with respect to any Buy/Sell Back Transaction as of any date, the aggregate amount obtained by daily application of the Pricing Rate for such Buy/Sell Back Transaction (on a 360 day basis or 365 day basis in accordance with the applicable ISMA convention, unless otherwise agreed between the parties for the Transaction) to the sum of (a) the Purchase Price and (b) Accrued Interest paid on the Purchase Date for such Transaction for the actual number of days during the period commencing on (and including) the Purchase Date for such Buy/Sell Back Transaction and ending on (but excluding) the date of calculation;

    (iii) *"Sell Back Price"*, with respect to any Buy/Sell Back Transaction, means:

    (x) in relation to the date originally specified by the parties as the Repurchase Date pursuant to paragraph 3(b)(iii) of the Agreement, the price agreed by the Parties in relation to that Buy/Sell Back Transaction, and

    (y) in any other case (including for the purposes of the application of paragraph 4 (margin maintenance) or paragraph 10 (Events of Default)) of the Agreement, the product of the formula $(P + AI + D) - (IR + C)$, where:

    $P$ = the Purchase Price

    $AI$ = the amount, equal to Accrued Interest at the Purchase Date, paid under paragraph 8 of this Annex

    $D$ = the Sell Back Differential

November 1995

IR = the amount of any Income in respect of the Purchased Securities payable by the issuer on or, in the case of registered Securities, by reference to, any date falling between the Purchase Date and the Repurchase Date

C = the aggregate amount obtained by daily application of the Pricing Rate for such Buy/Sell Back Transaction to any such Income from (and including) the date of payment by the issuer to (but excluding) the date of calculation

5. When entering into a Buy/Sell Back Transaction the parties shall also agree the Sell Back Price and the Pricing Rate to apply in relation to that Transaction on the scheduled Repurchase Date. The parties shall record the Pricing Rate in at least one Confirmation applicable to that Buy/Sell Back Transaction.

6. Buy/Sell Back Transactions shall not be terminable on demand.

7. In the case of a Buy/Sell Back Transaction, the Purchase Price shall be quoted exclusive of Accrued Interest to the Purchase Date on the Purchased Securities and the Sell Back Price shall be quoted exclusive of Accrued Interest.

8. For the purposes of paragraph 3(c) of the Agreement, in the case of a Buy/Sell Back Transaction, the Purchased Securities shall be transferred to Buyer or its agent against the payment of the Purchase Price plus an amount equal to Accrued Interest to the Purchase Date on such Purchased Securities.

9. In the case of a Buy/Sell Back Transaction, paragraph 3(f) of the Agreement shall not apply. Termination of such a Transaction will be effected on the Repurchase Date by transfer to Seller or its agent of Equivalent Securities against the payment by Seller of (i) in a case where the Repurchase Date is the date originally scheduled by the parties pursuant to paragraph 3(b)(iii) of the Agreement, the Sell Back Price referred to in paragraph 4(iii)(x) of this Annex plus an amount equal to Accrued Interest to the Repurchase Date; and (ii) in any other case, the Sell Back Price referred to in paragraph 4(iii)(y) of this Annex.

10. If the parties agree that a Buy/Sell Back Transaction is to be repriced in accordance with paragraph 4(i) of the Agreement, they shall at the time of such repricing agree the Purchase Price, the Sell Back Price and the Pricing Rate applicable to the Repriced Transaction.

11. Paragraph 5 of the Agreement (relating to Income payments) shall not apply to Buy/Sell Back Transactions.

12. References to "Repurchase Price" throughout the Agreement shall be construed as references to "Repurchase Price or the Sell Back Price, as the case may be".

13. In Paragraph 10(c)(i) of the Agreement (relating to Events of Default), the reference to the "Repurchase Prices" shall be construed as a reference to "Repurchase Prices and Sell Back Prices".

# Annex IV
## Transactions Entered into as Agent

1.  Subject to the following provisions of this Annex, either party may enter into Transactions as agent for a third person (a "*Principal*"), whether as custodian or investment manager or otherwise (a Transaction so entered into being an "*Agency Transaction*"). In this Annex the party entering into an Agency Transaction as agent is referred to as the "*Agent*" and the other party is referred to as the "*other party*".

2.  A party may enter into an Agency Transaction if, but only if:

    **(a)** it specifies that Transaction as an Agency Transaction at the time when it enters into it and in the Confirmation;

    **(b)** it enters into that Transaction on behalf of a single Principal whose identity is disclosed to the other party (whether by name or by reference to a code or identifier which the parties have agreed will be used to refer to a specified Principal) at the time when it enters into the Transaction; and

    **(c)** it has at the time when the Transaction is entered into actual authority to enter into the Transaction on behalf of that Principal and to perform on behalf of that Principal all of that Principal's obligations under the Agreement.

3.  A transaction shall not be entered into under the Agreement and this Annex if both parties specify that they propose to enter into that transaction as an agent.

4.  Each party undertakes that, if it enters as agent into an Agency Transaction, forthwith upon becoming aware:

    **(a)** of any event which constitutes an Act of Insolvency with respect to the relevant Principal; or

    **(b)** of any breach of any of the warranties given in paragraph 8 below or of any event or circumstance which has the result that any such warranty would be untrue if repeated by reference to the current facts;

    it will inform the other party of that fact and will, if so required by the other party, furnish the other party with such additional information as the other party may reasonably request.

5.  **(a)** Each Agency Transaction shall be a transaction between the relevant Principal and the other party and no person other than the relevant Principal and the other party shall be a party to or have any rights or obligations under an Agency Transaction. Without limiting the foregoing, the Agent shall not be liable as principal for the performance of an Agency Transaction, but this is without prejudice to any liability of the Agent under any other provision of this Annex.

    **(b)** All the provisions of the Agreement shall apply separately as between the other party and each Principal for whom the Agent has entered into an Agency Transaction or Agency Transactions as if each such Principal were a party to a separate agreement with the other party in all respects identical with the Agreement as supplemented by the provisions of this Annex other than this paragraph, but with the following additions and modifications:

(i) if there occurs in relation to the Agent an Event of Default or an event which would constitute an Event of Default if the other party served a Default Notice or other written notice under any sub-paragraph of paragraph 10 of the Agreement, the other party shall be entitled by giving written notice to the Principal (which notice shall be validly given if given to the Agent in accordance with paragraph 14 of the Agreement) to declare that by reason of that event an Event of Default is to be treated as occurring in relation to the Principal. If the other party gives such a notice then an Event of Default shall be treated as occurring in relation to the Principal at the time when the notice is deemed to be given in accordance with paragraph 14 of the Agreement;

(ii) if the Principal is neither incorporated nor has established a place of business in Great Britain, the Principal shall for the purposes of paragraph 17 of the Agreement as so applicable be deemed to have appointed as its agent to receive on its behalf service of process in the Courts of England the Agent, or if the Agent is neither incorporated nor has established a place of business in the United Kingdom, the person appointed by the Agent under paragraph 17 of the Agreement, or such other person as the Principal may from time to time specify in a written notice given to the other party.

(c) The Agent shall do all such things and provide the other party with all such information as may be necessary to identify any Transaction Exposure which may arise in respect of any Principal.

(d) The foregoing provisions do not affect the operation of the Agreement as between the other party and the Agent in respect of any Transactions into which the Agent may enter on its own account as a principal.

6. Paragraph 9(b) of the Agreement shall be deleted and replaced by the following:

"(b) it will engage in this Agreement and the Transactions contemplated hereunder as principal or, subject to and in accordance with of Annex IV, as agent and the conditions referred to in Annex IV will be fulfilled in respect of each Transaction into which it enters as an agent;".

7. At the beginning of the last sentence of paragraph 9 of the Agreement there shall be added the words "Subject to Annex IV,".

8. Each party warrants to the other that it will, on every occasion on which it enters or purports to enter into a transaction as an Agency Transaction, be duly authorised to enter into that transaction on behalf of the person whom it specifies as the Principal in respect of that transaction and to perform on behalf of that person all the obligations of that person under the Agreement.

# Annex V
## Names, Addresses and other Details for Communication Between Parties

**1.** Party A

**2.** Party B

November 1995

# Annex VI
## Name and Address of Party A's Agent for Service of Process

# Annex VII
# Name and Address of Party B's Agent for Service of Process

# THE UK GILT REPO ANNEX

## PSA/ISMA GLOBAL MASTER REPURCHASE AGREEMENT
### Supplemental terms and conditions where repurchase transactions are to be effected in UK gilt-edged securities
### Annex 1, Part 2

### 1. Interpretation

1.1 In this Part of this Annex:

**(a)** the "**Agreement**" means the Agreement dated       substantially in the form of the PSA/ISMA Global Master Repurchase Agreement for Gross Paying Securities of which this Annex forms part;

**(b)** "**Central Gilts Office Service**" or "**CGO Service**" means the computer-based system for the transfer of gilt-edged securities by exempt transfer (as defined in the Stock Transfer Act 1982) operated by the Central Gilts Office of the Bank of England;

**(c)** "**CHAPS system**" means the same day payment system operated by the CHAPS Clearing Company Limited;

**(d)** "**gilt-edged securities**" means securities which are gilt-edged securities for the purposes of section 51A(7) of the Income and Corporation Taxes Act 1988.

1.2 Terms to which a defined meaning is given in the Agreement have the same meanings in this Annex.

### 2. Scope

2.1 The parties have agreed that the Transactions to which the Agreement applies may include Transactions in respect of gilt-edged securities.

2.2 The terms and conditions set out in this Annex apply to Transactions in respect of gilt-edged securities and, to the extent and in the circumstances provided in paragraph 3.4(c) below, Transactions wholly or partly in respect of such other securities as are referred to in that paragraph.

### 3. CGO Service

3.1 The CGO Service shall be an agreed securities clearance system for the purposes of paragraph 6(a)(iii) of the Agreement.

3.2 Where under the rules and procedures of the CGO Service the delivery of any Securities from a securities account in the name of one party or its nominee or agent ("**the transferor**") to a securities account in the name of the other party or its nominee or agent ("**the transferee**") gives rise to an assured payment obligation by which the settlement bank acting for the transferee is obliged to make a payment to the settlement bank acting for the transferor, the creation of that assured payment obligation shall for the purposes of the Agreement and any Transaction be treated as a payment from the transferee to the transferor of an amount equal to the amount of the assured payment obligation.

**3.3** Where any transfer of Securities under or for the purposes of the Agreement or any Transaction results, under the rules and procedures of the CGO Service, in a payment (whether under paragraph 3.2 above or otherwise) which is not required to be made by the Agreement or the terms of the relevant Transaction:

(a) where the amount of the relevant payment is less than £100, the payment shall be treated as made by way of margin adjustment under paragraph 4 of the Agreement;

(b) in any other case the party receiving such payment shall, unless the parties shall have agreed otherwise, cause an irrevocable payment in the same amount to be made to the other party for value the same day through the CHAPS system or another guaranteed payment system agreed between the parties.

**3.4 (a)** Subject to and in accordance with the following provisions of this sub-paragraph, the parties may agree to enter into an overnight sale and repurchase transaction (a "**DBV Transaction**") to be effected under the "delivery-by-value" facility of the CGO Service.

(b) The Confirmation relating to a DBV Transaction:

(i) shall specify the Transaction as a DBV Transaction;

(ii) shall not describe the Purchased Securities;

(iii) shall specify as the Purchase Price the consideration to be input in respect of the delivery of the Purchased Securities through the CGO Service.

(c) The Purchased Securities under a DBV Transaction shall be such Securities (which may include Securities which are not gilt-edged securities) as shall be selected and delivered by the CGO Service on the apportionment of securities to the relevant delivery in accordance with the rules and procedures of the CGO Service.

(d) The amount by which the Repurchase Price under a DBV Transaction exceeds the Purchase Price shall be paid by Seller to Buyer on the Repurchase Date on or as soon as practicable after the delivery of Equivalent Securities through the CGO Service from a securities account of Buyer to a securities account of Seller. Such payment shall be made outside the CGO Service in same day funds.

(e) If on the Repurchase Date of a DBV Transaction Equivalent Securities are not delivered to Seller by reason of the fact that:

(i) either party's membership of the CGO Service has been terminated or suspended; or

(ii) overnight collateral chits issued by the CGO Service at the request of Buyer have not been returned to the CGO Service on the Repurchase Date by the latest time fixed for such return by the rules and procedures of the CGO Service;

then, unless before the latest time for delivery of such Equivalent Securities under the rules and procedures of the CGO Service an Event of Default has occurred under paragraph 10 of the Agreement in respect of either party, such non-delivery shall be deemed to constitute:

(A) where Buyer's membership of the CGO Service has been terminated or suspended or sub-paragraph (ii) above applies, a failure by Buyer to deliver Equivalent Securities on the Repurchase Date;

**(B)** where Seller's membership of the CGO Service has been terminated or suspended, a failure by Seller to pay the Repurchase Price on the Repurchase Date.

**(f)** if after an Event of Default has occurred under paragraph 10 of the Agreement Equivalent Securities to the Purchased Securities are delivered to a securities account of Seller against the creation of an assured payment obligation in accordance with the rules and procedures of the CGO Service notwithstanding the termination of the relevant DBV Transaction, such delivery shall give rise to the following obligations, each of which shall be conditional on the simultaneous performance of the other:

**(i)** an obligation on Seller to deliver to Buyer on demand securities equivalent to the securities so delivered; and

**(ii)** an obligation on Buyer to pay to Seller on demand a sum equal to the amount of the assured payment obligation so created.

**3.5 (a)** The parties may agree to enter into a series of DBV Transactions to be confirmed by a single Confirmation, each such DBV Transaction being for the same Purchase Price and each such DBV Transaction other than the first commencing on the Repurchase Date of the previous Transaction. Such a series of DBV Transactions is in this paragraph referred to as:

**(i)** an **"Open DBV Repo"** if the Repurchase Date of the last Transaction in the series is not specified in the Confirmation but it is instead provided that, if either party gives to the other notice of not less than a stated period, the DBV Transaction which will be due for Termination on the date specified in the notice will be the last Transaction in the series and the series will be limited accordingly;

**(ii)** a **"Term DBV Repo"** if the date on which the last Transaction in the series is due for Termination is specified in the Confirmation.

**(b)** Subject to the following provisions of this sub-paragraph, paragraph 3.4 above shall apply in respect of each DBV Transaction forming part of an Open DBV Repo or a Term DBV Repo.

**(c)** it shall not be necessary for any Transaction forming part of an Open DBV Repo or a Term DBV Repo to be evidenced by a separate Confirmation and, subject to sub-paragraph 3.5(d) below, each such Transaction shall be deemed to be entered into on the Repurchase Date of the preceding such Transaction.

**(d)** Notwithstanding the preceding provisions of this sub-paragraph, a transaction which would otherwise be deemed to be entered into on any day and would form part of an Open DBV Repo or a Term DBV Repo shall be deemed not to be entered into if before the parties have taken the steps necessary to effect delivery of the Purchased Securities under that Transaction on that day in accordance with the rules and procedures of the CGO Service:

**(i)** an Event of Default has occurred in relation to either party; or

**(ii)** an earlier Transaction forming part of that Open DBV Repo or Term DBV Repo has been terminated under paragraph 10(e) or 10(f) of the Agreement.

**(e)** In any case where sub-paragraph 3.5(d) above applies, no further Transaction forming part of the relevant Open DBV Repo or Term DBV Repo shall arise.

**(f)** Subject to sub-paragraph 3.5(h) below, and save in so far as the Confirmation relating to an Open DBV Repo or Term DBV Repo may otherwise provide, that part (if any) of the Repurchase Price in respect of each Transaction in the relevant series (other than the last such Transaction) which exceeds the Purchase Price shall not be payable on the Repurchase Date, but shall instead be deferred until, and shall be payable on, the Repurchase Date of the last Transaction in the series. Such payment shall be made outside the CGO Service in same day funds.

**(g)** Any amount payable in respect of a Transaction forming part of an Open DBV Repo or Term DBV Repo payment of which has been deferred under sub-paragraph (f) above shall, until it is paid or the relevant Transaction is terminated under any provision of paragraph 10 of the Agreement, be treated for the purposes of paragraph 4(c) of the Agreement as if it were an amount payable under paragraph 5 of the Agreement.

**(h)** If any Transaction forming part of an Open DBV Repo or Term DBV Repo is terminated under any provision of paragraph 10 of the Agreement, any amounts payable in respect of any earlier Transactions forming part of that Open DBV Repo or Term DBV Repo payment of which has been deferred under sub-paragraph 3.5(f) above shall become due and payable immediately.

## 4. Transactions in partly paid Securities

**4.1** This paragraph applies where:

**(a)** the Purchased Securities under a Transaction are Securities on which a call or instalment remains to be paid; and

**(b)** the due date for the payment of any such call or instalment occurs before the Termination of the Transaction.

**4.2** Seller shall pay to Buyer, for value on or before the due date of the call or instalment, an amount equal to the call or instalment payable on that date in respect of Securities equivalent to the Purchased Securities.

**4.3** No adjustment to the Repurchase Price shall be made in consequence of the call or instalment or of the payment made by Seller under paragraph 4.2 above.

**4.4** On and from the due date for the payment of the call or instalment the expression "Equivalent Securities" shall with respect to that Transaction be taken to mean Securities of the same issuer, forming part of the same issue and being of an identical type, nominal value, description and amount as the Purchased Securities but after payment of the call or instalment in question.

## 5. Exercise of rights of conversion

**5.1** This paragraph applies where the Purchased Securities under a Transaction are Securities in respect of which a right of conversion (whether arising under the terms of issue of the Securities or under a conversion offer made after such issue) becomes exercisable before the Termination of the Transaction.

**5.2** Seller may, not later than a reasonable period before the latest time for the exercise of the right of conversion, give to Buyer written notice to the effect that, on Termination of the Transaction, it wishes to receive Securities in such form as will arise if the right of conversion is exercised or, in the case of a right of conversion which may be exercised in more than one manner, is exercised in such manner as is specified in the notice.

**5.3** With effect from the latest time for the exercise of the right of conversion the expression "Equivalent Securities" shall be taken to mean:

**(a)** if a notice has been given under paragraph 5.2 above not later than the time specified in that sub-paragraph, such amount of such Securities of such description as fall to be held by a holder of Securities of the same issuer, forming part of the same issue and being of an identical type, nominal value, description and amount as the Purchased Securities if he has exercised the right of conversion in the manner specified in the notice;

**(b)** In any other case, such amount of Securities of such description as fall to be held by a holder of Securities of the same issuer, forming part of the same issue and being of an identical type, nominal value, description and amount as the Purchased Securities if he has not exercised the right of conversion.

## 6. Termination of on demand Transactions

**6.1** Paragraph 3(e) of the Agreement shall not apply, but shall be replaced by the following:

"(e) In the case of on demand Transactions, demand for Termination shall be made by Buyer or Seller, by telephone or otherwise, and shall provide for Termination to occur as soon as reasonably practicable after such demand or on such date (being at least one Business Day after that on which the demand is made) as may be specified in the demand: provided that, unless otherwise agreed between the parties, a demand which is made before 10 a.m. on a Business Day may provide for Termination to occur not later than the close of business on that day."

## 7. Dividend entitlements: effect on margin provisions

**7.1** This paragraph applies where:

**(a)** the ex-dividend date for the payment of any dividend on any Purchased Securities occurs before the Termination of the relevant Transaction; or

**(b)** the ex-dividend date for the payment of any dividend on any gilt-edged securities which have been delivered to a party as Margin Securities occurs before Equivalent Margin Securities have been delivered to the other party.

**7.2** For the purposes of paragraph 4 of the Agreement:

**(a)** where paragraph 7.1(a) above applies, from the period from the ex-dividend date until the Termination of the Transaction, Buyer shall be deemed to have received a payment of Cash Margin equal to the amount of the dividend payable on the Purchased Securities by reference to that ex-dividend date;

**(b)** where paragraph 7.1(b) above applies, the party which has received those Margin Securities shall, from the period from the ex-dividend date until Equivalent Margin Securities are delivered to the other party, be deemed to have received a payment of Cash Margin equal to the amount of the dividend payable on those Margin Securities by reference to that ex-dividend date.

# Notes to supplemental terms and conditions for repurchase transactions in UK gilt-edged securities

*Gilt Repo Legal Agreement Working Party*

1.  These supplemental terms and conditions (referred to in these notes as "the Supplemental Terms") have been prepared by a working party of market practitioners and regulators and are recommended under the Gilt Repo Code of Best Practice for use in respect of repo transactions in UK gilts, subject to users taking further legal advice where appropriate, for example in the circumstances referred to in these notes and in the guidance notes to the PSA/ISMA master agreement.

*Purpose of supplemental terms*

2.  The Supplemental Terms are designed to be incorporated in Annex I to the PSA/ISMA master agreement, together with any other supplemental terms and conditions agreed between the parties. The Supplemental Terms have, like the PSA/ISMA master agreement itself, been drafted with a view to legal, regulatory and taxation provisions applicable in the United Kingdom, and they are intended to cover those matters which are thought likely to be common to most gilt repo transactions or to most such transactions of particular kinds. They are not intended to limit parties' freedom to deal with parties outside the United Kingdom or to incorporate other terms, subject to appropriate consideration of and advice on the additional issues which this may raise.

*Securities which may be covered*

3.  The PSA/ISMA master agreement to which the Supplemental Terms form an annex may, if the parties so decide, cover repos in both gilts and other securities.

*Combination with other agreements*

4.  It would be possible to provide for a master agreement incorporating the Supplemental Terms to be operated in combination with another master agreement for other transactions (for example a gilt-edged stock lending agreement in a form approved by the London Stock Exchange, which includes events of default and close-out and netting provisions substantially identical to those of the PSA/ISMA master agreement). However, the Working Party took the view that any such linkage should be left for parties to agree if they chose rather than recommended as a matter of course.

*Confirmations*

5.  The Annex does not vary the provisions of paragraph 3 of the PSA/ISMA master agreement relating to confirmations. Parties who wish to do so, for example by making express provision for the status of taped telephone conversations (which are permitted by the PSA/ISMA master agreement), are free to add specific provisions.

*Central Gilts Office Service and "delivery by value" transactions*

6.1 Paragraph 3 of the Annex contains provisions relating to the use of the CGO Service. Paragraph 3.4 modifies the application of the Agreement where the parties agree to use the CGO "delivery by value" facility, under which the parties may agree an overnight transfer of securities having a specified value. The securities will be selected by the system in accordance with a predetermined procedure laid down by the rules of the system and the transaction will be reversed automatically the following morning unless in the meantime the CGO membership of one of the parties has been suspended or terminated. The consideration used by the system for the reversal will be the same as that of the original delivery; paragraph 3.4(d) therefore provides for any agreed premium element of the repurchase price to be paid separately outside the CGO system.

**6.2** Paragraph 3.5 enables the parties to enter into a single agreement for a series of successive DBV Transactions, each following on immediately from the preceding transaction in the series, and for any premium element in the repurchase price of each individual DBV Transaction in the series to be carried forward and settled together at the end of the series.

*Transactions in partly paid securities*

**7.** Paragraph 4 of the Annex makes provision for transactions in partly paid securities. Where a call or instalment becomes due while a repo transaction is outstanding, the seller is obliged to fund it by making an equivalent payment to the buyer. There is no increase in the repurchase price, but the seller's obligation is to repurchase the securities in the paid-up form. The value of the securities in the paid-up form will increase on the due date for the call or instalment and it is likely that this will trigger a margin transfer from buyer to seller.

*Exercise of rights of conversion*

**8.** Paragraph 5 of the Annex makes provision for transactions in securities on which a right of conversion becomes exercisable during the term of the transaction, whether under the terms of issue of the securities or because the securities are the subject of a conversion offer. In these circumstances the seller is entitled to give notice to the buyer specifying in what form it wishes to receive securities on termination of the transaction. It will then be for the buyer to ensure that it is able to deliver such securities, whether by exercising the conversion right on securities which it holds, purchasing securities in the converted form or exercising a corresponding right under a matching repo agreement into which it has entered as seller. If the seller does not give a notice, the securities deliverable at the maturity of the transaction are securities in the form which will be held by a holder who has taken no action.

*Termination of on demand transactions*

**9.** The Annex varies the normal timing laid down by the PSA/ISMA master agreement for the termination of on demand transactions by giving either party the right to call for same day termination provided that the call is made before 10 a.m. (The general position under the PSA/ISMA master agreement is that termination will occur after not less than the minimum period customarily required for the settlement or delivery of money or securities of the relevant kind. In the case of a repo of gilt-edged securities, this would mean that a termination notice must be given by close of business on the business day before that of the intended termination. Parties who prefer this position may wish to amend the Annex so as to exclude paragraph 6.)

*Ex-dividend dates: effect on margin provisions*

**10.** The length of the ex-dividend period for most gilt-edged securities has been reduced to seven working days. In spite of this reduction, gilt-edged securities will continue to differ from most securities used in repo transactions in having a significant ex-dividend period. During this period the market value of the securities is likely to fall to reflect the fact that they have gone ex-dividend. Normally this fall would be taken into account in the calculation of margin under the PSA/ISMA master agreement and would trigger a margin payment to the party holding the securities. This is thought to be inequitable, given that that party is entitled to receive the amount of the dividend from the Treasury. The Annex therefore provides that for the purposes of margin calculation that party is treated as having received a payment of cash margin equal to the dividend entitlement.

*Taxation*

**11.** Like the PSA/ISMA Agreement itself, the Annex is drafted to cover only repos in respect of which "manufactured dividends" are to be paid without deduction of tax, whether or not actual interest on the securities is received subject to deduction of tax. Under the new taxation arrangements introduced under the Finance Act 1995, corporate holders of gilt-edged securities who are resident in the UK for tax purposes may elect to receive interest on those securities gross; such holders will be required to operate quarterly accounting arrangements for payments on account of tax and to hold their gilt-edged securities (directly or indirectly) in specially identified CGO accounts.

*Special counterparties*

**12.** The Annex does not include provision for counterparties with a special status such as trustees or partnerships. Parties will need to form their own view as to whether special investigations or additional provisions are appropriate when dealing with such counterparties.

# APPENDIX 2
# A Summary of Market Day/Year Conventions

| Instrument | Day/Year Basis | Yield or Discount |
|---|---|---|
| **Belgium** | | |
| OLO | 30(E)/360 (annual) | Y |
| T-bill | ACT/365 | Y |
| Repo | ACT/365 | Y |
| **France** | | |
| BTF (T-bill) | ACT/360 | Y |
| OAT, BTAN | ACT/ACT (annual) | Y |
| Repo | ACT/360 | |
| **Germany** | | |
| Depo/CD/Bubill | ACT/360 | Y |
| Bund, OBL | 30(E)/360 (annual) | Y |
| Repo | ACT/360 | Y |
| **Italy** | | |
| Depo/CD/T-bill | ACT/365 | Y |
| BTP | 30 (E)[1]/360 [accrued interest] ACT/365 [yield calculation] (semi-annual) | Y |
| Repo | ACT/365 | Y |
| **Japan** | | |
| Depo/CD/T-bill | ACT/365 | Y |
| JGB | ACT[2]/365 (semi-annual) (exclude February 29) | Y |
| Repo (domestic) | ACT/365 | Y |
| Repo (international) | ACT/360 | Y |
| **Spain** | | |
| Depo/CD/T-bill | ACT/360 | Y |
| Bono | ACT/ACT [accrued interest] ACT/365 [yield calculation] (annual) | Y |
| Repo | ACT/360 | Y |

**UK**

| | | |
|---|---|---|
| Depo/CD/£CP | ACT/365 | Y |
| BA/T-bill | ACT/365 | D |
| Gilt | ACT/365 (semi-annual) | Y |
| Repo | ACT/365 | Y |

**US**

| | | |
|---|---|---|
| Depo/CD | ACT/360 | Y |
| BA/$CP/T-bill | ACT/360 | D |
| T-bond/note | ACT/ACT (semi-annual) | Y |
| Repo | ACT/360 | Y |

**Euromarket**

| | | |
|---|---|---|
| Depo/CD/ECP | ACT/360 (except ACT/365 for GBP, IEP, BEF/LUF, PTE, GRD) | Y |
| Eurobond | 30(E)/360 (annual) | Y |

*Notes*

1. Accrued coupon calculation adds one day to the usual calculation (the start date and end date are counted inclusively).

2. One day's extra coupon is accrued in the first coupon period.

# APPENDIX 3
# A Summary of Calculation Procedures

## 1. Accrued coupon/accrued interest

$$\text{Accrued rate} = \text{coupon rate or interest rate} \times \frac{\text{days}}{\text{year}}$$

Remember that in all calculations $\dfrac{\text{days}}{\text{year}}$ is not necessarily the same for repo rates or money market instruments as it is for accrued bond coupons in the same currency.

## 2. Discount to true yield

$$\text{Yield} = \frac{\text{Discount rate}}{\left(1 - \text{Discount rate} \times \dfrac{\text{days}}{\text{year}}\right)}$$

## 3. Price of a Treasury bill

In most currencies, price = 
$$\frac{\text{Face value of bill}}{\left(1 + \text{yield} \times \dfrac{\text{days to maturity of bill}}{\text{year}}\right)}$$

In USD or GBP, price =

$$\text{Face value of bill} \times \left(1 - \text{discount rate} \times \frac{\text{days to maturity of bill}}{\text{year}}\right)$$

## 4. The cashflows in a classic repo (securities-driven amounts)

Cash paid at the beginning =

$$\text{nominal bond amount} \times (\text{clean price} + \text{accrued coupon})/100$$

Cash repaid at the end =

$$\text{cash paid at the beginning} \times \left(1 + \text{repo rate} \times \frac{\text{repo days}}{\text{repo year}}\right)$$

## 5. The cashflows in a buy/sell-back

Cash paid at the beginning =

$$\text{nominal bond amount} \times (\text{clean price} + \text{accrued coupon})/100$$

*(The same as for a classic repo)*

Total cash repaid at the end =

$$\text{cash paid at the beginning} \times \left(1 + \text{repo rate} \times \frac{\text{repo days}}{\text{year}}\right)$$

*(The same as for a classic repo)*

Forward price (clean price) = forward dirty price − accrued coupon at end =

$$\frac{\text{total cash repaid at the end}}{\text{nominal bond amount}} \times 100 - \text{accrued coupon at end}$$

## 6. The cashflows in a buy/sell-back with a coupon payment

Cash paid at the beginning =

$$\text{nominal bond amount} \times (\text{clean price} + \text{accrued coupon})/100$$

*(The same as in 4 and 5 above)*

Value of intervening coupon = nominal bond amount × coupon rate ×

$$\left(1 + \text{repo rate} \times \frac{\text{days from coupon payment to end of repo}}{\text{year}}\right)$$

*(Use $\frac{1}{2} \times$ coupon rate if coupons are semi-annual)*

Total cash repaid at the end =

$$\text{cash paid at the beginning} \times \left(1 + \text{repo rate} \times \frac{\text{repo days}}{\text{year}}\right) - \text{value of intervening coupon}$$

Forward price (= clean price) = the same as in (5) above

## 7. The cashflows when there is a haircut

Cash paid at the beginning =

$$\frac{\text{nominal bond amount} \times (\text{clean price} + \text{accrued coupon})/100}{(1 + \text{haircut rate})}$$

Then continue as in 4 to 6 above

(Note that this method of calculating a haircut assumes, for example, that a "2 percent haircut" means that the value of the collateral must be 2 percent more than the value of the cash loan: value of collateral = value of cash loan × 1.02. This is consistent with the PSA/ISMA agreement. Market dealers sometimes work in reverse, however, interpreting a 2 percent haircut as meaning that the value of the cash loan must be 2 percent less than the value of the collateral – that is: value of collateral = value of cash loan ÷ 0.98. This results in slightly more collateral.)

Also note that it is possible for the lender of securities to demand a haircut from the lender of the cash, rather than the other way round. If this is the case, you should change all the formulas here to *multiply* by (1+ haircut rate) instead of *dividing*, and vice versa.)

## 8. Cash-driven deals

The amount dealt in a repo may be driven by a "round" amount of cash at the beginning, rather than by a "round" nominal amount of security. In this case,

$$\text{nominal bond amount} = \frac{\text{cash paid at the beginning}}{(\text{clean price} + \text{accrued coupon})/100} \times (1 + \text{haircut})$$

*(This is just the reverse of the formula in 7)*
Then continue as in 4 to 6 above.

## 9. Mark-to-market/margin calls

$$\text{New value of cash loan} = \text{cash paid at the beginning} \times \left(1 + \text{repo rate} \times \frac{\text{days so far}}{\text{year}}\right)$$

(A) new nominal amount of collateral required =

$$\frac{\text{new value of cash loan}}{(\text{new clean price} + \text{new accrued coupon})/100} \times (1 + \text{ haircut rate})$$

(B) Margin call = difference between (A) and the collateral previously transferred.

If the margin call is settled in cash rather than securities, then cash transferred =

$$\text{B} \times (\text{new clean price} + \text{new accrued coupon})/100$$

## 10. Close out and repricing (adjusting the cash amount)

*(Alternative to calculating a margin call as in 9)*

(C) Close-out amount on original repo =

$$\text{cash paid at the beginning} \times \left(1 + \text{ repo rate } \times \frac{\text{days so far}}{\text{year}}\right)$$

(D) New cash amount = new value of collateral adjusted for haircut =

$$\frac{\text{nominal bond amount} \times (\text{new bond price} + \text{new accrued coupon})/100}{(1 + \text{haircut rate})}$$

The cash difference between (C) and (D) is transferred and a new repo is then in place for the new cash amount from the new start date.

## 11. Close out and repricing (adjusting the securities amount)

(*Alternative to calculating a margin call as in 9*)

Cash interest is paid on loan so far = cash paid at the beginning $\times \left( \text{repo rate} \times \dfrac{\text{days so far}}{\text{year}} \right)$

(E) Nominal bond amount now required as collateral =

$$\frac{\text{cash paid at the beginning}}{(\text{new bond price} + \text{new accrued coupon})/100} \times (1 + \text{haircut rate})$$

The difference between (E) and the original collateral is transferred in order to change the nominal amount of security lodged as collateral, and a new repo is then in place for the same cash amount from the new start date.

## 12. Cross-currency repo

For a security-driven deal, convert the all-in market value of the security into the currency of the cash loan at the spot rate. Then continue as in the procedures above.

For a cash-driven deal, convert the value of the cash amount into the currency of the collateral at the spot rate. Then continue as in the procedures above.

## 13. Substitution

The procedure is exactly the same as when marking to market in 9 above, but using a different security:

Nominal amount of new collateral required =

$$\frac{\text{new value of cash loan}}{(\text{clean price of new collateral} + \text{accrued coupon})/100} \times (1 + \text{ haircut rate})$$

## 14. Cash-and-carry arbitrage

Assume the arbitrage is achieved by buying the cash bond and selling the futures:

(F) Cash cost at start = nominal bond amount $\times$ (cash bond price + accrued coupon at start)/100

(G) Total payments = (cash cost at start) $\times \left( 1 + \text{repo rate} \times \dfrac{\text{days to futures maturity}}{\text{year}} \right)$

(H) Total receipts = nominal bond amount $\times$ (futures price $\times$ conversion factor + accrued coupon at maturity of futures)/100

Profit= (H) − (G)

Expressed as interest rate $= \dfrac{(H) - (G)}{(F)} \times \dfrac{\text{year}}{\text{days to futures maturity}}$

This assumes there is no intervening coupon on the bond.

# APPENDIX 4
# Glossary

**Ask**

Same as **offer**.

**Base currency**

(As defined in the **GMRA**) the currency for margin calculations, and for settlements when there is a default. *See* **contractual currency**.

**Basis**

The difference in price between a futures contract and the underlying cash market price. In the case of a bond futures contract, the futures price must be adjusted by the conversion factor for the particular cash bond in question.

**Basis trade**

Buying the **basis** means selling a futures contract and buying an underlying bond. Selling the basis is the opposite.

**Bid**

The rate at which the buyer of the collateral in a repo is prepared to lend cash – it is the bid rate for the collateral, not the bid rate for cash. *See* **offer**.

**Bilateral repo**

A repo with only two parties involved, the **seller** (lender of securities) delivering the securities to the **buyer** (lender of cash) rather than to a third party. *See* **triparty repo, hold-in-custody**.

**Bobl**

Or OBL, Bundesobligation, a German government bond.

**Bono**

Bono del Estado, a Spanish government bond.

**Borrower**

Same as **buyer** in a repo. It is the borrower of the securities, not the borrower of the cash. In a securities lending transaction, it is the borrower of the **special** rather than the borrower of the **general collateral**. *See* **lender**.

**BTAN**

Bon du Trésor à Taux Fixe et Interêt Annuel, a French Treasury fixed-interest bill.

**BTF**

Bon du Trésor à Taux Fixe et Interêt Précompté, a French discount bill.

**BTP**

Buono del Tesoro Poliennale, an Italian Treasury bond.

**Bund**

Bundesanleihe, a German government bond.

**Buy/sell-back**

Separate spot purchase and forward sale of a security, with the forward price calculated to achieve an effect equivalent to a **classic repo**.

**Buyer**

The buyer in a repo is the party lending cash and borrowing securities (the temporary buyer of the securities).

**Cash-and-carry**

A round trip where a dealer buys bonds, repos them out for cash to fund their purchase, sells bond futures, and delivers the bonds to the futures buyer at maturity of the futures contract.

**Cash-driven**

When a repo trade is cash-driven, the amount of cash lent is a round amount and the nominal amount of collateral will be an odd amount. *See* **stock-driven.**

**CCT**

Certificato di Credito del Tesoro, an Italian Treasury credit certificate.

**CGO**

The Central Gilts Office, run by the Bank of England, through which **gilts** are settled.

**Cheapest to deliver**

In a bond futures contract, the one underlying bond among all those in the basket of bonds which are eligible for delivery, which is the most price efficient for the seller to deliver.

**Classic repo**

Or "repo" or "US-style repo." Repo is short for "sale and repurchase agreement," whereby a dealer borrows money against a loan of collateral. A **reverse** repo is the opposite. The terminology is usually applied from the perspective of the repo dealer. For example, when a central bank does repos, it is lending cash (the repo dealer is borrowing cash from the central bank).

**Clean price**

The price of a bond excluding accrued coupon. The price quoted in the market for a security is generally a clean price rather than a **dirty price.**

**Close out and repricing**

When a repo is **marked to market** and the value of the collateral is found to have changed, the parties may either adjust the nominal amount of the collateral accordingly or terminate the repo early and re-establish it at the original repo rate but reflecting the new market price for the collateral. The latter is "close out and repricing."

**Collateral**

Or "security"; something of value, and often good credit-worthiness such as a government bond, given temporarily by the **seller** in a repo to the **buyer** to protect the buyer in the event of the seller defaulting on the cash loan. Also given by the **borrower** to the **lender** in a securities lending transaction. *See* **general** and **special collateral.**

**Contractual currency**

(As defined in the **GMRA**) the currency of any one particular transaction. *See* **base currency.**

| | |
|---|---|
| **Cross-currency repo** | A repo in which the currency of the cash is different from the currency in which the collateral is denominated. |
| **CT** | Certificat du Trésor, Belgian Treasury bill. |
| **CTO** | Buono del Tesoro con Opzione, Italian Treasury certificate with an option. |
| **Customer repo** | When the US Federal Reserve ("Fed") does a repo with the market on behalf of one of its own customers, such as another central bank or supranational organization. *See* **Fed repo, system repo.** |
| **DAC – RAP** | Delivery against collateral – receipt against payment. Same as **DVP.** |
| **Day-to-day repo** | Same as **open repo.** |
| **DBV** | Delivery by value, a **CGO** mechanism for overnight loans against **gilt** collateral between CGO members. |
| **Deliver-out repo** | A repo in which the collateral is delivered – that is, a **bilateral** repo. |
| **Deliverable bond** | One of the bonds which is eligible to be delivered by the seller of a futures contract at the contract's maturity, according to the specifications of that particular futures contract. |
| **Dirty price** | The price of a security including accrued coupon. *See* **clean price.** |
| **Dollar repo** | A repo in which the buyer may return at maturity a security which is different, within agreed limits, from the original collateral. |
| **Dollar roll** | **Buy/sell-back** (in the US). |
| **Double-dipping** | The illegal practice of a repo seller using the same security to collateralize two separate repos in an **HIC** repo (not possible where the collateral has to be delivered). |
| **Due bill repo** | Same as **hold-in-custody** repo. |
| **DVP** | Delivery versus payment, in which the settlement mechanics of a sale, or loan against cash, of securities is such that the securities and cash are exchanged against each other through the same clearing mechanism and neither can be transferred unless the other is. |
| **Equivalent securities** | The normal arrangement in a repo, whereby the securities to be returned to the seller at maturity of a repo are |

required to be exactly the same issue as the securities delivered at the beginning, but not necessarily exactly the same numbered holding.

| | |
|---|---|
| **ESLA** | Equities Stock Lending Agreement. |
| **Fed repo** | When the US Federal Reserve ("Fed") initiates a repo or a reverse repo with the market, the terminology is viewed from the market's viewpoint and not from the Fed's. Thus a repo is when the Fed is lending money to the market against collateral and a reverse is the opposite. *See* **customer repo, system repo, matched sale-purchase.** |
| **Fed reverse** | Opposite of a **Fed repo.** Also "matched sale-purchase." |
| **Flat basis** | When a repo is transacted with no **margin.** |
| **Flex repo** | A classic term repo with the added feature that the cash is repaid to the buyer in instalments. |
| **Forward-start repo** | A **repo** where the start date is for value later than the normal settlement date for the security concerned. |
| **GC** | Abbreviation for **general collateral.** |
| **GEMM** | Gilt-Edged Market Maker, a dealer in the **gilt** market required to quote two-way prices (make a market) in gilts. |
| **General collateral** | A repo dealt for general **collateral** can be secured by any acceptable collateral – *see* **special.** |
| **Gensaki** | A repo in the domestic Japanese market. |
| **Gilt** | Gilt-edged security, a UK government bond. |
| **GMRA** | The Global Master Repurchase Agreement, developed jointly by the **PSA** and **ISMA**, is the standard documentation under which repos are transacted internationally. |
| **Gross-paying securities** | Securities where coupons are paid without deduction of withholding tax. *See* **net-paying securities.** |
| **Haircut** | Same as initial **margin.** |
| **HIC** | *See* **hold-in-custody.** |
| **Hold-in-custody (HIC)** | **Repo** in which the security continues to be held by the seller on the buyer's behalf, in order to avoid settlement costs and facilitate **substitution.** |
| **Hot stock** | A security in general demand in the market. |

**Implied repo rate**  The break-even **repo rate** at which it is possible to sell a bond futures contract, buy a deliverable bond, and repo the bond out. *See* **cash-and-carry**.

**Indexed repo rate**  Where the repo rate in a classic repo is periodically reset with reference to some benchmark such as LIBOR.

**Initial margin**  *See* **margin**.

**International repo**  A **repo** in the international or domestic European markets, rather than the US market.

**Investor**  Same as **buyer** in a repo.

**IRS**  An interest rate swap.

**ISLA**  International Securities Lenders' Association.

**ISMA**  The International Securities Markets Association (formerly the AIBD), the international professional body governing dealing in securities. *See* **PSA**.

**JGB**  Japanese government bond.

**Lender**  Same as **seller** in a repo. It is the lender of the securities, not the lender of the cash. In a securities lending transaction, it is the lender of the **special** rather than the lender of the **general collateral**. *See* **borrower**.

**LIBOR**  London Inter-Bank Offered Rate, the rate at which banks in the London market are willing to lend to other banks of top creditworthiness.

**Manufactured dividend**  When a coupon is paid on collateral during the term of a **classic repo**, it is received by the **buyer** but repaid to the **seller**. The repayment is called a manufactured dividend.

**Margin**  Initial margin (or "haircut") is the extra collateral or cash required to allow for a potential subsequent change in the collateral's market value. Usually required by the buyer to protect against a fall in the collateral's market value, but sometimes required by the seller to protect against a rise in the collateral's market value. *See* **variation margin**.

**Margin call**  A call by one of the parties in a **repo** for **variation margin**.

**Margin ratio**  (As defined in the **GMRA**) the all-in market value of the securities divided by the cash loan, so that if the **haircut** is 2 percent, the margin ratio is 1.02.

**Mark-to-market**  The process of continually revaluing collateral to ensure that its market value is the same as that of the cash loan, adjusted for accrued coupon, accrued interest and any initial **margin**. Also refers to the process of then increasing or decreasing the collateral.

**Matched book trading**  Offering two-way prices in **repos**. Does not imply that the dealer doing so in fact has a matched, or square, trading book.

**Matched sale-purchase**  Same as a **Fed reverse**.

**Net exposure**  (As defined in the **GMRA**) the net total of: the **transaction exposures** on all outstanding deals, the **net margin** paid or received on all outstanding deals, and any **manufactured** payments which are due but not yet paid or received. This calculation gives the amount of margin transfer which may be called for.

**Net margin**  (As defined in the **GMRA**) the amount of **variation margin** paid (including margin securities, margin cash, and accrued interest on margin cash) from one party to the other, netted against the amount of variation margin paid or repaid in the other direction.

**Net-paying securities**  Securities where coupons are paid net of withholding tax. *See* **gross-paying securities**.

**OAT**  Obligation Assimilable du Trésor, French Treasury bond.

**OBL**  *See* **Bobl**.

**Off-side date**  The value date for the second leg of a **repo**.

**Offer**  The rate at which the seller of the collateral in a **repo** is prepared to borrow cash – it is the offered rate for the collateral, not the offered rate for cash. *See* **bid**, **ask**.

**OLO**  Obligations Linéaires Obligaties, Belgian government bonds.

**On-side date**  The value date for the first leg of a **repo**.

**Open repo**  A **repo** with no fixed maturity. The repo is generally rolled over each day at a new repo rate, although the rate could instead be refixed at longer intervals, such as monthly. Same as day-to-day repo.

**OSLA**  Overseas Securities Lenders' Agreement.

**Overnight repo**  A repo from today until the next working day ("tomorrow").

| | |
|---|---|
| **Pension** | Short for "Pension Livrée." **Classic repo** in the French domestic market. |
| **Prêt de titres** | **Securities lending** in France. |
| **Price differential** | (As defined in the **GMRA**) the accrued interest on the cash lent in a repo. |
| **Pricing rate** | (As defined in the **GMRA**) same as the **repo rate**. |
| **PSA** | The Public Securities Association, a US-based association which developed the standard repo documentation used for domestic repos in the US. *See* **ISMA**. |
| **PSA/ISMA agreement** | *See* **GMRA**. |
| **Purchase price** | (As defined in the **GMRA**) in a **classic repo**, the cash originally lent (effectively the **dirty price** adjusted for haircut). In a **buy/sell-back** the original **clean price** transacted at the beginning. |
| **Rebate** | The lending fee in a **securities lending** transaction deducted from interest paid on cash collateral. |
| **Repo rate** | The short-term interest rate for borrowing/lending at which a **repo** is transacted. |
| **Repo** | Usually refers in particular to **classic repo** or **US-style repo**. Also used as a term to include classic repos, **buy/sell-backs**, and **securities lending**. |
| **Repurchase price** | (As defined in the **GMRA**) in a **classic repo**, the current value of the cash loan – that is, the original cash loan plus accrued interest on it so far, at any time during the transaction. *See* **sell back price**. |
| **Reverse to maturity** | A **reverse repo** with the same maturity date as the security used for collateral. |
| **Reverse** | Reverse repo; the opposite of a **repo**. |
| **RP** | Abbreviation for **repo**. |
| **Securities-driven** | Same as **stock-driven**. |
| **Securities lending** | When a specific security in particular demand is lent against securities (**general collateral**), cash, or some other form of **collateral**. |
| **Sell/buy-back** | Opposite of **buy/sell-back**. |
| **Sell back differential** | (As defined in the **GMRA**) the accrued interest on the cash loan at any time during a buy/sell-back (equivalent to **price differential** in a classic repo). |

| | |
|---|---|
| **Sell back price** | (As defined in the **GMRA**) calculated for the original repurchase date in a **buy/sell-back**, the clean forward price. Calculated for any other date, the all-in price for close-out. *See* **repurchase price**. |
| **Seller** | The seller in a repo is the party borrowing cash and lending securities (the temporary seller of the securities). |
| **Special collateral** | A repo dealt for special **collateral** can be secured by only one particular security; the **buyer** enters into the transaction precisely because it needs that specific security rather than any other. If a security "goes special," it means that there is particular demand to borrow it, so that it commands a lower **repo rate** than usual. *See* **general collateral**. |
| **Specific collateral** | Similar to **special collateral**. A buyer may insist on a specific security rather than general collateral, because he needs that particular one. |
| **Spread trade** | A strategy involving the **repo** of a security (possibly a special) at a lower interest cost to borrow cash which is then invested at a higher interest rate through a **reverse repo**. |
| **SPVTs** | Spécialistes en Pension sur Valeurs du Trésor (French primary dealers in repo). |
| **Stock-driven** | When a repo trade is stock-driven, the nominal amount of the collateral is a round amount and the cash is an odd amount. *See* **cash-driven**. |
| **Stock lending** | Same as **securities lending**. |
| **Substitution** | A repo dealt for **general collateral** may allow the seller to substitute one security for another as **collateral** during the term of the repo. |
| **Synthetic repo** | A series of transactions which is economically equivalent to a **repo** (for example, a bond sale in the cash market, purchase of a bond call option, and sale of a bond put option at the same strike, all undertaken simultaneously). |
| **System repo** | When the US Federal Reserve ("Fed") does a repo with the market on its own account, in order to adjust the supply of cash in the market, or to signal a change in interest rate policy. *See* **Fed repo, customer repo**. |
| **Tail** | The exposure to interest rates over a forward-forward period arising from a mismatched position (such as a two-month **repo** against a three-month **reverse repo**). *See* **matched book trading**. |

| | |
|---|---|
| **Taishaku** | Uncollateralized **securities lending** in the domestic Japanese market. |
| **Term repo** | A repo dealt for a specific length of time, as opposed to an **open repo**. |
| **Third party repo** | Same as **triparty repo**. |
| **Threshold** | The level below which parties to a transaction agree not to make **margin calls**. *See* **variation margin**. |
| **TMP** | Taux Moyen Pondéré, a daily average of the interbank overnight rate (itself a weighted average of the rates actually dealt), used as a floating-rate benchmark in France. |
| **Tom/next** | A **repo** or other transaction from the next working day ("tomorrow") until the day after ("next" day). |
| **Transaction exposure** | (As defined in the **GMRA**) the difference between the current value of the cash loan (including accrued interest) plus margin, and the current market value of the securities (including accrued coupon) for any particular transaction. |
| **Treasury bond** | A bond of over ten years' maturity issued by the US government. *See* **Treasury note**. |
| **Treasury note** | A bond of up to ten years' maturity issued by the US government. *See* **Treasury bond**. |
| **Triparty agent** | The third-party custodian in a **triparty repo**. |
| **Triparty repo** | **Repo** in which the collateral is delivered to and held by a third party custodian on behalf of the **buyer**, against cash settled through the same third party via **DVP**. |
| **Trust-me repo** | Same as **hold-in-custody** repo. |
| **US-style repo** | Same as **classic repo**. |
| **Variation margin** | Generally, the amount of cash or **collateral** which must be transferred when there is a change in the value of the collateral, in order to bring the ratio between the values of cash and collateral back to that required under the repo agreement. In **gilt** repos, variation margin refers to the fluctuation band or threshold within which the existing collateral's value may vary before further cash or collateral needs to be transferred. *See* **margin**. |

# SELECT BIBLIOGRAPHY

BACOB Bank (1996) *The Belgian Repo Market*, BACOB Bank, Brussels.

Bank of England (1995) *Gilt Repo Code of Best Practice*, Bank of England, London.

Bank of England Quarterly Bulletin (November 1995) *The Gilt Repo Market*, Bank of England, London.

Corporate Finance (February 1994) *More Repo Lessons Please*, Euromoney Publications, London.

Corporate Finance (May 1995) *Make Sure You Use The Right Repo Agreement*, Euromoney Publications, London.

Corrigan, D., Georgiou, C. and Gollow, J. (1995) *NatWest Markets Handbook of International Repos*, IFR Publishing, London.

*International Securities Lending*, (Various articles).

Merrill Lynch (eds) (1996) *A Treasurer's Guide to Repo*, Treasury Management International, London.

PSA (1996) *Master Repurchase Agreement*, Public Securities Association, New York.

PSA (1996) *Repo Trading Practices Guidelines*, Public Securities Association, New York.

Risk Magazine (November 1995) *Repo, A Risk Special Supplement*, Risk Publications, London.

Stigum, M. (1989) *The Repo and Reverse Markets*, Dow Jones Irwin, Illinois.

Stigum, M. (1981) *Money Market Calculations: Yields, Break-Evens and Arbitrage*, Dow Jones Irwin, Illinois.

Union Bank of Switzerland (1995) *The International Repo Market, An Investor Guide*, Union Bank of Switzerland, Zurich.

# INDEX

# MARKETS INTERNATIONAL LTD

## Training, consultancy, and publishing for the international financial markets

Markets International Ltd is an independent company providing training to banks and companies on financial markets and mathematics, risk management techniques, analysis and management policy, credit analysis, technical analysis, and other financial subjects. The company also publishes currency and interest rate forecasts which are sold worldwide. In addition, it specializes in advising international companies on treasury risk management. Services range from reviewing management policies and procedures, through the development of appropriate hedging strategies, to short-term market advice on foreign exchange and the international money markets.

Among the subjects covered in Markets International Ltd's workshops on financial markets and banking are:

- Financial mathematics
- Foreign exchange and interest rate risk management
- Repos
- Corporate exposure management
- Technical analysis
- Accounting for derivatives
- Credit analysis

The company also runs workshops aimed specifically at the following ACI exams:

- The ACI Diploma
- Pre-Diploma (Introduction to Foreign Exchange & Money Markets)
- Repos
- Financial Calculations
- Fundamentals of Swaps

For further information on in-house training opportunities, or open courses, please contact:

Bob Steiner,
Managing Director,
Markets International Ltd,
111 The Promenade, Cheltenham, Glos GL50 1NW, UK.
Telephone: 01242 222134;
Fax: 01242 260793.

# The ACI Fellowship/Associateship Examinations

## Level One:
## The ACI Foundation Programme

*Four subjects – All subjects compulsory*

| Subject | Forex Association Examination Board | Partner organization | Date of first examination | Status |
|---|---|---|---|---|
| 1 Introduction to Foreign Exchange & Money Markets | Forex London | To be appointed | Available now | Compulsory |
| 2 Code of Conduct & Market Practice | Forex Singapore | Institute of Banking & Finance, Singapore | Available now | Compulsory |
| 3 Back Office Operations | Forex London | To be appointed | Dec–96 | Compulsory |
| 4 Risks & Controls in the Dealing Room | Forex Suisse | To be appointed | Target Jun–97 | Compulsory |

## Level Two:
## Leading to the status of fellowship (for ACI members) or Associate (for non-members) of the ACI Institute

*Six subjects (one compulsory and five options to be chosen from ten)*

| Subject | Forex Association Examination Board | Partner organization | Date of first examination | Status |
|---|---|---|---|---|
| 1 The ACI Foreign Exchange Simulation | Forex Australia | To be appointed | Available now | Option |
| 2 Options | Forex France (AFTB) | MATIF SA & ITM | Available now | Option |
| 3 Futures | Forex France (AFTB) | MATIF SA & ITM | Available now | Option |
| 4 Swaps | Forex France (AFTB) | MATIF SA & ITM | Available now | Option |
| 5 The Repo Market | Forex Luxembourg | Institute de Formation Bancaire, Luxembourg | Available now | Option |
| 6 Financial Calculations | Forex Norway | To be appointed | Available now | Option |
| 7 Risk Management using Derivatives | Forex Singapore | National University of Singapore | Dec–96 | Option |
| 8 Technical Analysis | Forex Suisse | To be appointed | Target Jun–97 | Option |
| 9 Treasury Risk Management | Forex USA Inc | Stern School of Business, Salomon Centre, NYU | Available now | Option |
| 10 Fundamental Analysis (Macroeconomics) | Forex South Africa | To be appointed | Dec–96 | Option |
| 11 Operational Risk Management | To be appointed | To be appointed | Target Jun–97 | Option |
| 12 The ACI Diploma | Forex London | To be appointed | Available now | Compulsory |

*Ten subjects are required altogether for Fellowship or Associate status – the four from level one and six from level two.*
Note: Holders of the ACI Diploma (formerly the Forex Association London Foundation Diploma) are exempt from the "Introduction to Foreign Exchange & Money Markets" examination.

**market editions**

The *Financial Times Market Editions* are authoritative and practical handbooks, written for market professionals by market professionals. These titles will introduce the reader to the financial markets and provide an in-depth look at their products, applications and risks.

OTHER TITLES IN THIS SERIES:-

# Mastering Derivatives Markets

ISBN 0 273 62045 2   Price £35.00
*Available now*

# Mastering Government Securities

ISBN 0 273 62416 4   Price £40.00
*Available now*

# Mastering Exchange-Traded Equity Derivatives

ISBN 0 273 61974 8   Price £40.00
*Available now*

# Mastering Foreign Exchange & Currency Options

ISBN 0 273 62537 3   Price £40.00
*Available now*

# Mastering International Capital Markets

ISBN 0 273 62200 5   Price £40.00
*Pub: March 1997*

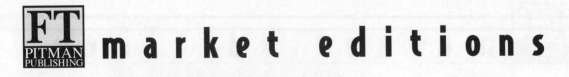
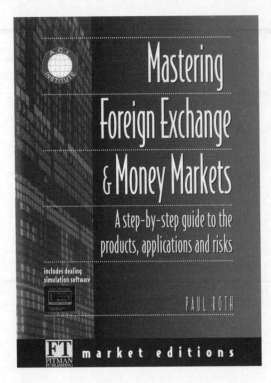

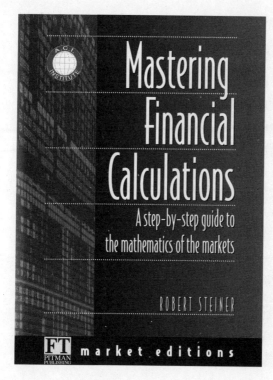

# Mastering Financial Calculations
## A step-by-step guide to the mathematics of the markets
ROBERT STEINER

Success in the financial markets requires a firm grasp of a range of financial calculations and mathematical techniques. A firm understanding and ability to manipulate and apply these tools with speed and confidence is an essential skill for any player in the markets. *Mastering Financial Calculations* helps traders and investors alike to master the essentials of pricing, evaluating and analysis across a core range of financial instruments and markets. It covers: money markets, foreign exchange markets, bond markets and derivatives; NPV calculations, yield calculations, pricing (including black scholes), marking to market and risk management volatility. Containing worked examples and exercises throughout, it reflects the style of professional exams.

ISBN 0 273 62587 X          Price £30.00
*Pub: March 1997*

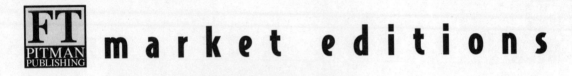

# Mastering Swaps Markets
## A step-by-step guide to the products, applications and risks
### ROBERT STEINER

*Mastering Swaps Markets* is a fully international, interactive book, which addresses market conditions, product characteristics, pricing and valuation calculations, trading strategies, risk management and settlement and compliance. It contains worked examples and exercises throughout which reflect the style of professional exams.

ISBN 0 273 62588 8     Price £50.00
*Pub: April 1997*